The Crisis Clinic

By John Farrell Ph.D., L.C.S.W.

ISBN: 978-1-945526-19-0

Library of Congress Control Number: 2017955350

Front cover photograph by Robert Farrell

Photo of author by Martha Sward

Dedication

To Martha, Kate, and Matt
for keeping my life full of love and joy

Acknowledgments

With her meticulous, tireless editorial skills, Martha Sward persisted in making this book cleaner, sharper, and better no matter how many times I told her not to. Thank you, Martha. I was also lucky to have two creative writers, Kate Farrell and Matt Farrell, contribute their thoughtful comments to the writing of this book.

Table of Contents

Introduction

I was asked to write an introduction to this book although I do not know the author well. He has admired me and wanted to be like me for a long time, so let me introduce him.

John Farrell does not share the history of many fine writers, the love of books and the need to write. In adulthood his lovely wife, Martha, had to push him toward the classics because he was only familiar with their CliffsNotes. He was a speed reader and a speed writer in high school and college, and he cared little for comprehension or coherence.

The one exception to his poor literary refinement was his genuine love for Ian Fleming's books on the life and adventures of James Bond. By the age of 13, he had read all of the James Bond books twice. At that young age John knew what he wanted to be in life: he wanted to be James Bond. He imagined the fast cars and sexy women and sexy cars and fast women and all the cool gadgets that could save his life or take the lives of others—evil others. Perhaps more than anything else, John wanted to possess the magical, priceless, ever-so-grown-up, black, gunmetal cigarette case that held 50 of James Bond's special Balkan and Turkish Moreland cigarettes. He searched for years without success for that cigarette case, although he did not smoke.

While he was still 13, John picked up the phone and called the British Secret Service, the SIS, the Secret Intelligence Service, and asked them how to best prepare to become a spy. He made many, many calls before reaching a human being who could answer his question. The woman on the other end of the phone, a spy John thought, immediately referred him to the CIA. He was impressed with how quickly she could tell he was an American just by talking to him. John's father was impressed by the large phone bill.

Only again after many calls, was John able to get through to a live person at the CIA who told him that life at the CIA was not what he imagined it to be, but she did say that they were always looking for people with good language skills. John had very poor language skills. No aptitude for languages whatsoever. He still cannot speak a coherent sentence of Spanish after years of formal training other than a few memorized phrases from his high-school Spanish recitations, phrases that will help him find a library should he run into a woman named Isabel in Guadalajara or help him order meatballs (albóndigas) from a waiter named Carlos in Oaxaca. John holds onto English for dear life.

Disappointed by a crushed dream, John went on a search, far and wide, for the meaning of life, although he did not leave the Berkeley, California area. It was more of an internal search. He decided to dedicate his life to finding God, and he pursued a path after college that led him to a graduate theological seminary. But he was too promiscuous in his religious tastes, feeling that all religions were right and all religions were wrong, so he was deemed unfit for ordainment.

John became a clinical social worker and a psychologist and worked in an emergency room because he wanted a life of excitement and danger, like James Bond's life, and a life focused on the search for meaning, like Siddhartha's life. He did not regret one day in his 43 years working for Psychiatric Emergency Services at UC Davis Medical Center, although he never drove a fast car, was generally ignored by sexy women, and never did find the meaning of life.

While he failed to become a super spy, he was surrounded by a new generation of super social workers and super psychologists who gracefully juggled psychiatric assessments in one hand and death notifications in the other, while child abuse, elder abuse, and domestic violence assessments hung in the air. He was always proud to be part of the clinical team.

Upon his retirement, John did locate and buy himself a black gunmetal cigarette case, although he does not smoke.

— Bond, James Bond

AUTHORS NOTE

This book is nonfiction, which is to say it is an accurate reflection of the life I lived, the patients I saw, and the staff with whom I worked at UC Davis Medical Center. I have, however, changed the names of, as well as some facts and features about, all the patients to protect their confidentiality, and I have also changed the names of some fellow professionals to reduce their irritation with me should they read this book.

—Farrell, John Farrell

Superman

He stood on the bank of the Sacramento River considering his options, which were bleak, and their consequences, which were deadly. He could keep on running, but he had run for miles and they still surrounded him: four men on the deck of the Mexican restaurant looking down on him, with margaritas in one hand and guns in the other, two or three men hidden in heavy vegetation on the riverbank, guns drawn taking aim at him, and a woman standing on a houseboat signaling to the men. He could dive into the river and swim for the other side, but the night was dark and moonless, the water cold, the river swift, and the distance far. They would cut him down before he took his first stroke. He could fight. He had a knife but they had guns. He could not see them well and they undoubtedly had night scopes. He was one man and they were many, but he did have one advantage: they were motivated killers, yes, but he was the one lit on fire, every cell of his body adrenalized, communicating, each cell fed from a potent well of chemical divinity.

He seized his advantage and dove into the river. His clothes were heavy, his arms immobile, and his legs were dragging. One shoe fell off, he swallowed water, and he sank to the bottom, but he was able to stand up as his feet sank slowly into the murky, muddy bottom of the river. He could see his enemies closing in on him, rushing to the river bank, guns drawn. His supercharged alertness made him risk death before capture: he ripped off his heavy black coat, fought off the suction of his feet in the mud, kicked off his other shoe, and waded out slowly toward the middle of the river. His skin was so cold that it stung and his body was heavy from his wet shirt and pants, but the heavy clothes were not his immediate problem.

The real worry was his breathing; he could not inhale because his chest was frozen and would not expand. As if on automatic, his body did make progress floating across to the other side of the river. It may have been the rapid current or possibly his forced, feeble attempt at swimming, his arms flailing about and his legs jerking, kicking, and flopping, that accounted for some movement toward the safe side of the river. He was not swimming, but he was not sinking either; he was afloat and moving.

When he came close to the other side, when he had no fight left, almost no life in his body, he stared up at the safe riverbank, hopeful, proud, triumphant, and very angry—angry that he was being persecuted, hunted down, violated, tortured, and almost murdered. He was angry about the listening device that had been implanted in his brain, hearing his every thought, angry about his food being poisoned, his house being gassed, his body being abused during his sleep, and angry that his family would be raped and murdered, if they had not been already.

With one more lunge of his arms and a kick with his legs he would be safe and alive, at least for this moment in time. But as he came closer to his intended escape route, the safe side of the river, he could see more of them standing on that shore, men in camouflage suits with rifles and spearguns. They would have no mercy and no intention of taking him prisoner. His only option now was to die and he did not want to die with the arrow from a speargun in his back. He floated back out toward the middle of the river so he could drown in peace. He could feel himself sinking below the deep, dark, cold surface of the water, and the last thing he remembered was a boat rushing toward him.

. . . .

When he awoke he found himself vomiting up blood, water, and something like green goo. He was placed on a gurney by people who appeared to be firemen, or so their uniforms indicated. The organization that hunted him was clever, however. They were not always obvious, like in the movies, tall muscular men in black suits with mirrored sunglasses driving big black Buicks, although sometimes they were exactly that. They could be and had been just about anybody: men with FBI jackets, police with SWAT team coats, soldiers with full body armor, even a small girl on a bicycle outside his bedroom window. They could be anywhere: outside his house, in

2

stores where he shopped and restaurants where he ate, in his bathroom, and in his bedroom watching him as he slept, which he could no longer safely do. There was no lock, no wall, no window, no weapon that kept them out. The gases in his house, the fumes, the metallic toxic taste in his mouth, the constant voices planted in his head, echoing outside his head; he could feel their persecution even when he could not see them. Their cruelty was relentless and unwarranted. He did not know what he had done, what he knew, or what he possessed that was of value to them, but they were willing to kill him, and his family and friends, to complete their mission. He was not close to his sister or his father, but he did not wish them dead, nor did he wish to bring this horrific tragedy down upon them.

As he lay on that gurney he cried, but it took only one moment for those tears to turn to rage, only an instant for him to spring from the gurney, sprint upstream, uphill, back to the Mexican restaurant, race through the dining room, escape to the balcony, and fly over the balcony guardrail onto the concrete parking lot below.

. . . .

This time, upon awakening, he was restrained to a gurney and was being rushed in a Sacramento Fire Department ambulance to the Emergency Department at the University of California, Davis, Medical Center, one of the largest trauma centers in California, located in the heart of the city of Sacramento. The ambulance was followed by Sacramento Police Department officers who would place an involuntary psychiatric hold, a 5150, on this frightened, wild man for being a danger to himself and gravely disabled.

The patient was observed by paramedics to have a golf-ball size swelling to the right side of his forehead, and a very bad attitude. He pulled frantically at his restraint belt, rolled vigorously to the left and right on his transfer gurney, screamed, "Help, murder!" to no one who could possibly assist him, and, in helpless rage, spat at the paramedics. In all fields of medicine, at every point of medical rescue and intervention, nobody likes a spitter.

He arrived in the ambulance bay in four-point restraints, both arms and legs tied to the paramedics' transfer board, a restraint belt around his waist, and a spit mask over his head, but he had fight left in him, plenty of it, enough to warrant a medical order for rounds of Haldol and Ativan for comfort and safety—his and that of the medical staff.

A typical trauma evaluation—an assessment of a patient from a motor vehicle collision, for example—is a careful, methodical, and thorough exam best performed on a calm and cooperative patient. It is made more difficult by a patient's pain and fear, and by the seeming chaos of so many medical people surrounding a patient: trauma doctors, emergency attendings, residents, medical students, X-ray technicians, medical technicians, social workers, nurses, highway patrol. The UC Davis Medical Center is a teaching hospital and it has a passion and promise to teach and heal; it says so in its motto. There are plenty of students of every kind in the treatment room, and it is a party, a bad party for the patient. But in the case of a volatile, combative, confused patient—well, then nobody is having fun.

Before patients are moved from a paramedic's hard transfer board to the larger, softer, hospital gurney, their restraints must be released from the board and then retied to the hospital gurney, and this transfer can provoke more violence from patients and more need for their sedation. Predictably, this patient erupted again during the untying and retying and needed more medication.

When a patient's identity is unknown to the Emergency Department staff, he or she is registered as a Doe, like John Doe, so that treatment can begin and medical information can be tracked. This patient was assigned the name, Walter Doe, and upon entry into the ED, he was agitated and fighting for his life. With the added calming help of medications, the techs, nurses, and doctors were able to cut off his wet, muddy, soiled, urine-soaked clothes as they re-belted lap belts and tied his punching, kicking hands and feet to the hospital gurney.

The medical staff listened to the paramedic's report, a report similar to many patient reports in the past—psychosis, paranoia,

4

agitation, combativeness, tachycardia, probable methamphetamine intoxication—but with the added complication of a head injury. The patient possessed a wallet with some ID, thank God, a cellphone that was wet and inoperable, and a knife. After everything useful from his wallet was xeroxed, his possessions— excluding his cut-up clothes that were trashed, and a ziploc bag of suspicious little crystal rocks, possibly methamphetamine, that was destroyed—were placed and locked in patient storage.

The trauma team does not miss any injury, that is their job. With the fall this patient had suffered, they would check head to toe— everywhere. It was when they stuck a finger up Walter Doe's butt that he rose from his heavily medicated fog and screamed piercingly and repeatedly, "Get out of my asshole." His words were clearly enunciated and perfectly heard well down the hallway, into the waiting room, where registered patients, many of whom had already waited many hours to have their non-life-threatening problems addressed, must have wondered if the Kaiser ED, just a few miles away, or Dignity Health, a walkable distance away, might be a better choice for them. The actual hallway patients, those who had already logged in many, many hours of waiting and were now seemingly abandoned to the hallway, one step further in line than the waiting room patients, but not yet in a treatment room, must have been tightening their buttocks just a little bit, because they were committed; there was no turning back for them.

Walter Doe presented a complicated yet common treatment dilemma. Since he had a large knot on his forehead, and he was confused and combative as someone with a head injury might be, and since he was a patient with a witnessed fall, he needed a CAT scan of his head. A head CT requires a calm, cooperative patient, or an unconscious one, so Walter Doe was medicated to the point of CT readiness, to near or full unconsciousness, and then intubated to protect his airway. His state of unconsciousness made it quick and simple for medical staff to slide a catheter up his urethra, an uneasy procedure for even the most cooperative, conscious man, and to more effectively place and secure his IVs.

5

The picture on his driver's license confirmed who he was: Tony Rootlieb, a 34-year-old white male who had long, unkempt, brown hair, possibly self-cut with the aid of a bad mirror, and a powerful build, 200 pounds on a 6 ft 2 in frame. I was surprised that with his size, his power, and his rage, he had not earned himself a tasing by the police. Some officer—or many—had been merciful in his restraint of Mr. Rootlieb, however, this patient had knocked himself out from the fall, so he was helpful to them.

When Mr. Rootlieb was first presented by paramedics to staff in the ED, I introduced myself to the police officers who had followed the patient to the hospital: John Farrell, Psychiatric Emergency Services. I told them I would be accepting their psychiatric hold and completing the psychiatric assessment. The police described to me a man they had received a dozen calls on throughout the night. He had been sprinting through people's yards, hopping over their fences, hiding in their bushes, gardens, and trash cans, dodging cars in traffic, and finally, irrationally if not suicidally, jumping into the Sacramento River with an attempt to swim to the other side. "And then this idiot tried to swim back," they said. "We had to pull his ass out of the river only to have him pop back to life, barrel through a restaurant, and dive off a balcony. "He's all yours," one of the officers said with relief, but added, "Oh, he had a knife which we gave to one of the nurses, and he even tried to camouflage himself by slapping mud on his face. In his mind he was in the middle of a combat zone."

This patient was lucky that he was not under arrest, since so many laws had been broken, not the least of which may have been illegal drug use, but a man like this is not welcome at the main jail where a modicum of decent, controlled behavior is expected. A patient like this presents a monumental management problem even for the most structured setting in the world: a jail. This is why the officers happily said, "He's all yours." Given the choice, I do hope that when I go berserk and light up a neighborhood with terrorizing, bad behavior, I will be taken to a hospital on a 5150 and not to jail. Not to my own hospital, mind you, not UC Davis Medical Center. No, I would rather go to jail. I will take confinement and prosecution over embarrassment and humiliation every time.

I did not see Mr. Rootlieb that day, or most of the next day. He was asleep—deeply so. But he had been a patient at the Medical Center a number of times before, and I was able to research his case on our electronic medical records, our EMR. His records contained emergency contact numbers for his sister, Peggy, and his father, George. In the past he had been treated for numerous fights resulting in many injuries dating back to his late teens and early 20s.

I called Peggy first and then George and explained the circumstances and my urgent need for information. When I am trying to determine the appropriateness of a psychiatric hold, the potential risk of death for the patient or the possible risk of harm to someone else, I do not have to give a damn about confidentiality; the law backs me up on that, giving me permission to do whatever I need to do in the person's and public's best interest. I can ask anyone for any information I need, and I can give out any information if that will yield additional useful history. In Mr. Rootlieb's case, I was making a decision where his life or other lives were at stake, and a decision that could possibly strip Mr. Rootlieb of his rights and freedom, if not his dignity and self-respect, for up to 72 hours, so I wanted to talk to Peggy and George before I made that decision.

. . . .

George was an alcoholic, 12 years, four months, and three days sober, he said, repeatedly. Peggy was living with George, as was her eight-year-old son. Peggy was separated from her husband who was also an alcoholic, three months, five days sober, exactly the amount of time he had spent in jail so far after his most recent assault on Peggy. Peggy's husband beat her regularly and unpredictably, but his drinking was regular and very predictable. When he was a free man he was tolerable sober, but he was rarely sober. His violence was coming close to their son, so Peggy had seized a rare moment of freedom and moved the two of them into her father's house the day her husband was cuffed and booked into jail. Peggy told me she would never return to this evil man. Her father told me she had said that many times before.

Peggy had lived too long with violence as an adult, but she had been no stranger to violence as a child either. As the older sister, Peggy witnessed her father beating Tony when Tony was little, and she witnessed Tony beating her father when Tony was big. She was the ineffective referee between the two and was often hit in the process. Peggy said that she was six years old and Tony was two when their mother died after a seizure. George reported that his wife was a lifelong drug and alcohol abuser who died of a drug overdose, leaving George to raise the children, work in a warehouse, fix the meals, and get the kids to school by himself. He had done this for all of his children's lives, with the help of alcohol.

"I did the best I could," he said several times, but it was evident that Peggy felt it was not good enough. Sometimes forgiving and generous children, when they become adults, come to the conclusion that their parents should be forgiven for all the bad times because their parents "did the best they could," but when the bar is set so low, it makes you wonder if they couldn't have done a little better.

George was trying to make amends to his adult children by his sobriety and support, and both Peggy and George had the desire to help Tony, but they were also afraid of him. Sometimes Tony showed up at the house in a rage, completely irrational, accusing Peggy and George of many things, bizarre things: conspiracy plots, murder attempts, weird stories of being followed and harassed. Other times he frantically came over to warn them to run for their lives because they were in serious danger. They knew he was a drug addict and that he ate, smoked, and shot up all kinds of drugs, and they were aware he was crazy, paranoid, and sometimes suicidal when he was on drugs or off of them. A month prior to this forced hospital visit Tony was on George's doorstep crying uncontrollably, begging God for the courage to kill himself. Occasionally, George

8

and Peggy would get an urgent call from him from another state where he had fled for his life.

Episodically, he had been in jails and in hospitals, but Peggy complained that they never kept him, they never gave him help, they always let him go. Peggy described a long and discouraging history of her begging hospitals to put him away for a long time and to make sure he came out better. "He needs to be locked up, maybe for good. He's going to kill someone and it will be your fault," she said to me. "He won't get help for himself, and he can fool you into thinking he does not need help." He was not really fooling anybody today; he clearly needed help. Her tone was one of frustration and anger as she said to me, "Why don't you people ever do anything?"

Tony's long run with drugs started in middle school with marijuana and alcohol. Peggy and her father never saw any signs of problems because all kids used marijuana and alcohol, including Peggy, and so did their father. From the age of 16, Tony stopped going to high school and started using drugs more seriously and more frequently. Peggy said he quit high school and turned mean and crazy. Once he discovered methamphetamine, it became his drug of choice. He did not use anything else, did not need to. He lived on his own, on the streets, or with fast-made friends, panhandling, stealing, and occasionally picking up temporary jobs. Sometimes the family would not hear from him for a year or two, and Peggy admitted that she did not miss him and neither did his father. Those were the rare times of family peace. They did care about Tony, but they could not have him in George's house, not with an eight-year-old boy living there. They thought Tony was dangerous, on drugs or off.

. . . .

Methamphetamine is no enemy to job security in the mental health field. I could say that methamphetamine has given me a job— not the selling of it, the cooking of it, or the using of it, but the attempted treatment of those who do use it. The staff of our Psychiatric Emergency Services will argue that Sacramento is the

9

methamphetamine capital of the world, although other cities are competing enthusiastically for and claiming that title. But Sacramento is a formidable contender, and I believe meth puts food on my table. It accounts for hundreds of psychiatric evaluations in our ED every year, all by itself, and it also forces instability onto schizophrenic, depressed, and bipolar patients, involuntarily landing them in emergency rooms needing urgent psychiatric help. No single drug, prescribed or illegal, is so potent a precipitant of psychiatric crises. Alcoholics can raise their hands here and ask the question, "What about me?", but meth users are the clear winners.

Ask patients why they use methamphetamine and they will tell you: because it works. Ask them why they discontinued their prescribed psychiatric medications and they will also tell you: because they do not work. The truth is that drugs work in different ways and prescribed medications are in there for the long run, not the short high. Methamphetamine, however, catapults the powerless into power; it makes the weak strong, the depressed euphoric, the exhausted tireless, the frightened fearless, the confused clear, the nervous confident, the shy social, the bored excited, and the sick well. One methamphetamine user told me that the drug raised him from the dead every day. What other medication can do that? And if he smoked the more potent crystal methamphetamine—glass, also called ice—he could "stay alive" all day long.

Methamphetamine is plentiful on the streets, is cheap, has immediate effects, and is intensely pleasurable. The user can eat it, snort it, smoke it, or inject it. Who doesn't need an occasional pick-me-up? But if you dance with the devil you will feel the fires of hell. You will get burned and you will have scars. Take methamphetamine long enough and the devotee starts seeing things, hearing things, smelling things—not pretty things. Grotesque bugs, more horrific than any nightmare can conjure up, start crawling through the skin, coming out of the eyes, ears, ass, vagina, penis, everywhere. Snakes eat out internal organs, worms travel freely throughout the body. Some patients collect these perceived parasites, which are tiny dug-out pieces of their own skin, in jars so they can prove their point to skeptical doctors who, of course, know that methamphetamine is the cause and the problem. Skin is destroyed by the user's constant picking, gums are diseased, teeth are brittle, broken, and falling out. The toothless look is a diagnostic clue for the beginning therapist because those big, visible, front teeth often go first. After a while there is a steady march toward dementia, and the patient progresses to an involuntary imitation of the walking dead—a zombie in mind, body, and soul.

Psychosis takes a firm grip on the meth patient and rational thought becomes a thing of the past. Some of these lost souls are paranoid people with fearful thoughts of a horrible death at the hands of sadistic strangers who hunt them down for reasons they do not understand. Sometimes meth addicts kill themselves to end their suffering, but others defend themselves and attack the perceived attackers. Mainly they land in jails or hospitals with a fantastic story of persecution and torture that, even to them, seems unbelievable. And it is true: no one will ever believe them. But the kind therapist will at least acknowledge the hellish world through which they travel because the paranoid delusions are very real to the addict.

I recognize that some people can occasionally, socially smoke crystal meth, then leave it alone for a while. Good for them. But the rush, the euphoria of crystal meth, is so intense that the craving to return to the experience is intense also, even after one trial, and tolerance builds quickly. For some, one time use can be a step off a cliff. I interviewed a wealthy, young, new mother on the newborn inpatient unit whose tox screen indicated that she and her newborn baby were positive for methamphetamine. This finding constituted a mandatory report by me to Child Protective Services, CPS.

The mother pleaded with me not to tell CPS or anyone else and said that she was a one-time user overwhelmed by family visits during this last month of her pregnancy. She was required to entertain many people and was exhausted, so she needed a little help, a lift. Surely I could understand that. But it was not for me to understand, it was for CPS to understand, and they are not very understanding about methamphetamine use in pregnant women. She

11

promised me that she had never used methamphetamine before and she would never use it again. That promise had been heard by CPS workers many times.

Imagine the family's surprise when this pregnant woman went into labor a month early, and imagine their excitement with the birth of a first grandchild, a healthy baby girl, and imagine the confusion when that baby was handed over from the hospital staff to a CPS worker, and then to a temporary foster-care mother. While every agency varies in capabilities, and every worker in every agency adds a unique plus or minus to that service, I would say, on the whole, that CPS in Sacramento does a very good job. Ultimately, they are invested in a new mother having custody of her new baby, and they will go to great lengths to make that happen.

Nobody loves a child like the mother does, especially not a temporary foster mother. But it was to a temporary foster mother that this new mother's child was given. To me, the foster mother looked like a 1950s roller-derby queen with, literally, a pack of cigarettes rolled into her t-shirt, and that foster mother taking care of that baby for very long seemed like a bad decision. The right decision was to place the child in the very short-term custody of CPS while the mother went through a mandatory drug treatment program which included unannounced visits from a CPS worker and unannounced urine tests to determine her drug use, and then quickly return the child to the anxious mother. All turned out well for this family, but life was never the same. The one thing I took away from that incident was that CPS needed a larger pool of foster mothers.

It is not ordinarily the one-time users who become psychotic, it is the long-time users, the injecting users, the crystal meth users, the committed users. They can be psychotic during intoxication, for hours or days after intoxication, and even for months after intoxication. It was evident to all staff in the ED that it was the incessant use of crystal meth that brought Mr. Rootlieb to our emergency room.

. . . .

12

Before I entered Mr. Rootlieb's room to assess him, some 16 unconscious and semi-conscious hours after he arrived, I was told by his nurse that the reward she received for untying his hand restraints was that he extubated himself, actually pulled the tubing to his lungs right out of his mouth, yanked the catheter tube out from his penis, and ripped out his IVs. Some of that must have hurt. She last entered his room, his tiny condominium-like private ED home, to find it splattered with his blood and urine, and to find him naked, with his finger up his rectum, accusing her and the doctors of planting a recording device up his ass.

I needed no more information nor any further graphic imagery to conclude he was still intoxicated on meth and overtly psychotic. Law enforcement was called again to re-restrain and re-medicate him. He met police with significant resistance, mainly because he did not believe they were real law enforcement, but also because he was angry about his sore throat, his painful penis, and his violated asshole. When I entered the room he was full-steam-ahead delusional and fighting off as best he could the newly administered medications: more Haldol and Ativan.

His blood pressure was high and his heart rate was racing, now more out of agitation and paranoia than the medical effects of methamphetamine, and his eyes darted about the room, suspicious of all its contents. His whole body was wet with sweat. Our UC Davis Police told me directly and clearly that they were tired of standing by to subdue and restrain this strong, naked, sweating, bloody, urine-soaked, crazy man. On another day, off methamphetamines and all cleaned up, Mr. Rootlieb might have looked like a handsome, clean-cut, muscular firefighter, but today was not that day. Today, he was the type of patient that made UC Davis police officers engage in long conversations about early retirement and "golden hand-shakes."

Everybody involved was frustrated with caring for this patient. In response to the patient screaming at his nurse, "You tried to kill me, you bitch," the nurse replied, "No, they don't just let us do whatever we want to here." High-maintenance patients bring out the

13

worst in all of us, and I do think, not to excuse lapses in professional behavior, that many nurses going into emergency medical care—care that saves lives—do not anticipate that emergency rooms are full of poorly-behaved, combative patients. But they are. Many counties have inadequately-funded mental health services offering no emergency psychiatric services and few beds in psychiatric hospitals. That leaves the two default services, jails and emergency rooms, for psychiatric patients needing emergency care, a guarantee of poor treatment in the wrong settings.

Mr. Rootlieb was in no mood to converse with me, he was eager to attack. He stared at my badge, repeated my name as if to remember it, and mulled over the letters Ph.D. and L.C.S.W. I introduced myself, John Farrell, said I had a doctorate in psychology and I was a licensed clinical social worker. I could have said anything, "I'm a zoologist"; it was not relevant or believable to him.

"You look like a fucking homeless man," were his first words to me. I think he was right about that. I attended UC Berkeley from 1966 to 1970, the active years, and like many of us from that era and location, I am stuck in a time warp of longish hair, casual clothes, and an unassuming, unimpressive presence. As a group, we are not believable as people of power, influence, and success, as well-dressed people who drive luxury cars are. Our hands are tied by an unspoken, long-ago promise to avoid the appearance of prosperity, and to change the world, possibly for the better, and so we are comically ill-prepared to be impressive. If you put us in a suit and tie we look like we are going to a costume party. At first glance, and second also, it would appear foolish to hand over large responsibilities to us. But we like to surprise people by our come-from-behind qualities, by starting from a place of low expectations and shooting up to mediocrity.

So, the fucking homeless man, me, who stood before this patient was a tall, thin, moderately long-haired, casually dressed, bearded, 1960s-looking man lost in a past decade. I could see Mr. Rootlieb's point, and the points of many observant patients who

14

came before him.

I explained to Mr. Rootlieb that he was on a psychiatric hold, a 5150, because it was determined by officers of the Sacramento Police Department that he was a danger to himself and gravely disabled. I said it was a hospital hold, not a criminal hold, meant to help him not harm him, meant to treat him not confine him. This explanation fell on deaf ears because Mr. Rootlieb was busy staring piercingly, with those big, dilated pupils, at all the strange, sharp, tubular, electronic, computerized equipment in the room. In his mind it was all there to poke, prod, puncture, torture, and kill him, or it was meant for the simple amusement of all these people pretending to be doctors and nurses in this fake hospital. Mr. Rootlieb knew, in his hyper-lucid state that this was no hospital; this was the mother ship, the home base of the organization, home to all the people who had brought agony to him and his family for so many years.

He told me that he was the winner, not me, because he was finally going to find peace, finally going to be allowed to die, but he did express sadness that we would hunt down his family. It was his strong chemicals that brought him to this hospital, and now it was our strong chemicals that induced his deep sleep. I watched him until he could not keep his eyes open or utter another word. The 5150 would remain in place, and I would see him the next day, which would be two days after his arrival, and counting.

. . . .

About 40 hours after he was brought to the ED, Mr. Rootlieb was awake, calm, unrestrained, eating lunch, and declared to be medically cleared, that is, cleared of all medical problems that would prevent his medical discharge or his transfer to an inpatient psychiatric hospital. The UCD Medical Center does not have a psychiatric inpatient unit; there are four in Sacramento, three private hospitals and one county facility. They are all obligated to take transfers from the many emergency rooms in Sacramento, but they do pick and choose patients based on many things, mainly available space, but also nurse staffing ratios, need for patient seclusion rooms, patient agitation levels, and plain old human preference. Some patients are more desirable than others; they may be more treatable, motivated, cooperative, docile, already familiar to the hospital staff, or rich with insurance. An uninsured, angry, unmotivated, uncooperative, drug-abusing patient, with no desire to change and no insight about the need to change, is not the first patient an intake worker at a psychiatric hospital is likely to pick from the pile. The pile is often big and the choices varied. A patient like Mr. Rootlieb is not likely to be picked up by anyone as a first-round choice.

There are many other emergency departments in the Sutter, Dignity, and Kaiser hospitals in Sacramento, and all have their own lists of psychiatric patients waiting to be placed into psychiatric hospitals. Each emergency department is staffed with round-the-clock, competitive discharge planners and social workers trying to sell their psychiatric patients to the psychiatric hospitals. Mr. Rootlieb would be a hard sell.

. . . .

"Remember me, I'm the homeless guy," I said to Mr. Rootlieb. "Sorry about the last 40 hours. I know they've been rough and confusing for you. I am here to figure out, with your help, what happens next."

"You get my clothes and I walk out of here. That's what happens next," he said.

"Good start. Let's talk about that." I said, as I sat down in one of those little round whirling chairs that do not make sense anywhere but in a hospital. "I have to make sure that you are OK before you leave."

Mr. Rootlieb was not OK. His eyes still darted from one piece of medical equipment to another, he periodically jerked his head around, certain there was someone in back of him, and he anxiously tried to control the automatic tics and reflexive movements of his face and body. There was some progress, some slow march toward sanity, and he was beginning to believe that he was in a real hospital

16

on a psychiatric hold, partly because he had faced this same circumstance before, an unwanted 5150, and partly because the methamphetamine was losing its tight grip on him.

"I don't have anything to say to you. I don't need to be here and you have no right to keep me here. I am going to leave right now."

His anger was returning like an old friend, ready to defend him. I was the enemy, but not more so than anyone else who participated in his treatment. I had one shot to help him, one shot, no mistakes. I would likely never see him again after today or so I hoped, and there was only one way to successfully ensure that—help him. The question does come up, for all of us working in an emergency department doing psychiatric assessments, about how much you can help someone in a single visit. I know people who have gone through six years of psychoanalysis, four sessions a week on the couch, and they do not seem to be much better to me—maybe a little worse. What can I do in a single visit?

. . . .

One day I was taking a walk in San Francisco—I am a long walker, both a city walker and a nature hiker—and a San Francisco police officer yelled at me, me specifically, singling me out from the crowd of strangers with whom I was standing. "Get back on the sidewalk, stupid. Cars are coming," the officer said to me, holding back no volume. I was standing just one step off the curb waiting for the light to change so I could cross the street when the officer yelled at me, and then, in my mind, lunged at me to push me back up onto the sidewalk. Even though I was not pushed or touched, I may have let out a subtle yelp before tripping on the sidewalk in back of me. My fear, I think, was justified. She was really frightening.

For the next hour or so I was filled with ugly thoughts: I hate San Francisco, the streets are dirty, the people mean, the crowds intense, cars honking, jackhammers assaulting my ears, people pushing, sun half-hidden by clouds, cold winds. Not for me.

17

Sacramento, country living, is my kind of town.

Not to excuse the police officer, because it should not make a difference, but I was more than my raggedy-looking self that day. My hair was windblown, maybe wild, and there was quite a bit of it, my clothes patched, or should have been, but they were comfortable and meant for hiking. I was worn out and hungry, walking since dawn, which is when I like to start my hikes. Perhaps, in the officer's mind, I was homeless, an alcoholic or a drug addict, or mentally ill, or just plain stupid. To an untrained eye, I could have been all those things.

A couple of hours after this incident, I was walking near Union Square, looking no better, and I nearly walked into a well-dressed man, a waiter standing outside his café, handing out sample waffles. He asked me in the most pleasant and inviting tone if I would like a waffle. I may have eaten that waffle quickly and with enthusiasm, as I had walked a long way with no sustenance. This man held my shoulders with both hands and said, "Wait right here. I'll be right back."

He brought me a large—not a sample—chocolate waffle on a paper plate with a plastic fork, a little container of maple syrup, and a bit of whipped cream on the side. He said to me, "I think you're going to like this. The chocolate waffle is my favorite." And then he changed my life in small measure, or gave me the opportunity to change it myself; he looked at me eye-to-eye, heart-to-heart, and said, "I wish you well, brother."

One shot, no mistakes, and this man made me see the world of San Francisco differently that day. The people of San Francisco were so friendly, so generous, so lively and happy. The architecture was beautiful, the vistas of the Bay magnificent, the sun peeking through the clouds welcoming me with its warmth. So great to be alive in the loveliest city in the world.

Can one person, on one day, with a single encounter, make a difference? Well, I know this: on one day, in a brief encounter, with few words spoken, a man with a waffle saw something of value in me. He looked me straight in the eyes and into my heart and said, I see beauty in you.

....

One shot, no mistakes, a chance to motivate Mr. Rootlieb to make a life change.

"If I don't get my fucking clothes right now, I am suing this hospital. Get me a god damn phone. I'm calling my lawyer."

Perhaps it was only a small chance to change Mr. Rootlieb's life. Methamphetamine addiction packs a punch and the urge to get back to crystal meth is particularly ferocious. Timing is everything. Mr. Rootlieb had to be ready to walk across a bridge, all the way to the other side, he needed to accept the fact that he had a serious, uncontrollable problem, he had to ask for help sincerely, urgently, and he had to knock on heavy doors and push through them to get the help he needed. It was also critical for him to see with great clarity the alternative to treatment: death or worse. For those people who are ready to make a change, to leap into open space, I want to encourage that bold step. For everyone else, for those not ready, for those stuck on the familiar, pathological, self-destructive spot on which they stand, off of which they will not move, I will not be of much help, even with maximum effort.

Sometimes the timing is right. I take my best shot, I hit the target, and I help someone move forward. One-shot therapy, crisis therapy, is more active, involved, supportive as well as confrontational, persuasive, and urgent than regular outpatient psychotherapy. As a crisis therapist I play both the good cop and the bad cop, the good and bad parent, the caring, supportive therapist, and the confrontational bully. Whatever I can do, I do, whatever works, I employ.

I start out by encouraging the horse to find the water by himself. If he can't find it I put him in the vicinity of the water. If need be I lead him directly to the water, and if I have to I ladle the damn water up to the horse's mouth. However, it is hard to engage someone who will not engage. I do have some power, some authority, and I do try to maximize my leverage to provoke change.

I can keep this patient on a 5150 and thus prevent him from leaving the hospital, and, in spite of his legal threats to the contrary, I can place Mr. Rootlieb into a psychiatric hospital against his will. I can take away many of his rights and freedoms if he is acting in his worst interests, likely to cause harm to himself, and I can be a roadblock between him and his urgent, compelling need to get back to crystal meth. I can outlast him until he realizes that it is in his best interest to talk to me. Waiting him out would take patience on my part because he was still threatening me with lawsuits, telling me that I would never work again, that I would be disbarred, which I think is a penalty for lawyers, not psychologists, and that I would be humiliated and thrown to the wolves, which I think is a penalty for medieval psychologists.

Some patients will start the negotiation process for leaving the hospital with a threat, often a litigious threat: if you don't drop the psychiatric hold, I am going to sue you. Sober and clever patients become aware of the futility of their threats early in the interview, so they are left with begging, bargaining, and persuading, all steps in the right direction. "I didn't mean to do this, you misunderstand, I will never do this again, I was drunk, I don't even remember saying I was suicidal, I am fine now, safe to go home."

Some people are fine when they say they are. Many people have said they were suicidal when heavily intoxicated, but they are not suicidal when they are sober. They were "drunkacidal," not the same thing as suicidal. I let these people go. I do not enjoy placing someone on a psychiatric hold who sees no value in it. I release psychiatric holds on many people when they fall down badly but have the motivation or the resources to get back up: the impulsive young woman who regrets swallowing pills after a fight with her boyfriend, a boyfriend who is now snuggling up to her, supportively but uncomfortably, on her small gurney in the ED hallway, the schizophrenic patient who claims his voices are getting worse, but who is really asking me to help him change his board and care facility, the angry adolescent who breaks his mother's best china and cuts himself in the process. Many problems, most problems, that

20

present in an ED can be resolved short of psychiatric hospitalization.

I let most people go, especially if they are in treatment, willing to stay in treatment, and have the support of their family and their mental health community. I want patients to legitimately meet the criteria of danger to self, danger to others, or gravely disabled before I place them or keep them on a psychiatric hold. It is understandable that the public can be frustrated and confused by the lack of consistency and reliability of the mental health professionals who place or choose not to place psychiatric holds on patients, because there is no absolute right or wrong in this decision. It is a judgment call and no two human beings have the same judgment. My decision may not be my colleague's decision.

It took an hour of Mr. Rootlieb shooting high-volume, threatening, insulting, vulgar, and patronizing arrows at me, and peppering me with impressively searing sarcasm, for him to understand that I would not get his clothes and he was not leaving the hospital, not yet. We were both worn out so I took a break and came back later to talk with him. In the new go-round I was prepared to talk with him rather than have him talk at me.

I summarized for him the entire story that the paramedics and police had told me: he was running from no one, senselessly jumping fences, sprinting through traffic, darting in and out of bushes along the Sacramento River, ultimately diving into the river, swimming across the river, and nearly drowning while attempting to swim back. That was not the end of it. He jumped off a restaurant balcony, hit his head on the concrete below, knocked himself out, came to, fought with paramedics, resisted the police, attacked the medical staff, and argued with me for a long, long time. He had said there was a listening device planted in his head, and that we stuck another listening device up his ass. As he was in and out of consciousness he talked about all sorts of dangerous people who were hunting him down to torture him and to kill his family.

Now this is a fantastic story, I told him, and one he would think I had never heard before, but I had heard many versions of this

21

story before, and always by people who used methamphetamine. I told him, and I was sure he was aware of this, that methamphetamine can make its user crazy, paranoid crazy, and that methamphetamine made him crazy.

"I don't fuck with meth!" he said.

"I have your tox screen. You are positive for meth. You do fuck with meth."

"Then somebody poisoned me," he said.

"You poisoned you," I said. "After you get crazy on meth once, it is a warning to you. Methamphetamine is poison to you and you will get crazy every time you use it. You may kill somebody, you may kill yourself. You will either die slow and ugly or you will die swiftly like the river you chose to drown in."

He stopped talking for a while and so did I, and then he asked me his first reasonable question: "Is my family safe?"

I told him that his family was fine, that I had talked to his father and his sister and they wanted him to get help. In fact, they wanted him to get help in a long-term, locked facility but I did not tell him that. I told him that they both wanted to visit him at the hospital, and I asked him if he wanted to see them. He said no, under no circumstances did he want to see his family.

Mr. Rootlieb did not feel he had any problem with drugs of any kind, and he emphatically stated that he did not want my help. He repeatedly reverted back to his statement that I could not legally keep him there and that I had to let him go. He was not about to cross a bridge into treatment that day. The same bridge would be there the next day, but I did not think that Mr. Rootlieb would notice it. He did have both sedative and antipsychotic medications on board, for what worth they were in dampening his agitation, and he still had some signs of paranoia, perhaps not flagrant signs like before, but symptoms that concerned me. I was aware of the possibility that the medication we gave him would be out of his system soon, and his paranoid symptoms would come rushing back like a second tidal wave. I have known patients with a methamphetamine psychosis return to near-normal states of lucidity only to become dangerously delusional again when their sedative and anti-psychotic medications completely wore off.

So I chose to keep Mr. Rootlieb on the psychiatric hold, and he was accepted by and transferred to a psychiatric facility the next day. His 72-hour hold was about to run out so I wrote another one in what would appear to be a contradiction to the law. Why even have a law that allows for a specific period of 72 hours when a designated mental-health professional can come along and just write another hold for another 72 hours? The loophole here is that an emergency room is not a county-designated 5150 facility. We are technically only holding patients until a psychiatric facility can accept them. But in our county, psychiatric facilities can take three or four or 10 days to accept someone, so we keep writing holds until a patient no longer meets the criteria for a 5150 or until a patient is accepted at a psychiatric hospital.

We try to treat psychiatric patients the best we can in an emergency room setting even though we do not have a structured treatment program for them. An actual psychiatric hospital would offer individual psychotherapy, occupational therapy, group psychotherapy, medication management clinics, educational sessions, and all of the recreational and social activities that accompany a comprehensive and intense treatment program. We do have in the ED a psychiatric consult team, the Psychosomatic Consult Service, made up of psychiatrists, psychiatric residents, and medical students, who have the job of treating psychiatric patients in a non-psychiatric setting. Since the ED setting is limited, the main treatment is reduced to medications and time. That was our treatment gift to Mr. Rootlieb during his stay at our hospital: medications and time. He was transferred to the overcrowded county psychiatric facility where his near-sanity would shine above the very psychotic population that surrounded him, and he would be discharged as soon as he could shake off his paranoia.

So, in extending his psychiatric hold, Mr. Rootlieb had even more reason to be angry with me, and he promised to keep his promise of suing me. I bought Mr. Rootlieb a little more time, two or three days, precious time that he did not volunteer to give, before he would be free again to seek out the only drug that had ever worked for him.

Voodoo Psychiatry

"I have had so many psychotherapists in my life you'd think I was crazy. I'm probably wasting your time."

"Well, this is where I work. I come here every day. I'm more concerned about wasting your time," I said. "Why did you come here?"

"It was my insurance if you want to know the truth. I'm a Davis student and my choices were the health center on campus or here. I've been to the health center, and they weren't helpful at all."

"For a start, you don't seem crazy to me, perhaps a little disappointed," I said.

She proceeded to tell me all of the reasons why she had not come in to be seen, all of the things she did not want to talk about, all of the idiotic advice therapists had given her in her life, and all of the ways therapists had not been helpful to her. If I were in a study that rated the quality of a large number of therapists, I would guess my rank to be in the middle, so I was sure that I would not be the one to climb to the top of this heap of failed therapists. At a future time, when she sat in the next therapist's office, I figured that I would be the discarded idiot, the target of her complaints.

She set some rules for me from the start. She did not want to discuss medications for anxiety, and definitely no medications for depression; one fool thought she was bipolar, another inept therapist thought she had ADHD, and yet another idiot thought she was a borderline personality disorder. The dope now sitting in the therapist's chair across from her thought she was unhappy, that's for sure.

We were not supposed to talk about school, talking about grades was off-limits, no talk about relationships, no talk about her social life, nothing about her promised jobs that never materialized, and nothing, absolutely nothing, "And I give you fair warning," she said, "nothing about my being fat." So, she ruled out work, love, play, school, and personal appearance. That left the weather and the upcoming NFL draft for the San Francisco 49ers. She hated sports. The weather was pretty good that day.

Beyond her distinct rules set forth to me, the good weather was all we established in that first session. I have done less in session one, so I was not defeated.

I worked for 43 years for the University of California, Davis, Medical Center, a teaching hospital, a medical school, and a level-I trauma center, a designation which means it provides high-level trauma care of all types at all times, and that equipment and staff are always on hand to provide that high level of care. It is an excellent hospital, nationally ranked, with specialty care in many fields, serving more than a million people in the Sacramento area and throughout Northern California. In those four-plus decades, I worked every mental health setting that UCDMC offered: inpatient, outpatient, intensive day treatment, aftercare, medication clinics, and, for about 35 of those years, the Psychiatric Emergency Services, also called Crisis Services, in the Emergency Department.

I have worked with young and old patients, couples and groups, the gravely ill and the worried well. I was young when I started and old when I left, eager and proud to work when first hired out of graduate school, and ready to retire when I did.

The outpatient clinic in the Department of Psychiatry was a pleasurable vacation from the intensity and rigors of the Psychiatric Emergency Services, PES, and I worked outpatient for years in between long stints with PES. In the outpatient department I supervised social work interns, psychology interns, medical students, and psychiatric residents, all of them bright, energetic, fun people, and I saw a caseload of patients myself. There were days when I went out for a cappuccino supervision session in the morning, at noon, and in the late afternoon, so eager was I to teach, so fond was I of cappuccino.

Students from the campus of UC Davis, including our own medical students and students from other professional programs, who presented to be seen for psychotherapy in our outpatient clinic, were often seen, out of courtesy, by staff and faculty, not by interns

26

or residents in training. The job of working with students is a therapist's dream; they are young, bright, motivated, and insightful. But my newly assigned patient, Bertha, was a handful, and that is no reference to her weight.

Prior to her leaving our first psychotherapy session, as she was standing and opening the door to leave, I told her to call me John, as most of my patients did, and asked her what I could call her.

"Big Bertha," she said. "Like the golf club."

"Are you a golfer?" I asked.

"No, I'm big."

"I can't call you Big Bertha," I said.

"I'm asking you to."

"No," I said.

"I'm paying you to."

"Not enough," I said.

"Then call me Bertha until you grow some balls."

"OK," I said.

Big Bertha was her self-declared name, which, I would later learn, was her method, employed from high school to the present time, of making fun of herself, her size, before people made fun of her. She made them laugh with her, not at her. She was over 250 pounds and of medium height and she would declare this poundage with the self-created name she gave to everyone before anybody knew anything else about her. In effect, she was saying to new people, "I'm Big Bertha, that's all you need to know." The "anything else" part of her was appealing: her tasteful manner of dress, her stylish, short, dark hair, her sad, intelligent eyes, her graceful, dancer's gait when she walked in and out of my office, and even her angry smile. Bertha was definitely angry about her long, failed history in psychotherapy and, for her, there was no such thing as a good psychotherapist. They talk too much, they talk too little, they give no advice, they give bad advice, they shove medications at you—sometimes one at a time, and sometimes a bunch—they diagnose you poorly and then treat you badly. They pretend to care, but do not care; they are paid to appear to care. While she expressly hated psychotherapy and disparaged therapists, she was dependent on them and kept going to them in spite of her protests. What alternatives did she have when she was so sad and mad and not yet ready to die?

"The name is Big Bertha please," she would repeat to me session after session as she slowly, resentfully, rolled out her life.

In Bertha's words, she was a fat kid, a sad, nervous, and shy kid, an angry kid prone to outbursts and prone to breaking things during outbursts, and a kid who did not like school and could not focus in school. As a fat kid she went through one diet after another, and as a depressed, eruptive, anxious, unfocused kid she was prescribed one or two or three medications after another.

Food was comforting to her and her obese mother knew that. Her mother worried constantly and deeply about her daughter's unhappiness and attempted to cure that unhappiness in the only way she knew how, through special treats, like a trip to the ice cream parlor or to the candy store. Her daughter's sadness was the mother's sadness so they went through treatment together, diet by diet, pill by pill, sometimes prescribed the same meds for the same symptoms. The mother blamed herself for her daughter's symptoms, a bad genetic load, and felt responsible to find some road back to happiness for her daughter, although it was clear that the mother had never found that road for herself.

"I'm an only child of a military father and a fat mother," Bertha said. "We moved a lot. I rarely went to the same school two years in a row and half the time we moved in the middle of the school year. It's hard enough for a pretty girl to move into a new school but when a fat girl moves, she moves from misery to hell. My father didn't give a shit. He never once told me he was sorry that we had to move again. And my mother cried. That's what she did best. She would say that at least we would all be together, one big, happy family. She had the big part right."

Bertha's mother was too helpless to be of much help to her child. The problems that Bertha suffered so reminded the mother of her own childhood problems that the mother became lost in her

28

double sadness for herself and her daughter.

As Bertha would tell it, there was never a good day in high school, never a single happy memory: no dating, no friendships, no party invitations, no pool parties—definitely no pool parties—no fun family vacations away from school. Vacations consisted of moving from their current house to a new house in a different city in a faw-away state where they were newly assigned to live. Bertha could remember the many sad times during the lonely school lunch hours when she sat by herself, not close enough to friends to eat a sandwich with them.

"A fat person might not want to eat in front of other people, but they want to sit with other people," Bertha said. "They didn't want to sit with me, so fuck them, I didn't want to sit with them."

Kids made fun of her, not so much directly but often with subtlety, and she developed a keen sensitivity to derision and scorn. When she was 16 or 17 she found that people laughed when she made fun of herself, so that is what she became good at. She practiced and she excelled.

Her mother tried to smother her with love and bought her things to show her that love: earrings, purses, cupcakes, and many other things. She encouraged Bertha to do anything that brought her happiness. Bertha did like to dance and her mother enrolled her in ballet and jazz classes from early childhood through high school. Bertha also liked to walk, which she typically did alone, and this did bring her some peace.

"I was good at dancing. Big, but good," she said. "And I'm a strong walker."

Her mother's hovering felt like pity, but Bertha thought her father should try to hover a little more. He was career military: disciplined, orderly, compulsive, and always on time. Bertha felt he was sometimes disgusted with her mother, ashamed of her, ashamed of her weight and the lack of discipline he thought created that weight. So Bertha assumed he was disgusted with her also, although he never specifically said as much. He rarely said anything to Bertha. He would say to his wife, "Life is not that tough. Just

29

don't eat so much." He would also tell his wife that she would not be so weepy all the time if she did not have so much free time on her hands. Life's problems may have had simple solutions to Bertha's father, but the father's life was not easy. There was little joy in the house.

Life was better for Bertha in college. "Not good, but better." She was an English major who enjoyed her classes and did well in them, and she met some students in classes whom she thought of as almost friends. In her first year at UC Davis she took a dance class both semesters. She lived with a roommate in the dorms, someone who became an actual friend, and they signed up together to become roommates as sophomores. She did see counselors at the Student Health Center that first year because she felt vulnerable to depression, "But they were limited in how many times they could see me and didn't know what they were doing anyway."

When summer came Bertha returned home and returned to a depression darker than she had ever experienced before. That deep sadness set in for the whole summer and Bertha had an impossible time shaking it off and it followed her into the beginning of her sophomore year.

"It was my roommate, Sandra, who told me to see you, maybe not you specifically, but someone at the Medical Center because the student health center wasn't working out."

"Sandra sounds like a good friend," I said.

"I think she is the only friend I have ever had, quite honestly. She said the Medical Center would have cutting-edge therapists. Are you a cutting-edge therapist?" she asked me.

"Yes," I said.

. . . .

"Aren't you ashamed to be in a profession where nobody gets better? Tom Cruise is right. Psychiatry is nothing but a cult," she said to me one session, although I thought things were going pretty well in her life, and she no longer complained of constant sadness.

"I feel pretty good," I said.

30

In truth my own feelings about psychiatry and psychotherapy are mixed. On the one hand, who wouldn't want a nice person to talk to, more objective and less invested than a friend, learned, non-judgmental, rarely over reactive, non-parental, with a nice smile and good teeth. Sure, we have our blind spots, our troubled areas, problems I fear that other people are able to see all too well, problems that we, as psychotherapists, are blind to no matter how much psychotherapy we have had. As a group, I would say we are no more and no less proud, arrogant, controlling, narcissistic, or intellectually limited than other professional groups. However, there is a subtle rumor circulating that psychiatry is the most disturbed branch of the medical profession. Most of us in the profession have had a lot of psychotherapy because we are human, we have problems, and we want to learn by living in the patient chair—and we seek out growth, emotional and spiritual growth. Some of us are broken and should not be practicing, but most of us are giving a good faith effort to learn as much as we can to be as helpful as we can.

. . . .

"My mother sent me to this psychoanalyst when I was in high school," Bertha said. "He thought I was oral. I thought he was anal. He was not yet a psychoanalyst but he was training to become one. He talked my mother into making me one of his cases, said I couldn't progress without psychoanalysis, said I would always be fat because I had a fear of intimacy."

"Did you find any value in the experience?" I asked.

"No. I quit. He had to start over with another training case. He was mad about that. I guess I saw a little something of value in that. It made me happy to kick him back to square one."

Bertha's mother never gave up. She took Bertha to one psychiatrist after another to try out one form of psychotherapy after another.

"My Gestalt therapist had me put my imagined mother in a chair and then had me talk to the chair, telling the chair all the things I've always wanted to say to my mother. I couldn't get it through that guy's head that my mother wasn't in that fucking chair."

"I'm beginning to get the picture," I said. "Nothing very helpful."

"That's the picture," she said. "My positive psychologist told me I'm too negative. He gave me homework to do at night before I went to sleep. Think of three positive things that happened to me that day and think of three things I am grateful for. I was grateful that my mother didn't push me into seeing him again."

"Was anyone helpful?" I asked.

"No, but some people were less helpful than others. The worst were psychiatrists. I am a living test tube of modern psychopharmacology. Everything tried, nothing worked. Sometimes they'd say, 'Oh, this is a new generation of antidepressants, much better than the old ones. Here, take this with this, and also this, and all these little enhancers, and everything will be all right.' Bullshit."

Long-term psychotherapy is not about forcing change; it does not have the urgency and demands that emergency psychotherapy has. It is about exploring change, and certainly one of the ways that psychiatrists have of exploring change is by playing with biology— change through better chemicals. But if a patient cuts out medication as an option, or, more commonly, if medication is not an appropriate option, then therapists are left with their most fundamental and powerful tool: themselves. The relationship inside the office becomes the instrument of change, and the honest and true exploration of that relationship, that unique microcosm of the real world, explored more deeply than it is in the real world, becomes the beacon of light illuminating new options for living, different choices to be made, alternative reactions to employ. If there is magic in psychotherapy, it is in using a small relationship in a little room to explore the world of relationships outside that room and, in so doing, test and challenge the fixed beliefs that we have about ourselves.

The process was not working well with Bertha. One reason was that Bertha set up too many rules, inflexible and impenetrable rules, about the content of our conversations. A second reason, at least for our rocky beginning, was that I was in a hurry to subvert those rules. It was not uncommon for me to ask Bertha the more common questions that move psychotherapy along and make it a unique relationship: tell me how you think we are doing in our work together in this room; it seems you have repeatedly had disappointing experiences in psychotherapy and I'd like to know your feelings about our experience in here; I noticed you were late today and seemed angry in the way you threw your backpack down and announced you had to leave early, and it makes me wonder if you are feeling angry with me? These kinds of comments and questions move the action of psychotherapy from the outside world, where a therapist has little control, to the inside world, where I can at least grapple for understanding. But I quickly found that these questions, even though delivered, I believe, with genuine affection and desire to move forward, were too direct and startling for Bertha, too abrupt for the fragile ground on which we stood together. I needed more patience and Bertha needed more control, and, at least for the time being, avoidance meant control. She carried within her an ocean of pain and she did not yet trust me with it.

Bertha had equally discouraging things to say about cognitive-behavioral therapists whom Bertha's mother gathered to help with Bertha's weight control, and Bertha had been to more than one expensive "fat camp." She might lose some weight at a fat camp only to gain it all back after she returned home.

"I admit it. I love food," she said. "I think about food all the time. I wake up each morning planning the rewards I will eat that day just for making it through the day. Food is addictive. But it gives me joy, pleasure, and comfort. The trouble is you can't quit food like you quit heroin. There is no such thing as going cold turkey when it comes to food addiction. See if you can get a heroin addict to cut down to three small hits a day for the rest of his life."

It was about the time when I was doubting my ability to be very helpful to Bertha when she asked me, "So what is your specialty? Why are you so cutting-edge?"

33

I cannot address that question very well because I do not have a specialty and I am not cutting-edge. I may try to put a pretty face on my abilities by saying that I am eclectic, but I worry that I do not know enough about any one system, belief, theory, or technique to do it justice. I have worked many different settings with different patient populations using different therapeutic approaches, and not all approaches are appropriate for all patients. I am, myself, guilty of belittling—not directly but in my own fantasy amusements—some therapists, especially young, new therapists, who embrace one and only one theory and practice of psychotherapy and apply it indiscriminately. I suppose these new therapists believe they are on their way to developing a specialty, an expertise, a cutting edge.

I recall a newly graduated psychiatric social worker who fell in love with William Glasser and Reality Therapy, a system of psychotherapy that is here-and-now, problem-solving, and focused on making better choices in life and taking responsibility for those choices. It seemed to me that several times a day I would overhear this therapist saying to a patient, in a paternal tone, "You have to take responsibility for yourself." In that one sentence he addressed all problems. He single-handedly made me feel comfortable telling people that I am eclectic.

But skipping from style to style, theory to theory, suits my personality. A supervisor once told me that I would never get to the other side of the river if I kept changing boats. He was right. I was always jumping ship, seeking a faster boat. But it has been my observation that the most effective therapists are flexible—perhaps another word for eclectic—and they have a deep understanding of a variety of approaches.

I admire many iconic figures in the field of psychotherapy. Irving Yalom is a gentle, humble genius, a philosopher-psychiatrist, comfortable with a group of schizophrenics but also in his element in discussing the meaning of life with future psychiatrists. I always wanted him to adopt me. Carl Rogers was the quintessential empathic master who could make patients feel he had gently stepped inside their heads and understood them as well as they understood themselves. As an outpatient therapist I am attracted to the old-style psychotherapy, the unhurried therapy of a relationship that builds— even though I worked most of my life in an emergency setting—as opposed to the new "empirically validated treatments".

I do not like the kind of documentation that insurance companies require in order to compensate therapists for the empirically validated treatments they employ. I want to feel free to fail in psychotherapy without consequence and without a drop in compensation, and free to succeed without measuring the unmeasurable. Growth, happiness, meaning, joy, and all their opposites seem to me intangible; they are vague constructs in the presence of a measuring stick. Most empirically validated treatments attempt to measure symptoms like bad behaviors, bad moods, and bad thoughts, or any combination of the three, and reduce them. I understand that insurance companies are in a hurry and want proof of progress, but mental health is a complicated field, frustrating, I am sure, to insurance companies.

So I am not a cutting-edge therapist and I said as much to Bertha. I confessed to her that many university hospitals have a great reputation for many good reasons but that a whole lot of ordinary people work there, too, and that I might be one of them.

"Well, I've lost 10 pounds since I started with you so you must be doing something right," she said.

I made a mental note that she had complimented me for the first time. I hadn't noticed that she had lost weight and would not have commented on it because it was a forbidden subject which I dared not approach. She would approach it at times and I had permission to listen, but never inquire. But I did venture out and say, "I wonder, Bertha, if you are feeling more comfortable in our relationship? It takes comfort to talk progress."

"You always have to spoil the moment," she said.

. . . .

Once Bertha gave me a homework assignment of looking at popular magazines at a grocery store and reporting back to her. Women's Health, Self, Vogue, Cosmopolitan, Shape, People, and Us all spoke the same language—sexy, impossibly thin, flawless, big-eyed, full-lipped, come-hither, young women—a delightful language that undoubtedly sold magazines. There was also the Oprah Magazine, O, with a lovely picture of Oprah on it, so the magazine rack was not a grand slam of seductively, although I personally found the picture of Oprah to be surprisingly erotic. These magazines were titillating and provocative beyond belief—actually beyond reasonable belief.

"That's what this world wants me to be," Bertha told me.

I suppose that men have many ways to be sexy—power, wealth, fame, and beauty—but we are not without our pressures. Nothing is less sexy than an unemployed man. But women have to be alluring, sexy, sensual, beautiful, and thin, and now many other things, so the bar is set impossibly high, to assure failure.

. . . .

"By the way, I ran five miles today," she said to me as she was walking out the door after one of our sessions.

"What?" I asked.

"Five miles," she said and smiled. I noted the smile because I could not remember her ever wearing one without anger.

"You always tell me important things when you are walking out the door," I said. "First point of discussion next week."

One week later she walked into my office and I said, "Five miles, that's a lot of miles. Do you want to talk about it?"

"No," she said.

At this point I had been seeing her for more than a semester and we were closing in on summer. She laid out her summer plan: go home, get depressed, come back as a junior, find a good therapist.

"Do you know where I can find a good therapist?" she asked.

"The best," I said. "I'll try to sharpen my cutting edge by the time I see you next."

We both thought that her plan would accurately and sadly predict exactly what would happen if she went home for the summer, so she did not go home. She stayed the summer in Davis, took classes, and by good fortune, paired up with her roommate, Sandra, in looking for an apartment. They planned to go off-campus to find an apartment for the summer and then keep it for the next year.

Bertha and I talked about it, and she chose to continue in psychotherapy with me during the summer.

Bertha leaked out her secret passion for running. She was officially a member of a Davis running group, many of whose members were training for a marathon. She started her training in a walker's group as an 18-minute-per-mile walker, but she soon worked up to a faster walk with an occasional short jog doing 16-minute miles. She would sometimes throw out a progress report as a tantalizing tease, but she did not want any follow-up questions to jinx her progress.

A primary focus of our psychotherapy over the summer continued to be her challenge of the value of psychotherapy itself.

"I read an article that said running is superior to both psychotherapy and to medication as an antidepressant," she said. "Does that bother you?"

"No, I'm glad to hear it," I said.

"I read an article that said yoga is superior to psychotherapy for anxiety," she said. "Did you know that?"

"No," I said. "But I can believe it."

"I read an article that said voodoo is more effective than psychotherapy," she said. "Twice as effective. Do you believe that?"

"Have you been reading the Voodoo Times again?" I asked.

"Have you ever thought that what you do is no better than voodoo?" she asked.

"I have had that thought," I said.

. . . .

37

I do not know if other therapists doubt their theories, techniques, or abilities as much as I do. I hope not. I make a lot of mistakes, and I remember most of them hoping not to make the same ones again. I once fell asleep while seeing a sight-impaired patient. In my defense, I saw him late in the day—he was always my last patient due to the bus schedule—and he talked in a slightly monotone voice, fluidly and without interruption, for long periods of time. I will admit I am not a high-stamina therapist. I have friends in private practice who can do ten 45-minute sessions a day, five and a half days a week, but I cannot do that. My energy drops off after four patients and my attention after five. Perhaps the actual exchange of money keeps the private practitioner upright, but I find psychotherapy to be hard work. At the University Outpatient Clinic, all the staff therapists had many meetings, teaching conferences, case conferences, and, in my case, cappuccino supervisions, so we only saw three or four people a day in psychotherapy.

While it may not sound like much at first that is a lot of attentive listening. My sight-impaired patient was remarkably forgiving even though he accused me of having fallen asleep for over a half-hour. He told me he spoke more softly during that time to make sure that he did not wake me up. I am certain he was exaggerating. I doubt I was asleep for more than 20 minutes.

Bertha was by no means my first patient who had weight problems, nor my first patient having weight problems with whom I made slow progress. I regularly and unintentionally irritated an anorexic patient whom I thought was stingy with praise. A full year after termination of psychotherapy she sent me this note which I kept and refer back to every so often:

"Dear John, I never thanked you for your hard work. At least you tried. I'm sure I deserve some of the fault for my lack of progress, although I seem to have done so much better after my termination with you. Nevertheless, I was never gracious in my goodbye to you. I did think about bringing you a box of candy for

38

our last hour, but at the time I thought you were too fat. Ha ha. That is me laughing. You once told me I needed to lighten up. You told me that that was a joke but I didn't get it at the time. I'm a year late, but now I see you are a funny man. I wish for you better success with future patients."

It is not difficult for me to see the mistakes that other psychotherapists make, and I suppose, unjustifiably, that allows me to forgive my own. Some therapists have become so monocular, focused, obsessed about one problem, that they see it everywhere: therapists molested as a child who see child molestation in all their patients, or therapists so fascinated with the diagnosis of multiple personality disorder, which is rare, that they have a whole practice full of multiples.

One of my former Emergency Department patients made an out-of-the-way trip back to the ED to tell me that her desperate feelings of being lost and alienated had nothing to do with depression, like I said it did. She had since seen a psychologist in town, a "brilliant" man, who believed that extraterrestrial aliens were walking into the bodies of unsuspecting people of Earth and living out their lives in those bodies. He told her she was a citizen of the constellation, Orion.

"Couldn't you see that?" she asked me. "Of course I am lost and confused. My people are from Orion. I am so glad that I found a competent psychologist in time."

Truth is, I could not see that, but her new psychologist could clearly see it in her and in others. There is no perfect therapist and there are many dysfunctional, imperfect ones: the obsessive-compulsive therapist who misses the big picture; the power therapist who must be in control; the anxious therapist who fears failure; the seductive therapist who needs to be loved, emotionally and sometimes physically; the avoidant therapist who will not take a new case; the expert therapist who cannot take criticism or supervision; the insecure therapist who needs respect; the good-mother therapist with all kinds of advice; the bad-father therapist, light on praise and heavy on punishment; the distant, professional therapist with a white coat and no emotions; the God therapist who needs to be worshipped—I could go on.

Perhaps Tom Cruise and Scientology are correct: psychiatry is a cult. Scientology has a mobile museum, quite interesting in fact, with fascinating films and all the free literature on the barbarism of psychiatry you could ever want. The day I casually passed the mobile museum they were giving out free, high-end bakery cookies, the aroma of which coaxed me in. The films and literature illustrated graphically the history of unique torture and deliberate sadism that psychiatry has inflicted on its unfortunate victims: surgeries, electric shock, many treatments meant to punish. The presentation included a detailed account of the early history of abuse in psychiatry, and it brought me right up to the present day where medications and, yes, electric shock, are still used for evil purposes and personal gain.

When a very polite Scientologist engaged me in a conversation about my interest in the museum and asked me about my work interests, I told a half-truth, also known as a half-lie. I told him I was a teacher. I did say, in full truth, I appreciated the peanut-butter cookies. I had some basic knowledge of Scientology, and I knew that I could not be a psychologist and a Scientologist at the same time. The whole field of psychiatry was the enemy to Ron Hubbard, the charismatic founder of Scientology. I was interested in Scientology in the late 1960s after reading the mesmerizing book, *Dianetics: The Modern Science of Mental Health*. I signed up for an introductory course on communication which I found to be useful. However, I was a psychology major in college, and I soon learned that my field of study was incompatible with Scientology, and I was told I should choose another major. Psychologists and psychiatrists, they said, were "enemies" of Scientology, "suppressive" people who meant to do the world, the organization, and ultimately me, harm. They said it would be wise to cut off all ties with any study or profession in mental health.

They taught me about a step-by-step process which semi-culminated in a high state of consciousness called "Clear," and went on to a second wave of evolutionary growth, a state of maximum freedom and power called Operating Thetan 8, described as a state of expansion so superior and with such extraordinary powers that this super-human being could function independent of a body. I believed, at the time, that this highly evolved state could come in handy, my spirit floating around outside my body. Frankly, I did not know anyone, even people with years of psychotherapy, who came close to living with the powers of an Operating Thetan 8, so I did consider "moving up the ladder." But I also heard about a sign-up contract, a commitment to Scientology for one billion years, which at first seemed like joke, which I quickly learned was not, and a billion years seemed like a long time for a young student, even in the context of eternity. Also, I would not only be required to surrender psychology as a major, but I would have to disassociate myself with anyone else connected to the field of mental health, which included my brother. The organization itself, and the people who were high-up running it, had an aggressive, military feel with a hard-sell approach and with follow-up calls and literature sent to your house that kept coming for years and years. I was scared off.

I am an expert in cults, having almost joined, or joined and quit, so many of them. I always sought out these experiences with the genuine desire to understand them and benefit by them, so I believe I am in a good position to answer the question, "Is psychotherapy a cult?" The 1960s were a time of explosive freedom—free sex, free expression, free drugs—and the power of pleasure merged with the freedom of expanded consciousness. But for me it was also a period of intense angst, an ongoing existential crisis, a desperate, harried search for the meaning of life.

I looked into the Hare Krishna movement; I liked the chanting, hated the haircuts and toga robes. I attended nude marathon encounter groups; we were told that in nudity we would shed our defenses. I took periodic pilgrimages to Esalen for the good food, the hot baths, and the good vibes, joined psychodrama groups, almost signed up for Werner Erhards's

41

"EST," and tried out many types of meditation—contemplation, concentration, and mantra techniques.

I threw myself into Western religions, taking a three-part religious study series at UC Berkeley, consecutively taught by a Protestant minister, a priest, and a rabbi. I was an ardent Presbyterian, a devout Catholic, and a reform Jew, each in its turn for about one college quarter apiece.

While other students were dropping acid or smoking marijuana, having fun with sex, food, and all the senses, I took hallucinogens by myself and recited passages from Timothy Leary's and Ralph Metzner's, *The Psychedelic Experience*, based on the *Tibetan Book of the Dead*, hoping to pass into the light of God. I was never attracted to alcohol or popular downers of the era, like Quaalude, because they dimmed the light of God, or so I thought.

I followed the "Perfect Master," 15-year-old Maharaja Ji of Divine Light Mission, to Las Vegas, then to San Francisco where I enthusiastically begged one of his disciples to initiate me into his secret techniques, only to find the meditation methods foolish. I threw myself into things, but, to my credit, I threw myself out of them, too. I was always ready to be launched anew if the practice had promise, if it was strong enough to catapult me into cosmic consciousness.

After a long and arduous search, I settled on Transcendental Meditation as taught by Maharishi Mahesh Yogi. The equation I use to evaluate a cult is simple: what do they give me, what am I required to give them. Transcendental meditation asked me for 35 dollars and a banana. The banana was part of the initiation process, as was some rice, which I think they provided, and a flower, which I picked from the yard of a private house on my way over to the initiation. I stood in line in the late 1960s with hundreds, possibly thousands, of other Berkeley students and Bay Area residents and was initiated into my new mantra technique by a beautiful, serene man named Jerry Jarvis. I have practiced Transcendental Meditation ever since that initiation, twice a day for 15 minutes— twice a day a dip into a most refreshing and rejuvenating pool of consciousness. I have never been asked to devote my life to Maharishi, never been told to believe anything, never been encouraged to recruit others. There is no requirement to give up family, friends, or field of study, no penalty for skipped meditations, no service requirement, no residential imprisonment, no haircut, and no dress code. Two exquisite dives a day into a fresh pond of energy for the price of 35 dollars and a banana.

I am not in cosmic consciousness, but I do feel clean, clear, and crisp after each dip into that pool. There are advanced techniques to be had if you want them and conferences to go to if you are so inclined, but people in the organization do not demand any of these things and will tell you that you can go the distance, all the way to the end, with that first simple mantra.

The application of my cult equation—what do they do for me versus what do they want from me—is more complicated when applied to organized churches. Some churches want a percentage of your income, some are intolerant of diversity of opinions, some may attempt to separate a member of the church from that member's family, and some may be punitive, harsh, and judgmental. But most people embrace a church for the community, support, and meaning it brings to their lives, and they make the decision that the cost is worth the return.

I have seen a number of parents and friends in the Emergency Department who are worried that their loved ones joined groups where the expected price, the giving, is way out of proportion to what the devotee actually receives. They believe that brainwashing has stolen their child or friend. Charles Manson required his followers to kill people, and other narcissistic, sociopathic leaders have killed their members. That is a steep price with a low return. Some organizations demand a surrender of your life, a dedication akin to slave labor, a belief system that is strict and carefully monitored; that is an unhealthy equation, my very definition of a cult.

Evaluating psychotherapy's cult status is muddy and complicated. Psychotherapy could be described as a mix of pseudoscience and science. It is an artful science. Therapy techniques can apply or not apply and medication can work or not work. Every therapist is different and the field is weak if judged by its reliability and consistency. On the right day, with the right patient, with an effective psychotherapist, and sometimes the right medication, psychotherapy can be helpful, very helpful to some. It can be disheartening and disappointing to others. The cost is relatively steep, I admit, but relief from pain and suffering, or enhancement of joy and peace, is a worthy return.

. . . .

"I think psychotherapy is a step up from voodoo," I told Bertha.

"Well I'm not giving up my pins and dolls just yet."

It was at the end of that summer when Bertha told me she had run her first half-marathon—the distance, not a specific race. It was a walk-run at a 16 minute-per-mile pace. She also said she had lost 35 pounds since starting psychotherapy, a change in her I could not help but notice, but it was still a taboo subject to explore in depth. Things were going well and I was thinking that if it ain't broke don't fix it, so I did not feel the need to explore more fully the reasons for her success. Sometimes psychotherapy is about forcing change, like in an emergency department, sometimes it is about encouraging change, and sometimes it is simply about witnessing change.

"I'm training for a marathon," she said as she stood up to leave.

"A marathon?" I asked. "What about a half marathon? Shouldn't you start with a half-marathon race? Achievable goals?"

"No, a marathon. It has to be a marathon," she said.

"Why?" I asked.

"I don't want to talk about it."

I added marathon to the long list of things we could not talk about. She did not want to jinx this goal by talking about it, but, almost against her will, she could not stop talking about it.

She told me about her training program and her supportive friends in the running club, and she talked most about the weekly long run, the building blocks of every marathon training program.

She even talked about the food she ate and the food she no longer ate. She set her mind to run in the California International Marathon, the CIM, Sacramento's largest and most prestigious marathon, run each year in the beginning of December. By the time she was eight weeks out from that race, she had gradually built up to a 17-mile run and was training her way up to an eventual 22-miler to be run as a final endurance preparation two weeks before the marathon. She had many aches and pain—balls of the feet, heels, ankles, shins, knees, hips, a black toenail—but she was happy. We talked less and less about her loneliness, her anger, and her sadness and more about this one goal, this one race. This was not only a race; it was her treatment plan, self-prescribed.

I have in the past suggested many paths, courses of action, helpful steps, and treatment directions for patients, and have often been countered or defeated for my self-perceived brilliant ideas. So when someone is walking their own road, their resistance to me and their resistance to psychotherapy dissipates. I had little to do with promoting or creating the changes I saw in Bertha, nothing to do with forcing them or willing them; I was a passenger witnessing the road we were driving down.

. . . .

Psychotherapy and voodoo have some things in common, certainly magic and the power of belief. If I change my belief about myself, it is possible I might increase my perception of my value, perhaps love myself more, feel the strength of more personal power, express my feelings more richly to others, accept and appreciate the feelings that others have for me. But changing that belief in myself, the value I hold, and the love I have for myself, is difficult, mystical, and elusive. It requires a bit of magic.

I wear a costume in life. I am a learned man with a Ph.D. and an L.C.S.W., an experienced therapist with a good, high-paying position at a university teaching hospital. There is magic in that costume and it makes me feel good about myself when I put it on. There are many potent costumes in life: the young woman who wears the cloak of the first in her family to go to college, the child who wins a national spelling bee, the amputee who learns to walk. These are powerful stories, meaningful stories, magical costumes. The grandmother who climbs Mount Everest—what a story she has to tell. She is no longer a bus driver or a teacher, noble professions in their own right; she is an Everest climber. She did not climb it because it was out there, she climbed it to put it in here; she tattooed it to her soul, never to be taken from her, an emblematic statement that she believes in herself. She is a conqueror.

Here is the voodoo of psychotherapy: if I believe in myself, others believe in me, too. I can step into a different world of my own creation, a new world that could be made manifest by a single act that fundamentally reframes how I see myself. A high school graduation, college graduation, or medical school graduation, a movement away from welfare and toward a job, the throwing away of the bottle, the needle, the cigarette, and the commitment to a rehab program, and maybe, possibly, a marathon, all redefining moments for some. Any of these giant steps can be the donning of a finer costume, a ticket to a better world, a world that recognizes my value because I recognize it myself.

I once notified a young African-American man of the death of his 58-year-old mother who died in the Emergency Department after a cardiac arrest and a prolonged period of CPR. He was the first in his family to graduate from college, a graduation that his mother had attended six weeks prior to her death. He graduated from college with no student loans, his mother saw to that; she worked two tough jobs, one as a housekeeper and another as a caregiver. As the medical team was working vigorously to save this woman, the young man begged out loud to our medical staff to do everything they could to bring his mother back. I stood with him near her bedside as they repeatedly pushed medications into her, shocked her with paddles, and resumed CPR over and over again.

He wanted us to know who his mother was and what she meant to him. He lost his mother that day but her courage, sacrifice and love for him lived inside him and defined him. He knew the truth: his mother lived for him and his mother died for him. She made him feel important and unique, and he wore that costume she gave him with pride. When all medical methods, medications, and procedures were exhausted, when her expiration was pronounced, and after the medical students, nurses, residents, and attendings wiped away their tears and gave their condolences, this young man, with his great strength and dignity, sat in his mother's room, holding her hand and crying for a long time. I checked in on him occasionally, and before he left her, before she was transferred to the morgue by the coroner's office, he said to her, "I promise you, Mama, I will do something good with my life. I will make you proud of me. Your hard work will mean something. I promise you."

As a therapist, I cannot predict the future, except for this one time: I guarantee this man will be something and do something important in his life. He will make a difference. His mother wove him a costume of royal purple and he understood its value.

. . . .

"I ran 16 miles today," Bertha told me. "I can't do any more. Everything is breaking down. Everything hurts. My ankles are swollen and my knees really hurt."

"Is it a good breakdown, like you've talked about, breaking down to build back up?" I asked.

"No. A bad breakdown. I am broken. My body can't do a marathon."

Bertha was mad, bitter, and tearful during our next three therapy sessions, three weeks which did not go well. She was particularly mad at me and at psychotherapy in general, and she argued passionately against my belief that she was less sad, more active, and more confident in these last months. While she expressed disgust with her progress, she never talked about wanting to leave psychotherapy, and she did not stop her training program for the marathon. By the first week in November she was supposed

47

to be up to 18 miles in her long run, but her longest run was still 16 miles; she said it was all she could do to run the 16 and even then she was risking injury. Where she had once recovered from the long runs by soaking her feet in a bucket of ice water, she was now taking whole-body ice baths to take down the pain and the swelling. Two weeks before the marathon she was supposed to have completed one run of 22 miles. She said she was able to make 18 miles of slow jogging, a lot of walking, and some despicable near-crawling. She announced to me that she had failed, the marathon was over.

Bertha's roommate, Sandra, bounced into their apartment on the day of Bertha's failed long run with a congratulatory cake, a happy smile, and a wrap-around hug for Bertha. Bertha was not in the mood, quite the opposite. She was in the middle of breaking dishes, throwing cups, slamming doors, and kicking furniture, a monumental effort for someone who was exhausted, beaten, and broken. Sandra wondered if she should call the police or an ambulance but she was able to reach me instead.

"What should I do?" asked Sandra. "She broke a bunch of stuff and she's still kicking things. Should I call the police? I'm afraid she's going to hurt herself."

I told Sandra not to call the police. I told her that I did not think Bertha would hurt herself, and that the stuff she broke is only stuff. "Let her go the distance," I said. "She needs this and she is probably nearly done."

. . . .

Even small failed goals can be humiliating. I was once on a Department of Psychiatry softball team. As a kid I was a good baseball player—a good hitter and a fair fielder. Our department softball team was in a league superior to our abilities, the C league in an A through F hierarchy. We were a little worse than F, but we had great pride in spite of our zero wins, seven losses record. Some of those losses were by a large margin, but I was consistently hitting well and I kept my head high.

In our last game of the season we kept the score close, and in the late innings we were within reach of winning. We were playing a tough-looking, blue-collar team who brought more to the game than the desire to play; they brought sexy, scantily-dressed girlfriends who trash-talked us during the whole game yelling things like, "This faggot can't hit!" We were desperately motivated to win.

I was playing third base and I made three errors in a row, all ground balls that I bobbled and threw wildly. I was replaced, mercifully, by a social work intern, a student, who played out the remaining innings with flawless skill. We lost that game, not entirely because of me, but mainly because of me. If I had won the title of "Psychologist of the Decade" that week it would not have soothed the wounded soul that inhabited me. Years have passed, many of them, but I still remember in great detail each one of those bobbled ground balls.

Bertha sat in my office five days before the marathon. She had, for the last nine days, tapered her runs down to just a few miles, and she reduced her widespread swelling and pain. Her longest run was the 18 miler she believed she had failed to complete, but she was prepared to line up at the starting line. It is an elegant philosophy in the culture of marathoning that the victory is not in crossing the finish line but in standing at the starting line. Bertha wore a T-shirt to our therapy session that said, in reference to the marathon, "There may come a time when I cannot do this anymore, but today is not that day."

Bertha was sweet and transparently vulnerable that session, two qualities uncomfortable and uncommon for her. She said she had some friends who were going to be at the finish line waiting for her to come in, waiting to support her. She shyly asked if I would be interested in being at the finish line in case she made it to the end.

"I know you must have other things to do," she said.

I told her the truth, that I was touched that she asked me, and that I would be proud to be at the finish line.

. . . .

It was a cold early morning on race day when the first African men crossed the finish line smoothly, elegantly, effortlessly. They looked like they could have easily run back to the starting line and on up to Lake Tahoe if they wanted to. I had never seen marathon winners finishing their race, and it was well worth the effort to fight the early spectator crowd. The runners' strides were like noiseless bicycle wheels rolling down the road, no visible energy expended. Now I understood the science of running a marathon: point your body in the right direction and let it silently fly for 26.2 miles. Easy.

After two more hours, about 10 AM, the runners crossing the finish line did not make the marathon look so easy. Men and women, all shapes and sizes, races and ages, clumped together in tight packs, came thundering down the last hundred yards. Legs were heavy, arms were pumping, feet slapped the pavement, and faces were pained, as people of courage gave all they had left to finish the race in style and dignity. These people were not about to run back to the starting line.

Some exulted in victory, pumping the air, screaming out, while others collapsed. I watched many runners, met by anxious loved ones, cry in the embrace of those who came to support them. In two more hours, when runners were coming in after six hours of pavement pounding, I could see many shades of human pain. There was no sign of Bertha.

In the next hour handfuls of people struggled in, walked in, limped in; they did what they could to cross that finish line, collect that medal, and change their lives. These were people who had run three times as long as the marathon winners, and a few carried almost twice the weight. There should be a special medal for that— long time running with heavy weight. It looked to me like these runners were committed to dying before quitting.

Bertha had said, and I had agreed wholeheartedly, that the real victory was lining up at the starting line. But once the starting gun is fired, marathon runners instinctively know that the victory lies ahead, and there is no telling what someone will do to finish the race. As is known and told in marathon folklore, there is no shame in quitting and living to race another day, but many do not adhere to such good advice. Bertha and I had a common love for the movie, "Cool Runnings," a film about the first Jamaican Olympic bobsled team. I reminded her that, "A gold medal is a wonderful thing but if you're not good enough without it, you'll never be good enough with it." She said to me, "I see pride, I see power. I see a bad-ass mother who won't take crap off of nobody." My parting words to her before the day of the race were, "Peace be the journey."

Crossing that finish line or not, Bertha was not the fat kid, the sad kid, the anxious kid that her parents had always known, and I doubted she would ever be again. She was a bad-ass mother and she was coming to believe it. I was not responsible for this change, she was, but I did have the privilege of witnessing it.

In a marathon race, the first mile is one mile long and the 25th mile is two miles long, or so it seems; with mile 26 comes hope and inspiration, light at the end of the tunnel and crowd energy to pull you through, but every mile after 20 is ugly. Time slows down, distances get longer, and the mile marker seems misplaced, far, far beyond where it is supposed to be. Sweat bead after sweat bead, men and women redefine themselves in the endless journey to 26.2.

One hundred yards away from me, away from the finish line, I saw a vision of a woman about to end that journey at just over seven hours, beyond the technical time the race had ended, but well within the definition of finishing a marathon. A group of women, about five of them whom I had not noticed before, held up a big sign, "Big Bertha, Our Hero," as they clanged loud cowbells and screamed boisterous, powerful chants of praise as Bertha headed home.

She was not running or jogging—it was more like an uncoordinated wobble—but she was moving toward the finish line. Her gait was more forced than a walk but not faster than a walk, and it did involve limping and leaning, near falling and flailing. It was not pretty, but she continued to come slowly toward us, toward the finish line, then across the finish line—and then came a hard fall to the ground. I saw all five of her friends pile on top of her like a football tackle, cheering, yelling, hooting. They sat her up as she looked stunned, they wrapped her with a space blanket, they gave her a banana, which she could not chew, and a bottle of water, which she could not swallow, and they had a race official come over and hang a medal around her neck.

These five women were ecstatic. For 10 solid minutes they hugged and cheered Bertha while they massaged her shoulders and legs. I sat next to Bertha on the sidewalk curb as her friends went to retrieve the victory car to take her home. They needed to get that car as close to her as possible because Bertha's walking was over for the day.

"So, how'd it go?" I asked.

"Very, very badly," she said. She could only utter small sentences.

"I see you crossed the finish line," I said. "I see you have a medal around your neck. If I'm not mistaken, that's the same medal that the man and woman who won this race have around their necks."

She smiled, paused a long time, and said, "I'm not Big Bertha anymore."

"No, you are a marathoner," I said.

She said, to my surprise, "My name is Violet."

"Really?" I asked.

"Yes, Bertha is my middle name," she said.

"Violet. That's a lovely name," I told her.

"I think I can take a break from psychotherapy for now," she said.

"I release you."

We sat in silence for a few minutes before she asked me, "Am I the worst patient you've ever had?"

I thought about that for a little while and said, "No, you were one of the best."

Therapists learn from their patients, sometimes valuable lessons never taught in graduate schools. I learned from Violet that running was right for me. I now run marathons very slowly, so slowly that fast walkers pass me by with words of encouragement. We are a friendly bunch in the back of the pack, all racing to beat that critical point where the race organizers take down the traffic blockades and leave us to fend for ourselves. My claim to fame is that I once placed third in the Silicon Valley Marathon for the 70 to 74 age group. I was 51 years old at the time and I ran a personal best. They got my birthdate wrong. In the last hundred yards my name came over the loudspeaker, "And here comes John Farrell from Sacramento. He is 71 years old. Give him a big hand." I looked good for a 71-year-old that day, but to this day I cannot compete with the excellent marathoners who are 20 years my senior.

Violet kept in touch by email for some time after we terminated psychotherapy. She received a master's degree, was teaching at a junior college, and she had run, when I last heard, over 20 more marathons, three or four a year. She told me she was not thin but she was really fit. She had met and married a man who said he could not understand why anyone would be so crazy as to run a marathon, repeatedly.

I understood.

Love and Work

I have started my day in the Emergency Department as part of a treatment team holding down one limb of a volatile, untreated, unmedicated, male schizophrenic patient, with the intent to medicate and treat him, and I have ended my day riding around in a UC Davis police vehicle hunting for a naked bipolar female, a woman who declared she was a member of the royal family, who slipped out of her restraints and AWOL'ed from the hospital. And in the middle of the shift I have seen and done much, much more, to patients and for patients, sometimes I'm not sure which. Psychosis, in its most exaggerated form, is a tragedy, a dark comedy, and a clear advertisement for the value of treatment.

There are schizophrenic patients and there are schizophrenic patients, there are bipolar patients and there are bipolar patients, or so the saying goes. The range in functioning, insight, type of symptoms, severity of symptoms, response to medication, and medication compliance is impressive. Sometimes things go right and outcomes are favorable; patients can recognize the need for treatment, consistently show up for treatment, and avoid the complications of drugs and alcohol during treatment, and these habits can be good predictors that outpatient treatment will not be interrupted by the need for inpatient treatment. It is also helpful, for a patient who has eruptive, psychotic episodes, to have an involved, supportive family and an intensive case management and treatment program. But sometimes things go wrong. In the absence of insight, treatment, and support, many schizophrenic and bipolar patients decompensate and require hospitalization. These patients are brought to the Emergency Department by family, friends, and treatment staff, usually voluntarily, or they are brought in by law enforcement, often involuntarily.

It is difficult to persuade a bipolar patients who are in a manic state, with their high energy, expansive moods, grandiose thoughts, activated sexual drives, sleepless nights, and big ideas for the immediate future, to go to an emergency room. They have things to do and they feel pretty good about doing them. A full manic episode is a wondrous thing to behold: boisterous, bellicose, flamboyant, overtly sexual, agitated, insulting, seductive, and oddly charming. Manic patients in the full bloom of mania can have any or all of these qualities and many more, and most often therapists do not see floridly manic patients voluntarily walking into an emergency room asking to be relieved of this state of apparent ecstasy. All of the therapeutic skills we have, all of the patience and kindness we employ, all the desire we have to do well for a patient can only minimally subdue some of the symptoms of this dramatic presentation.

Good therapists are thrown into the role of agents of control, enforcers of restraint, and few therapists enter the profession with this role in mind. However, staff can learn much when the mind of a patient is dramatically off-center and we are, after all, a teaching university, which is the same as saying we are a learning university. We have the privilege in an emergency department of seeing the entire range of psychopathology, all of its expressions, moods, behaviors, and distorted and delusional thoughts. It is not only a great teaching environment for the young and inexperienced, it is a great teaching environment for the old and accomplished. For my 35 years in the ED I kept on learning new skills, kept on seeing fresh and unique presentations, but the early years were particularly instructive.

I was working in the Emergency Department when paramedics brought in a tall, slender, African-American man in his 30s, Joseph, who had sullied their ambulance by repeatedly vomiting in it. The paramedics were irritated, but the patient was in a glorious mood. He lived in Sacramento but he took a cab about a hundred miles, a cab he could not pay for, to a Fisherman's Wharf restaurant in San Francisco he could not afford, ordered three lobster dinners consecutively, and ate them all. I do not know how he got that far

55

in executing his marvelous plan, but he did.

The restaurant wanted him arrested, and they detained him, called the police, and then watched the drama unfold. I would imagine that the staff at the restaurant had to be at least partially responsible for the events of that night because each time this overly convivial patron, this socially engaging, loquacious man, was asked by his attentive waiter if he wanted anything else, this appreciative patron said, "Why thank you, I'll have another lobster." And another lobster came, no questions asked. As the police attempted to corner him, this entertaining and friendly man flitted about from table to table talking about the cure for AIDS that he had discovered, his upcoming appearance on the Oprah Winfrey show, and his likely nomination for the Nobel Peace Prize in medicine. Joseph was at that restaurant on that night celebrating what was to become his entry into fame and fortune. He had insisted to the cab driver earlier in the evening and to the restaurant staff after dinner that he was funded by Oprah Winfrey and that she had promised to pick up the tab. He had given some payment, all the money in his pockets, some 28 dollars, to the cab driver, but it was not enough, and the cab driver was still mad at him and attempted to locate him long after his quick exit from the cab.

The police were able to see what the cab driver and the restaurant staff were unable to see, that this man needed psychiatric help more than he needed a long cab ride and three lobsters. He needed to be on a 5150. As it turned out this was a good night for Joseph, not all that expensive except for the cab ride, because his dinners were complimentary, not paid for by Oprah herself, but subsidized by the exhausted and frustrated staff of a quality fish restaurant.

Joseph was taken to San Francisco General Hospital where the triage staff immediately assessed one of the most important features of Joseph's history—he was from Sacramento. Therefore, he was treated to luxury transportation, his own ambulance transport, to UC Davis Medical Center. He was presented in our ED with an accompanying 5150 documenting his grave disability. The transport paramedics, whose clothing was soiled by regurgitated lobster, quickly headed back to San Francisco. In the ED we admitted this cooperative and very charming patient into a psychiatric hospital over his objection that he would miss his appearance on the Oprah show.

Prior to his hospitalization, I called Joseph's family and friends, people who really cared for him, who expressed their frustration over Joseph's lack of insight and his resistance to treatment when he was manic. They were grateful that we were taking his illness seriously, and they were innocently unaware that we had no choice but to do so given his dramatic presentation. Poor insight and resistance to treatment go hand in hand with many of the patients we see in the ED. Paranoid schizophrenics know that people are following them and are convinced that their voices are real, and it is difficult to talk some manic patients into treatment when they feel so naturally high. It makes sense that family members are pushed away and resented when they deny the patient's reality and present an alternative one.

. . . .

While in my training as a psychiatric social worker, during my second year of internship field placement, heading toward a master's degree in social work, I was placed with Psychiatric Emergency Services in the ED. We had a legal procedure at that time called a pre-petition screening that allowed psychiatric staff to make home visits for the purpose of psychiatrically assessing individuals who reportedly needed help but refused to get help on their own. I completed many of these screenings during that internship year because I enjoyed the process of leaving the hospital by signing out the mobile unit, and driving around the city having a shared experience with a colleague. We always went out in pairs, and I considered myself to be the expert in pre-petition screenings even though I was a student in training. My expertise was based on my sheer enthusiasm and willingness to do the

57

evaluations and the large number of them I had completed.

In the right circumstances, given the right patients, these psychiatric assessments in the home could be educational for me and exceedingly helpful to family members who had been unable to get their loved ones help in any other way. I was comfortable and confident, and I believe impressive, in my role as a mobile crisis consultant. My supervisor disliked doing these home evaluations himself and he trusted me to not only charge out into the community to clean up the town, but he also trusted me to train others to do the same. He believed that the blind could, in fact, lead the blind, and so did I.

When a new psychology intern, Susanna, arrived in the ED for a twelve-week training rotation through our service, I was enthralled and mesmerized by her, so much so that I became a different person, one who had never emerged before, virtually unrecognizable to me, a person with desperate longings that bespoke uncontrollable desires provoked by love potions. During her first week I hardly spoke to her; I was afraid to, yet I remained her captive servant. She looked like a goddess, had the mesmerizing, soft voice of a Greek siren, and smelled like Shangri-La, and I am not generally hypnotized by mythology.

Our first conversation, days after her arrival, followed an orientation speech I gave to new medical students rotating through our service, a speech that was supposed to be given by my supervisor, but my supervisor had become less and less available for work, so much was his trust in me. Others told me it was my supervisor's natural aversion to work. The fact that I rarely sat down with him for supervision after my first few weeks in training and never observed him actually seeing a patient did not necessarily, in my mind, point to laziness on his part. I felt he thought I was an exceptional intern, capable of independent work, but those who knew him best thought that he somehow always had "exceptional" interns capable of doing their work and also his work with little to no supervision.

"I like what you said to the medical students," Susanna told me, and she smiled at me when she said it.

"I like you, too," I said, like a robot, not the intelligent kind.

"I'm sorry?" she asked.

"I mean thank you," I said.

That was our first conversation, me at my best, top of my game, confident, articulate, although possibly perceived as being slightly stupid. My life with Susanna was over before it began if first impressions were as powerful as people say. I had a long way to go to redeem myself, and that would take time and less anxiety. I asked her to do a pre-petition screening with me, to go out with me on a home visit. She said she would be excited to; she actually used the word "excited." I was pleased with myself that I did not say, "I like you, too," again.

Unfortunately, but understandably, I was not the only male smitten with Susanna. Dr. Von Bernigan, one of many psychiatric residents who rotationally provided medical back-up for us during evening shifts in Psychiatric Emergency Services, was clear and persistent in his intent to win Susanna over. Most of the rotating psychiatric residents, including Dr. Von Bernigan, took their call from home when they were on call at PES, but Dr. Von Bernigan, the evening he met Susanna, decided to remain in-house rather than go home. He had never done that before, and I was well aware of why he did it now. He had no reason to be there, but there he was, talking and laughing with Susanna on a slow night, and then asking her down to the cafeteria for dinner.

. . . .

Up until that moment in time, I can honestly say that jealousy was an unfamiliar emotion to me. I had lived with women, loved women, I think, but it is possible that I had never fallen in love, not uncontrollably. I was not a jealous person, I thought, because I was a stable person, mature and anchored to solid ground.

In my relationship with a girlfriend I lived with prior to meeting Susanna, I occasionally pretended to be jealous so as not to be cold, casual, or insulting. My girlfriend came to me one day and said she

59

had an opportunity to study overseas for a year. I supported her. It was, after all, a good opportunity. She thought I supported her too enthusiastically. I thought I was being a good boyfriend. I offered to take care of her dog, her plants, everything, but she thought I was no kind of boyfriend, not one who actually cared. For weeks she said provocative things to me, but at the time I did not hear their meaning.

"A year is a long time. Chances are we will fall in love with other people," she said.

"I think we'll be fine," I said.

"You'll probably forget all about me," she said.

"No way, I'll have your dog."

This is how stable I was, like a rock, always philosophical about separations; they were meant to be, better for all of us, it will all work out.

....

Susanna was thoughtful enough to invite me to go down to dinner with her and her new psychiatric resident friend, Dr. Von Bernigan. He liked to be addressed by all with the title, "Doctor," a little unusual for our casual setting and ridiculous when talking across a dinner table. Dr. Von Bernigan communicated clearly to me, by his talented facial expressions, that he did not want me to go down to dinner with them. He should have spoken up.

"I am told that the cafeteria lost more people last year than the nine critical care units," I informed Susanna. "Critical care lost many of their patients only because they ordered from the cafeteria."

"We should go off grounds to eat sometime," she said to me. I wanted to jump to my calendar and set up times—dinner, Susanna, every day this year—but that was premature.

Dr. Von Bernigan made it a point to sit across from Susanna at the table. He spent most of his time talking about himself and his tennis matches in England, his golf games in Hawaii, his skiing in Banff, his racquetball right here in Sacramento, his Porsche, and his

BMW motorcycle. Dr. Von Bernigan was training to be a psychoanalyst and we both knew what he was really talking about; he was talking about his penis.

One of the psychiatric nurses on my shift, Terri, was training to become a clinical nurse practitioner. Terri asked Susanna to do her a "huge favor" by letting her perform a practice physical exam on Susanna to help Terri prepare for a test she was about to take. Susanna was kind in agreeing to stay late to help. Dr. Von Bernigan overheard this exchange and, playing the role of a professional medical doctor and wise mentor, offered to supervise Terri during the exam. Terri said she was thankful for his help.

I was unprepared and unfamiliar with the nature of the emotional seizure that came over me, a complete "mental breakdown" you could say; it was jealousy on fire with all the symptoms of panic, heat, sweat, and smoke. Then things got worse: I saw the three of them enter an exam room and shut the door. By any standard—psychiatric, employee behavior, legal—I was certifiable.

I was in a no-man's-land of crazed willingness to cross all boundaries of normal and respectable behavior. Like a zombie, but one with passion, I walked into the room next to their room and forcefully pressed my ear against the common wall so I could listen to them. I banged my head pretty hard against that wall causing my ear to bleed from a slight cut. I did not give a damn, I was in the mood to bleed. I imagine my head would have gone right through a normal wall, but these were ancient hospital walls capable of inflicting serious head injury before yielding. I tried listening in with a cup against the wall, tried sticking my head out the window to see what I could see, looked mindlessly for a pocket mirror so I could attach it to a stick and poke it out the window to give me a better angle, but there was no hope for me. I did not want to see what they were doing, but I needed to know what they were doing, such was my loose hold on sanity.

....

For half my internship year I trained on the evening shift from 3

61

p.m. to 11:30 p.m., and Susanna was rotating through on that shift, the busy shift, the one best for training. The night shift came in at 11 p.m. and worked until 7:30 a.m. It would appear that there was very little overlap between the two shifts, but we on the evening shift had many occasions to stay late or work double shifts, and the night shift had many occasions to come in early, and so we did get to know one another.

Jerry Douglas was the supervisor of the night shift. He was a brooding, ominous man with porcelain white skin and evil good looks, a mutant, a night person, probably dangerous. He was powerfully strong and could easily be mistaken, with the slightest change in costume, for a handsome Dracula. I admired his look because someone once said to me that I looked like Archie from Archie Comic Books and that I had the fear-provoking capability of a stuffed Koala bear. People say I have a pleasant face with a natural smile, and that can be easily mistaken for a friendly person. There was no mistaking Jerry; he was what he appeared to be.

Jerry, in addition to being in charge, did the same thing on the night shift as I did on the evening shift only he did it unmolested, during the dark hours, when managers and administrators were afraid to venture out. He was a clinical social worker, but not really, not in his heart. He spent his early adult life in military intelligence, and he received a master's degree in social work on the GI Bill after his discharge from the military. I once asked him how he got to be the manager of the night shift, since he had been there long before I started training at the Medical Center. He told me that the other manager died.

"Did you kill him?" I asked. I thought it was within the realm of possibility. He never answered me.

I was beholden to Jerry because he had saved my life, possibly several times, in my first six months at the ED. More than once he appeared, magically, when I was threatened by an aggressive patient. He would calmly and fearlessly bring violent patients to the ground and within his control without hurting them while I cringed, resigned to take a beating. He did this before I even knew he was there.

In the beginning, I was afraid of Jerry. He did not speak easily or well to people or about people. He had no skills at normal conversation. I told him outright that there was no one I had more respect for than him, but I was afraid that if I ever said the wrong thing to him, he would kill me.

"If I wanted you dead, I'd stop saving your life," he said. He had a good point there.

Jerry was an avid reader, a hoarder of books, a man who recited the dark, suicidal poetry of Sylvia Plath and quoted the jaded passages of H.L. Mencken, and he was a superior hiker, survivalist, and wilderness man. He did not like people in general, but if he liked a person in particular he was a loyal brother. As time passed and as we overlapped on shifts, Jerry became a friend and I went on many hikes with him, and because of him I came to intimately know and appreciate the phrase, "he's got my back."

But his having my back was edgy sometimes. I was driving Jerry back from Pt. Reyes National Seashore to Sacramento late at night after a long hike when a large pick-up truck with possibly four rancher men started riding our tail, flashing their bright lights. We were the only two cars on a lonely road, there was no place to pull over to let them pass, and they rode our tail for a long time flashing those lights before they finally did pass. After they passed and after they were far ahead of us, I foolishly flashed my brights at them, and they turned around as if they were coming back to us. Jerry told me not to worry. He was traveling, as he always did on his hikes, or possibly everywhere, with his hidden companion, an impressively large handgun he had named "Mr. Friendly." He took out the gun from his jacket pocket, grabbed a box of bullets from another pocket, and then dropped the box, scattering the bullets throughout my car.

"Don't worry," he said. "I only need a couple of bullets."

I told Jerry we could not shoot anybody. It would not look good for mental health people to shoot somebody. Jerry assured me he would not need the gun or use the gun, but he had so little opportunity in life to load the gun, that he was having a little fun.

The pick-up truck passed us now going the other way, and we never saw it again. Over the next several weeks I kept finding a stray bullet in my car here and there.

On another hike we were on a mountaintop in a heavy rain with incessant, terrifying bolts of lightning surrounding us. I was flat on the ground, face in the mud and rocks, cowering, ill-prepared to die but knowing death was near, while Jerry was standing tall and straight, his walking staff held high in the air, commanding the lightning to leave us be. He owned that mountain and controlled the lightning that day, I am sure of it.

It was Jerry I turned to for help that night Susanna drove me mad; I confessed to him my irrational, jealous love for a woman I hardly knew and the predicament over which I had no control. I was lost to rational thinking, I was not functioning well, and I was not inspiring others to function well either. Jerry solved the problem with the same ease as he would subduing a violent patient. He paged Dr. Von Bernigan over and over and over again to every part of the hospital for all kinds of emergencies. Some patients were reportedly AWOLing, others were out of control, and all of them needed Dr. Von Bernigan's attention immediately.

Jerry used his excellent and devoted staff to make it appear that there were emergencies for the psychiatric resident all over the hospital, none of which Dr. Von Bernigan ever found, all of which caused the poor doctor much confusion and frustration.

I was not pleased with myself as I walked Susanna out to her car late that night.

"How did the exam with Terri go?" I asked.

"Oh, I didn't know you knew," Susanna said. "Terri had to do an ear, nose, throat exam and we didn't get past the ear."

"Just ear, nose, throat?" I asked.

"What did you think?"

"Oh, I just thought Terri needed to do a full exam," I said.

Susanna laughed. "I think Dr. Von Bernigan has prurient interests in my body. Did you think that's what we were doing?"

"No, not really. I got called away. I forgot all about it until now,"

64

I said.

And with that single lie I was transformed from a man who previously in life pretended to be jealous when he was not, to a man who pretended not to be jealous when he was. For what it is worth, given the choice, I think living on the edge has some merit, being fully alive, but vulnerable to humiliation.

"So, when do we go on that pre-petition screening?" asked Susanna.

"Tomorrow," I said. I was hoping by the next day to be visited by a spontaneous cure and to return to the world of normalcy, but I suspected I was the victim of a serious, unyielding virus.

. . . .

A pre-petition screening starts with a complaint, a report by a concerned family member or friend stating that someone is at risk due to a serious mental illness, and that same someone needs help but refuses to get help. Days before Susanna and I did our actual home visit, I took a report from a minister in Rio Linda who said one of his parishioners had a family member who needed help. The man needing help was a bipolar patient in his 50s who lived in a dilapidated cabin on several acres of barren land who had barricaded himself inside his cabin and was holed up in there refusing to come out, even for family. His family reported that he was alone out there, possibly with no food and water, potentially sick, and not answering his phone. He did not have a history of violence, a fact that was always most important to me when doing a home visit, and he had no hostility toward his family, but he would not let them into his cabin and he would not come out to meet them.

In the event that we cannot make contact with our intended patient, when that patient will not open the door or minimally cooperate with our assessment, we have little option but to petition the court to pick up the patient and bring him or her to the Medical Center for a psychiatric assessment and a possible 5150 hold. If we complete our assessment in the field, and the patient does not meet the criteria of a danger to himself, a danger to others, or gravely disabled by virtue of a mental illness, then we send our assessment to the court recommending no pick-up or transport. We might recommend treatment options directly to the patient if the patient is amenable.

Due to the extreme resistance this man reportedly had to any contact with others, I thought it was unlikely that he would open the door for us; we would petition him into our hospital without an assessment, and Susanna and I would reward our hard work with an intimate dinner. She would get to know me, she would fall in love with me, I would be very happy, and I would regain my sanity. Life is simple sometimes.

Rio Linda was in our legal jurisdiction, but I do not know why. We drove forever, way out into farmlands, far from civilization, and far beyond any directions we were given. I had to call the minister who talked me through the wilds of rural America to the location of this isolated cabin. There was no driveway to the cabin, and it was getting dark and ominously cloudy as we walked through a field and approached the cabin. We were in Kansas, it appeared, and this was my first attempt at ultra-rural psychiatry. The word cabin would have been a prettied-up description of this shack which had boarded-up windows and uneven slats of wood covering gaps in the walls. The shack stood on acres of undeveloped grounds, mainly weeds and brush. It was cold and damp and now dark outside, and likely to rain, a true scene from the Midwest of an abandoned farmhouse on abandoned land, ripe for a tornado.

Most of the pre-petition screenings I had completed were quite straightforward: family was present, patient was psychotic, cookies and cake were offered, I was helpful, family thanked me, patient got treatment. I do not think the minister adequately prepared me for this odd farmland trek.

"Should we knock?" asked Susanna.

"I don't know. I'm not sure," I said.

"Aren't you supposed to know?" she asked.

"I don't know," I said again. How could I know? The whole surroundings were surreal and knocking on that door might make things worse.

"What do you think?" I asked Susanna.

"I don't know," she said.

I told Susanna that the minister said he was gentle as a lamb, but I wondered if that was pre-manic or post-manic or just biblical babble.

"We came a long way," said Susanna. "And it's getting really cold out here."

I knocked on the door but there was no answer. I knocked again with more force. I yelled out, "Mr. Ludley, Mr. Ludley, Mr. Ludley." Three times I shouted out his name, each time louder. There was no answer.

"I guess we should go," I said.

"Are you sure?" asked Susanna.

"No."

"I think your confidence will get us through this," she said.

"Mr. Ludley," I shouted, now putting every bit of energy I had into a last effort. "We are here to help you. We know that strange things are happening out here. Tell us how we can help."

Silence again. As we started to walk away the door swung open. I turned, looked, and involuntarily, with surprising force, screamed. Susanna opened her mouth to scream, but nothing came out but a strong push of air. Not so for me; you could hear my scream from miles away. Neighbors could hear my scream and there were no neighbors.

"Hey, I'm glad you guys finally made it," said Mr. Ludley.

Mr. Ludley was wrapped from head to foot in an armored suit of tinfoil. He was a silver knight, a nightmare Tin Man from the Wizard of Oz. He had two little peepholes for eyes and a slit for his mouth, the only outlets to the outside world. Everything else was covered by layers and layers of tinfoil, with fingers and toes individually wrapped and foil carefully rolled around his arms, legs, and trunk. I had seen in the past possibly three or four delusional patients who used tinfoil for protection from imaginary radiation or radio waves or some harmful influence, but never to this state of total perfection, complete coverage.

He beckoned us into the cabin, said we were in danger, gamma rays were particularly intense that night, powerful enough to change the weather and cause a storm. He told us that the dark, thick, black cloud that was, indeed, parked right above his house was hiding a hostile ship from another solar system. He said they were Pleiadians and their deadly gamma rays were beaming down right into our heads. He told us that he had long studied gamma rays and that short exposure caused symptoms and illness, which he was now suffering, but extended exposure meant death. We hesitated, I more than Susanna, being the more experienced, and then we entered the shack.

Inside his glittering, candlelit cabin was a fortune in applied tinfoil, the only known protection, as he understood it, from the corrosive effects of gamma rays. There was not one inch of wall, window, floor, or ceiling that was not covered with multiple layers of tinfoil. The Pleiadians were apparently beaming down gamma rays into his house, intentionally, meaning to do him, and now us, harm. He explained that the electrical outlets, the heating and ventilation ducts, and the pipes were reinforced with extra layers of tinfoil.

Mr. Ludley was worried about Susanna and me, and he offered to protect us as he pointed to large stacks of unused, unrolled, aluminum foil.

"Suit up," he said.

We politely declined saying we would not be staying long, and that, in fact, we were there to rescue him and to treat him in the hospital for his illness and his symptoms. But Mr. Ludley was genuinely and persistently worried about the effect the gamma rays were having on us, and he insisted that we cover ourselves with tin-foil which I, for one, resisted out of my odd need for dignity. I would not be able to predict the future of my relationship with Susanna after she saw me in tinfoil. However, his unyielding focus on our health, and his kindness and sense of new-found friendship with us, compelled me, and also Susanna, to cover our heads with

68

large sheets of tinfoil.

Susanna and I spent an hour trying to convince Mr. Ludley to accompany us back to the hospital arguing that he, at the very least, needed to be treated for gamma-ray exposure. He spent that hour telling us how the government, "our own government for Christ sake," was working with the Pleiadians to shut him up because he was one of the very few people who knew what was going on. He told us that government hospitals already had a history of forcing medications on him, like lithium and Haldol, to silence him. He was not going near a hospital, but he would appreciate it if we could deliver to him a gamma-ray detector from the hospital. "Anything that measures electromagnetic fields will do," he said.

The more Susanna and I moved our talking strategy from support to persuasion to coercion, the more suspicious and resistive he became. I had never actually taken someone back to the hospital in the mobile unit before, but I was willing to take him if he was willing to go with us. He was not. He had prepared well with stored-up canned and packaged foods and gallons of water. He had many boxes full of Snickers bars, and he generously offered one to us. Strange what comes to mind at times like this: I was hungry, I like Snickers, so I thought about taking one. But I declined.

We thanked him for his concerns for us, wished him well, and walked the long, wet path back to the mobile unit while rain poured down on the large sheets of aluminum foil he insisted we wear over our heads. We would petition the court to bring him to the Medical Center and we would in the future, when he arrived at the hospital, be filling out a psychiatric hold, a 5150, on him for grave disability.

It never feels good to reach out to someone in an attempt to help them, and then betray them after they trust you.

. . . .

The science of psychopharmacology has progressed. It has steadily moved away from a pseudo-science and marched toward greater precision: the prescribing of specific medications within categories of illnesses for specific genetic and biological abnormalities. But even with advancements in science, the practice of prescribing psychiatric medications is still dominated by trial-and-error: if not this, then let's try this. Newer anti-psychotic medications, the atypicals, have replaced older anti-psychotic medications, initially with exalted, exciting news of results, only to have more extensive reviews doubt the greater efficacy of the newer medications. The science still struggles to explain why some patients respond better to one medication over another or to two medications over one. Some patients need additional medications to act as catalysts or enhancers to the original medications in order to make the original ones work better or work at all, and too many patients do not respond well to any medications. Medication strategies can be complicated, and three or four medications may be prescribed for a single goal of reducing depression, or stabilizing mood states, or dampening psychotic symptoms. Side-effects can be troublesome and sometimes dangerous. Many medications only reach their peak efficiency after three or more weeks, a long time in a life with psychosis or deep depression, and no medication is effective if taken improperly or irregularly.

There is much riding on the outcome of treatment. A markedly manic individual is at risk with his poor judgment, uncontrolled sexual drive, wild spending sprees, impulsive travel, and dangerous behaviors, while a severe depression can mean suffering and death. A schizophrenic patient can lose herself and descend into hell.

I saw a schizophrenic patient who, twice, nailed himself to a large wooden cross, his two feet and one hand nailed to that cross. He asked his neighbor each time to nail the other hand to the cross but the neighbor called the police instead. Paramedics brought him to the ED nailed to the cross, and there he lay mumbling about Jesus and the guilt and sin of man. The trauma team was not sure how to remove large nails pounded through flesh into thick boards. They called a man from Engineering and Construction, a perfect model of Clint Eastwood with a large tool belt, who sauntered in, removed a large hammer from his belt, and coolly removed those nails with the claw end of that hammer. The patient did not even wince. Our local Clint Eastwood ambled on out of the treatment room, a man of few words, a hero to all of us observing him. He was not paid nearly enough for what he just did, but he had no complaints. I guess, for him, it was all in a day's work.

I saw a schizophrenic woman who beat up her schizophrenic mother because she thought her mother was stealing her "nipple fat." The patient was delusional, thinking she was pregnant, and believing that her breasts were getting bigger. But then she noticed her breasts were shrinking in size just about the time, she observed, that her mother's breasts were getting bigger. She believed her mother was stealing her baby and her breasts. Her long-time postmenopausal mother thought that maybe she, herself, was pregnant, but the mother adamantly denied stealing her daughter's nipple fat or her daughter's baby. The mother was convinced she was having a baby of her own.

Life can become dangerously chaotic for schizophrenic and bipolar patients who stop taking their medications, alter their medications, develop an epiphany and start self-medicating, mix their medications with drugs and alcohol, or take medications that do not work for them. While there is no absolute cure for bipolar disorder and schizophrenia, and there is no precise formula for prescribing specific medications to any one person or illness, there are smart psychiatrists with extensive biological knowledge and trial-and-error experience who, with the help of supportive families and treatment programs, can make life more livable for many patients. So the apparent betrayal of the trust I have developed with a schizophrenic patient or a bipolar patient who is in dire need of treatment but will not get help, is something I am able to live with.

. . . .

In the elegant first-date environment of Jimboys Tacos, although I do not believe Susanna viewed this as a first date, we sat in a booth, damp and cold, eating a bowl of corn chips. They tasted remarkably good.

"Well, I'm impressed," said Susanna.

"Was it the mad skills I showed under fire?" I asked.

"No, I mean that scream. You have a healthy pair of lungs," she said.

"Oh, that. I start from the diaphragm."

"I am grateful," she said. "You likely saved our lives."

"Maybe," I said. "But I'm not one to take advantage of gratitude in the event you feel the urge to fall all over me with affection."

"Well, I was thinking of paying for the chips," she said.

"I'll take it. Debt paid."

. . . .

Working in pairs is fun, and working with new rotating interns or medical students, teaching them to do what I had only recently learned to do, placed me at a great advantage: what I did, sometimes repeatedly, they had never done before. Almost always it made me look wise and competent even in an emergency room, perhaps especially in an emergency room, where intensity and anxiety are high and predictability is low. But when I worked with Susanna I was jinxed, a practical joke in God's hands. I did not have confidence and I did not instill confidence. I suppose, in the end, God had a plan for me because the more humbled I was by my ineptitude with difficult cases or my uncanny ability to make simple cases complicated, the more affection Susanna gave to me. She had a genuine sympathy for the poor, the helpless, and the suffering, and I was all those and then some. I can only imagine how distant she would have felt toward me had I been competent.

An emergency department is an intimate environment with multiple instances of life and death moments, extreme volatility, and terrible fear in the same day. There is a sad imbalance between the frequent delivery of bad news versus the occasional delivery of good news. I rarely or never get to announce something like, "Mrs. Johnson, you have a new baby boy," but I do have to explain, "Mrs. Johnson, I believe your son is having a first psychotic episode." Our ED patients, and their families, are in a fragile state, in a frightening place, hearing terrible news.

Some of our staff and interns almost always deliver the best of human compassion to frail and frightened people who have experienced great loss, while other staff have unresolved anger which is marginally disguised. Susanna was the former, consistently caring and kind, even to the most confrontational and frustrating patients.

She never overreacted to bad behaviors, never mocked bizarre presentations, and never, ever displayed arrogant attitudes or controlling demands. There was no narcissism in her, no hubris in her performance when working with other interns or with staff, no exaggeration of her abilities; there was always a humble, kind person available.

In a setting where great harm has already been done, a setting of trauma, death, and psychosis, the staff of Psychiatric Emergency Services, at the very least, wish to do no more harm. Susanna did so much more: she entered a dark room and brought her light. In her future, she would never rise (or fall) to the status of an iconic, popular, thespian-therapist, like the stage-driven Salvador Minuchin who dazzled students with his brilliant psychotherapy demonstrations; she had no need for applause or self-congratulations. She was the gentle wave of peace that enters a war zone, always calming, always de-escalating. She was incapable of self promotion or bragging, and, inexplicably, unlikely to fully realize the power and the value of her work. Her modesty blocked her own view of her brilliance, and her brilliance lay in that unmeasurable quality of profound human presence, the art of being there, presence without judgment, presence with palpable tolerance and acceptance. Although she was a psychology intern and not a seasoned staff member, she was the one on my shift who was best suited to take that fragile person in our frightening emergency room who just received terrible news and cushion that shock, clear that confusion, and quiet that pain.

Although I had more experience than Susanna, having been in the Emergency Department at UC Davis for a slightly longer period of time and having been given a bigger-than-intern role by an absent supervisor, I was never Susanna's mentor; she was always mine. I was more entertaining as a teacher, but she was more effective as a healer. I had the edge of experience, she had the natural ability, ability that you cannot teach. She was the one who could de-escalate the agitation of a terrified paranoid schizophrenic or be present with a young mother who had just lost her baby. I have trained and observed many psychotherapists over the past 40 years, therapists who were bold and brave, some who were dramatic and theatrical, some confident beyond their capabilities, and some, like Susanna, capable beyond their confidence. I admit there can be a role for the crashing surf in the profession of psychotherapy, but I admire most the power of the quiet rolling wave.

....

In regard to love: it is an astonishing, harrowing thing to fall in love, to feel deeply, to lose control, to think obsessively, to live unproductively, to behave badly, to be raw, exposed, and vulnerable. I wish this curse upon everyone.

Hello Darkness,
My Old Friend

—Paul Simon

Horizontal psychiatric interviews, which we conduct in the Emergency Department with patients who are clothed in purple hospital gowns, not the "normal" white gowns, can distort the dignity and power of a patient. When patients are vertical, fully clothed, and leaving the hospital they appear different from their horizontal selves; vertically they look solid, normal, and without psychiatric problems. This mismatch of the vertical therapist to the horizontal patient adds to the inequality of the interaction, adding bigness and power to the therapist while diminishing the size and authority of the patient.

When I periodically checked in on Sarah Headley for the first six hours of my 12-hour shift, she looked like a sweet, diminutive pre-teenager, peacefully asleep, no cares, no worries. It was her overdose on Benadryl, an anti-histamine commonly used as a sedative, that placed her in that halcyon state. At hour seven into my shift I knocked outside her cubicle-condominium   more than a cubicle, less than a condominium. The patient treatment cubicle is a relatively attractive, private, roomy treatment space, and there are about 50 of them in the Emergency Department. I found Sarah to be vertical, fully dressed, ready to go. Standing up she looked more like an adult.

"Hi, I'm John Farrell from Psychiatric Emergency Services," I said to her in a friendly, first-encounter greeting.

"I have to go," she said, and she appeared to be in a hurry.

Having shaken off the look of a sleepy pre-teen awakening after a slumber party, she presented herself more like her true self, a 20-year-old, professional, determined, young, smart woman on a tight schedule, annoyed at being late, who had not one more minute to waste. Her thin, small frame did make her look younger than she was, as did her long, beautiful, red hair which she frantically brushed as a last preparation before leaving.

"I see you are in a hurry, so I wonder if we could talk a little before you go?" I said to her.

"I'm sorry, I really have to go," she said.

"I'll be quick then. I am available right now."

"I don't have time. I'm really sorry. I have to get back to school. I have finals," she said.

Sarah's nurse had no idea that Sarah was up and dressed, having checked on this sleeping "child" just 10 minutes before.

"Can you take this thing out. It hurts," Sarah said to the nurse, referring to her IV. "I have to go."

Psychiatric evaluations in an emergency department do not resemble the orderly 50 minute interviews of an outpatient department. In the Emergency Department we have unscheduled, disorderly emergencies, and we gather information in multiple stages, sometimes over many long hours or even days. We are not in a hurry and we force our patients to be not in a hurry because there is much riding on our decisions, sometimes life and death. We want all the information we can get from all the sources which are helpful to us before we recommend a treatment plan that could range from an involuntary psychiatric hold to simply letting a patient walk out the door.

Sarah had been unceremoniously rushed to the ED from her boyfriend's apartment by paramedics responding to a call about an overdose. Her boyfriend, Jason, a student like Sarah, came home from his job on the Sacramento State campus to find Sarah unconscious with an empty bottle of Benadryl on the floor. She had vomited on the bed and on the floor. Jason had arrived at the hospital five minutes after the ambulance, and had patiently waited the whole six hours while she slept. He was an appealing young man with staying power who appeared committed to stand by her side, by her gurney, for however long it took.

I was working that month with a social work intern, a second-year graduate student in social work from Sacramento State who was assigned to UC Davis Medical Center for her internship field placement. One enjoyable responsibility built in to working at a university medical center is teaching students, and this student, Alison, reminded me of just how much fun that part of the job was every day I worked with her. A good student like Alison does your job for you, or at least helps you do less work and higher quality work, and also adds much to the morale of the team and to the enthusiasm and humor with which we approach our work. It is a win-win proposal, and we are grateful to Sacramento State for sending the social work interns and they are grateful to us for providing an internship. On the other hand, a difficult student, or an unseasoned one, can slow things down, and no one can afford to be delayed in the ED.

Alison spent a lot of time with Jason collecting the story, and she gave me the phone numbers she had obtained from Jason for Sarah's parents, who lived in Santa Monica, and Sarah's sister, who was a medical student at UCLA, so I could call them and add to this history. I talked to Sarah's mother and father and asked Alison to call Sarah's sister, and when we both had finished on the phone, all three family members were headed on the next available plane to Sacramento. This was an involved, concerned family, something I liked to see.

Sarah's sister, Rebecca, four years older than Sarah, was in her second year of medical school at UCLA. Rebecca was not only bright and articulate, but also insightful about herself, about Sarah, and about their parents, possibly due to her own recent psychotherapy for panic attacks. Jason also provided helpful information, having known Sarah since middle school and having been her boyfriend since late high school. Sarah's parents were nervous, worried, and distressed, each taking ample time to provide a full family history, each having many questions themselves about what had happened. By the time Alison and I talked to Sarah for the first time, we had an encyclopedia of background information about her.

77

Jason first said he was Sarah's boyfriend, and then he said, "not really." They had known each other since the seventh grade, and it was only in their last year of high school that they went out on one date, neither having dated anyone before.

They went to a high school prom, they kissed twice, and they both assumed this meant something, having nothing else to compare it with, so in their minds they were boyfriend and girlfriend, they guessed.

Sarah was an excellent student in high school, according to Jason, but she always worried about her grades. Jason said he thought that Sarah's mother would be very disappointed in Sarah if she received any grade lower than an A, but Sarah would also be disappointed in herself.

"The weird thing is that every test she ever took she thought she flunked," said Jason. "Her head hurt, her stomach hurt, she got sick, but she always got an A. Always. Never one B."

Sarah was admitted to UC Berkeley, and, like her UCLA sister before her, prepared for medical school by taking pre-med classes. Rebecca told Alison that their father was a physician and their mother was a woman who wanted her children to be physicians.

Jason, on the other hand, was a good student, with his share of B's, who entered Sacramento State at the same time Sarah started at Berkeley. They kept in touch their entire first year by phone and email but they rarely saw each other.

"Whenever I went to Berkeley she was too busy studying, and she never came to Sacramento because she was too busy studying," said Jason. "She had the same pattern in college that she had in high school. She was certain she had flunked every college test she took and would get very depressed about it, but then she would get an A. She would text a lot and talk a lot on the phone after a test before she got her grade, and I really worried about her. She seemed so down. After she got her

78

grade, her A, everything was OK until the next test."

After her first year at Berkeley, competing with the best and the brightest in pre-med courses, Sarah had all A's and one B+. She felt defeated and deflated about the B+ and was convinced, since the grade was in a chemistry class, that it would bar her from getting into any medical schools. She did not tell her mother about the B+ and she did not forgive herself for getting it.

Things got worse for Sarah during her second year at Berkeley, the year of organic chemistry. She received a B in her first semester of organic chemistry, "O-chem" as she called it, her only B that semester, and it was surrounded by a field of A's. However, she was absolutely certain that she would flunk the final of her second semester of organic chemistry, a final that she was just about to take.

Jason was tearful when he told Alison that he had not taken Sarah's sadness seriously enough this time. "I thought it was just Sarah being Sarah. She always thought she was flunking. She wouldn't be Sarah unless she thought she was flunking. But she always got A's. If I tell you I'm flunking, I'm flunking. But not Sarah."

Sarah took the train from Berkeley to Sacramento two days before her organic chemistry final to tell Jason she was flunking out of Berkeley and that she was not going to take any of her finals. However, she did study organic chemistry furiously all the way up on the train, and she spent most of her hours in Sacramento studying chemistry.

"I didn't believe her," said Jason. "I thought she'd go back to Berkeley, take the O-chem final, and get an A. She asked me not to go to work last night, but I had to go to work. When I got back, I couldn't wake her up."

It seemed to me and to Alison that Jason genuinely loved Sarah; he was certainly not breaking up with her as I commonly see in relationship-related suicide attempts. He actually wanted more of a relationship with her, wanted to do fun, recreational things with her, maybe take a trip together right after finals, something they had never done before. He was worried that Sarah's parents would think all of this was his fault, and he worried that maybe it was.

"I never should have gone to work," said Jason.

"You couldn't have known, Jason, not by her history," said Alison.

"I should've known," he said.

Jason knew that Sarah's parents did not like him. He said they did not actively dislike him, but Sarah would occasionally, affectionately tease him about the things her parents would say about him: "He's not going anywhere. He'll be a heavy weight around you. You don't have anything in common. He doesn't even know what he wants to be and he'll never get there anyway." In fact, Jason wanted to be an engineer and he was getting mainly A's and B's in his freshman and sophomore years at Sacramento State. He was getting there.

. . . .

Rebecca, it seemed, was eager to talk about her parents, eagerness that bespoke long, bottled-up frustrations. She was a gold mine of knowledge and insight. Rebecca's most recent, "overly-long" conversation with her mother, mainly a one-way talk, was described as her mother's "diatribe" about which branches of medicine Rebecca and Sarah should specialize in.

"You know Sarah is not even in medical school, don't you, Mom?" Rebecca had said.

Their mother historically had argued in favor of the high prestige and lucrative specialties in medicine, argued for the girls to be like their father, an orthopedic surgeon. But recently, after their mother's appointment with an internal medicine physician, she worried about what that physician told her: many of the specialties in medicine were not doing that well in this competitive insurance environment, and family practice and internal medicine were faring better. Her physician did say that dermatology and ophthalmology were commanding high compensation and had good working hours, but these specialties were highly competitive so top grades and distinguished clinical performance while in medical school were imperative.

"Honey, you have to think about these things," Mrs. Headley had said to Rebecca. "You should be asking faculty members." Mrs. Headley, herself, was never remiss in thinking about these things.

Since the time they were in the first grade, Mrs. Headley, a high school mathematics teacher, had been advising her children about their future careers in medicine. She never said they were required to go into medicine, but both children knew there was only one road to take in life. When the children were in high school, Mrs. Headley would casually remark to other mothers, "Rebecca and I haven't decided which branch of medicine she should pursue." The father believed orthopedics would be best, and envisioned his daughters working right alongside him.

The Headley children would be well-prepared. They lived in a world of science, of disciplined study, of planned intellectual growth, of excellence and accomplishment. Even before formal schooling began, homework was built into the evening and weekend schedule. Play time was precisely and carefully chosen for its learning value; enjoyable pleasure was an acceptable byproduct but unnecessary. Trips were planned based on their educational value and the only games played were ones that made children think.

"No Chutes and Ladders?" Alison asked Rebecca.

"What's Chutes and Ladders?" she asked.

Chess was acceptable, as was Trivial Pursuit and Brain Quest. The mother took pride in how well her children answered the sixth-grade questions from Brain Quest when they were only in the first grade. Toys had to be instructional and gifts were monitored and exchanged if inappropriate or silly.

The Headleys preferred like-minded parents whose planned play activities for children were purposeful. There were many questionable invitations that needed careful consideration—birthday parties to laser tag, a high school party to a paint-ball war game, a sleepover party with video games—many of these invitations needed to be declined. This exercise of parental guidelines could cause bitter disappointment, but good parents had to be parents, disappointment and all.

Dr. and Mrs. Headley thought alike and presented a united front. Books and movies were the classics only and both young children were guided to read appropriate adult literature. Television was invariably a brain buster. Harry Potter was irrelevant as were the whole genres of fantasy and science fiction. Dr. and Mrs. Headley were parents who had values, not just opinions, and these values were set in stone. Mrs. Headley took seriously the responsibility of teaching her children what the best choices in life were in work, study, and play. Rebecca said, with some sadness, that her parents taught her that there was only one right way for all decisions, whether big or small, like which way to roll the toilet paper, over or under, or which ice cream to choose from the 31 flavors. Bad choices led to bad habits led to an unhappy life.

. . . .

My brother, Bob, who is two years older than I am, taught me, when I was five years old, that chocolate ice cream was better than vanilla. He was embarrassed when I ordered vanilla in the company of others, and he told me that kids who liked vanilla were stupid. In high school, after 10 years completely off vanilla, faithful to chocolate, I rediscovered vanilla ice cream. For me, it was better than chocolate. But to this day I look around to see who is watching me when I order vanilla. I do not want people to think I am stupid.

. . . .

In high school, Rebecca's and Sarah's lives were "ultra-structured." Professional college counselors were hired to guide them and to help guarantee their acceptance into the best colleges.

Long ago, Dr. and Mrs. Headley had met each other while attending an Ivy League college, and they were both emotionally wedded to that college. They never missed a yearly reunion, their most valued friends were college friends, and they knew the lifelong advantages of a quality college.

Both of their children attended private schools from kindergarten through high school, and additional, professional counselors were hired to guide their course-work all through high school to make sure they had ample advanced placement courses. These counselors also recommended specific types of community service and extracurricular activities that were impressive and useful for college admission. Rebecca and Sarah were busy children with no time to waste. Sarah played soccer since early childhood and was an excellent high school player. She also played tennis and golf proficiently and took weekly lessons for each. She practiced an hour a day on the piano and performed consistently well at her teacher's recitals. Her ballet instructors raved about her talent, too.

Homework was almost always stressful for Sarah. She had natural qualities of self-discipline, orderliness, and compulsive perfectionism, and she had no need of a demanding, ambitious mother hovering over her and rooting for her to be "the best she could possibly be." Sarah was born to be the best she could possibly be, born to strive for excellence, and she was severely disappointed in herself when she did not achieve it. When her classmates in the second grade handed in their term project of a drawing of the world, most turned in vague, sloppy, but colorful sketches of three amorphous continents and an ocean, but Sarah turned in a precise drawing of continents, countries, capitals, bodies of water, and mountains. She drew in longitudes and latitudes. Her mother helped her, of course, as any good helicopter parent would, but it was in Sarah's bones to be the best.

Sarah consistently got the highest praise, the best grades, and the most awards for all of her hard work, and if anybody gave an award for the most worried girl in high school, she would have been the clear winner. She often wept at night during her long, exhausting hours of homework and her self-imposed imprisonment of perfectionism, and her mother's high standards also drove her into deep spells of sadness.

Children are different from the get-go. Some need careful supervision and a push, some need wide space and a pull back. The combination of a perfectionist child and a tiger mother can be a recipe for great achievement or for great depression. Nobody needed to push Sarah; she drove herself hard. Some parents worry that their child is not doing enough or being enough, while other parents worry their child is not happy enough. There is the right philosophy for each child in there somewhere, but the balance and ratios may be favored differently by each parent.

The Headleys wanted each of their children to be somebody, to do something important, specifically, to be a physician. They believed, sincerely, that their children would never be happy until they were successful doctors. These parents sacrificed, planned, plotted, and fought to that end.

The parents knew that only the best students were admitted to the best colleges, that only the best college students were accepted at the best medical schools, that only the best medical students entered the best residencies, that the best residents were selected for the best jobs, and, finally, that the best jobs gave their children the best chance of happiness. The Headleys knew that this long road to happiness was difficult, but it was a prerequisite for fulfillment in life.

Personally, I have seen just as many depressed people with advanced degrees from prestigious colleges as I have seen sadness in people who stopped their education with a high school diploma. I have treated as many elite university students for depression as I have community college students, and I have seen more depressed physicians than I have seen depressed carpenters. Once you step on that train headed to "being the best," it is hard to hop off. It takes a crisis sometimes, a wrench thrown into the merry-go-round machinery to change course. This young, smart, accomplished Berkeley student, with her overdose, may have thrown in the wrench.

"Sarah, I have to make sure you are safe before you leave," I said.

"I'm fine."

"I have to be sure."

I explained to Sarah what happens when somebody makes what appears to be a suicide attempt; I told her that I needed to be comfortable that she was safe, both medically and emotionally, before she left. After many repetitions of "I am fine," and "I have to go now," and "I have finals tomorrow," the disappointing news sunk in that she was not completely free to leave, as did the shocking news that her mother, father, and sister were all on their way to Sacramento to be with her.

Sarah's family was not scheduled to arrive at the hospital for hours, and Alison and I had the time and the strong motivation to do our best to help this fragile woman who was doing her best not to cry and not to lose her dignity.

"Jason has been here since you arrived, Sarah," said Alison. "He was not able to wake you up so he called 911."

"I didn't mean to take pills. I did mean it for a second, but I got scared and stuck my fingers down my throat and vomited it all up into the bathroom sink. Whole pills came out. I thought I was OK so I went to sleep."

Sarah could not remember vomiting again on the rug and in the bed. She must have digested some pills because she was heavily sedated when Jason arrived at home. She was treated in the ED and was soon to be medically cleared for discharge pending our required psychiatric evaluation.

· · · · · · · · · ·

The last thing I want to do is make my patients' lives worse and more complicated than they already are, but "dead" is the final definition of worse, a worst-case outcome that I do not want to face. So I am cautious. I do not want to trample on someone's life with an involuntary psychiatric admission, but I also do not want to free suicidal patients who are at risk for leaving the hospital with the intent to kill themselves. It is not an easy decision or a formulaic one. I cannot plug in risk factors and arrive at a guaranteed answer. For example, I may know certain statistical risk factors: women make suicide attempts more frequently than men but men are more successful, women more often use pills while men jump from high places or use guns, divorced patients pose more danger than married patients, seriously sick patients are a higher risk than healthy ones, substance abuse is worse than clean and sober, psychosis is never a good sign, isolation is worse than healthy support, prior psychiatric history and suicide attempts are red flags, a concrete and methodical plan for suicide is worse than an impulsive attempt; I know all this and much more, it is all through the literature. But when it comes down to this one decision about this unique individual, the theory, the statistics, and the demographics play only a small part. Each case is its own study requiring its own careful consideration separate from the common generalizations.

With each patient I am assessing, I take a close look at their suicide risk—at their background, history, support, suicidal ideation, planning, type of attempt, quality of attempt, motivation behind the attempt, and regrets for having made the attempt versus regrets over not being dead. I want to know how seriously they willed their death, how severe their pain is, and how promising relief and treatment might be for them. Most patients know that I mean them no harm, even though I have power over them, and most can sense that I genuinely like them and will advocate for them. I think Sarah knew this about both Alison and me, and she was able to talk about her sadness, the sadness that went way back in her life, and the fear that attacked her now.

"For a moment I thought I'd rather die than flunk organic chemistry. If I flunk O-chem I don't get into medical school and everything I've ever done will be for nothing."

"And that would be worse than death?" I asked.

"Yes, worse than death. You don't fail in my family."

"Your boyfriend thinks you are brilliant," said Alison. "He thinks you're the smartest person he's ever known."

"My boyfriend is not my parents," she said.

Sarah's fears of flunking chemistry were real to her even though everyone who knew her doubted she would flunk. Fears or not, it was quickly evident that Sarah had not given up on her chemistry final; Jason was sent back to his apartment at her request, as soon as she realized that she would be in the ED for an undetermined period of time, to gather up her study material and her organic chemistry book. This was a good example of "forward-thinking," something healthy to see in a suicidal patient, evidence that she was invested in a future and was planning for it no matter how pessimistic she was.

"Will your parents be so disappointed about a grade?" I asked. "When I talked with them on the phone, their whole focus was on your health and well-being."

"My parents, mainly my mother, were picking out my medical career before I was born," she said.

I had been struck by the depth of worry, love, concern, and desire to help that her parents revealed on the phone, and by their immediate plan to fly to Sacramento to rescue and nurture their daughter. Almost every question the mother asked me was appropriately tender and leaked no hint of disappointment. However, I did note that Mrs. Headley asked me, casually, not a critically important question, if I knew the grade point average and typical MCAT scores for medical students accepted at UC Davis.

"Is it all about your parents?" I asked. "Seems like you have high expectations of yourself. An A or death, the best or nothing at all. Not much wiggle room there."

. . . .

I am familiar with the American philosophy and the American way of life: set your goals high, strive to be the best, failure is not an option, winners never quit and quitters never win. The Olympics is the goal and the only acceptable prize is the gold medal.

Personally, I fail at these standards. I cemented in my life philosophy long ago: set your goals low in life and forgive yourself when you fail to achieve them. I am attracted to the wonderful marathon runners' phrase, for the back-of-the-pack runners, "Pace yourself at the start and then taper off." I want it said on my tombstone, "He died happy. He never expected much of himself." This is a personal philosophy not meant for all, but I have found that while achievement can bring me happiness, happiness can bring me happiness better. I want to live a meaningful life, but the meaning of my life is joy and love, big goals indeed, and elusive ones, too, particularly if you get distracted.

I do not have a need to be the best, and I am not haunted by the competition for recognition and awards. If I drive down that road by mistake, I turn around quickly because the road to perfection, for me, brings self-doubt, self-criticism, and depression.

I like to think I passed this trait on to my children, this passion to pursue joy, much like the Headleys wanted to pass on their highest values, their secrets to a good life, to their children. When my son was nine years old, a student of the piano, sitting down to practice, he said to his mother, my wife, a fine pianist, "I'm sorry, Mom. I quit. I can't live your dreams." I thought that was healthy at the time. I still do. He does, however, as an adult, regret giving up the piano. To shape or not to shape a child, that is the question.

I know I cannot convince Mrs. Headley that her philosophy of achievement is too rigid, nor can she kick start me into striving for excellence. It may be possible, however, for us to reach a compromise, on this one occasion, for this one crisis. I know that I am not fixed on the idea that any one philosophy or ideology is the truth, the best for all children. I am willing to give a little. It may well be that if I had a drug-addicted, unemployed, penniless adult son, a parasite living in my house way into his 30s, I might be persuaded to give him a little push. But I also think the perfectionistic child needs a lesson in lazy, unproductive, unadulterated joy.

I appreciate the fact that my own parents were never particularly interested in shaping me into anything, and that quality of theirs may be the foundation of my attitudes. I was a kid prone to Walter Mitty fantasies who presented to my mother frequent pronouncements of what I was going to be when I grew up. At the age of 13, having read all of Ian Fleming's James Bond books, I told my mother I was going to be a spy. I assumed spies in America had the same high-performance cars and cool cigarette holders that the British Secret Service had. I would introduce myself to people as, "Farrell, John Farrell," and I practiced a British accent to say those words even though I would apply to the CIA. I even hunted everywhere for a similar cigarette case to the one so suavely held by James Bond, and asked my mother to be on the lookout for it. My mother's only comment was, "Well, that's nice, dear. A spy you say. Well you know, we don't want you to smoke cigarettes. Maybe you could put chewing gum in that cigarette case." I could go to my mother and tell her I was going to raise pigeons for a living and she would say, "That's nice, honey. Try to keep them out of the house."

My father did have his preferences, but he put up little fight in defending them. He always repeated to me his heart-felt occupational truth that "the business of America is business." At one point in time, when I was still a child, he was the president of Hires Root Beer. He made a lot of money, and we drank a lot of root beer. We were happy. Although it is hard to find a Hires Root Beer now, and it must be special-ordered, it is the only root beer I will drink, the only root beer that has magical mood-elevation effects on me. Sometimes, when I am in a melancholic mood about my profession, having realized that I do not make a lot of money nor do I get to drink a lot of root beer at the Medical Center, I wonder if I made the right decisions in life.

If it is not bad enough that we expect ourselves to rise to the top of our profession and stay at the top, we also want our heroes to go out at the top of their game. We do not admire the struggling old athlete trying to swing away for one more season. I say no, don't go out at the top of your game, go out at the bottom.

I thought it best for me to leave my job with nothing left on the playing field. Absolutely nothing. Carry me off. I am not going voluntarily. I just wanted to spend my last couple of years in Psychiatric Emergency Services enjoying my work friends and colleagues, appreciating each of my final patients, and feeling the joy that new students feel upon entering the profession, the wonder and freshness of it all. I was not interested in the glory of research projects, and I had no need for recognition or awards. I had two great final years, and I am not ashamed of nor diminished by my lack of ambition. But I am blessed with unearned, irrational self-esteem and that almost always helps.

....

"I know I push myself, but I have to," Sarah said to Alison and me. "I can't get into medical school with B's. Not in chemistry."

"I am not as sure about that as you are," I said, "but we can talk about that. First, tell us more about your life in Berkeley as a whole. Where do you live, what do you do for a break or for fun?"

Sarah told us she had lived in a dorm her first year. She summarized that year in one sentence: "I went to classes and I studied." She was pre-med so her academic schedule was structured with sequences of chemistry, physics, and biology classes. She also had to work into that rigorous schedule her general education requirements like English and history. It was her perception, and I believe a very accurate one, that her roommates, her floor mates, and her dorm mates had more time and more fun than she had. They drank, smoked marijuana, had girlfriends and boyfriends, hung out together, had sex, sometimes in her dorm room. They made noise in her room and on her dorm floor, they went to football games, then basketball games, and they had parties, planned and impromptu ones, while Sarah went to classes and studied. She saw everyone around her having fun, and she wanted to have fun, too, but she was too worried and had too little time to surrender and relax, even for a moment.

Sarah did allow herself a diversion or two but not without worrying about the impact these activities would have on her study time and on her grades. She pursued her interest in ballet

90

by taking classes at Berkeley, she was a member of a pre-med society which occasionally met socially, and she frequently talked to Jason who several times took the train from Sacramento to Berkeley to visit her.

During her second year at Berkeley, Sarah lived off-campus.

"Off-campus housing in Berkeley is super expensive and pretty shabby for what you get," she said. "But my parents were paying for everything, and I went in with three other girls on a nice two-bedroom apartment on the north side of campus."

"Is that better for you than the dorms?" I asked.

"In some ways," she said. "The north side of campus is quiet, but two of my roommates have boyfriends who are over all the time and it is still crowded and noisy."

The second year of chemistry, the dreaded organic chemistry, was more difficult for Sarah than the first year of general chemistry, and she studied furiously—I had no doubt about that—but the material was more complex and the competition fiercer. Jason wanted more of a relationship with her, and she was not opposed to this, but she had no time to give him. Sarah's life was once again all study, all classes. She lost weight on her already small frame because she would forget to eat or be too nervous to. Jason was coming up to visit her only to watch her study. This was the life that Sarah always lived, observing others live life with pleasure, but claiming no rights to a good time for herself.

"I guess I am used to it. It's not like we had a playful family," Sarah said. "We learned that life was hard work and leisure was a waste of time. That was my mother's favorite phrase: 'What a waste of time.'"

"Did you have the feeling that you missed out on a lot?" Alison asked. "Were there things that you would have wanted to do, things you still want to do?"

"When I was a senior in high school, Jason wanted to take me to Disneyland," Sarah said. "His family had season tickets to Disneyland, if you can imagine. His family was so different from mine. As a little kid Jason's father told him that there is a heaven, and

91

it is in Anaheim, California, and its name is Disneyland. Jason is crazy about Disneyland. If it was up to him he would go every day."

"Did you go?" I asked.

"No. What a waste of time," Sarah said, quoting her mother.

Sarah's parents believed in the truth, the scientific, verifiable truth. They did not believe in lying to their children about Santa Claus or the Easter bunny or elves or dwarfs or witches or other silly fantasies. Children deserved the truth and a clear picture of the world so they could navigate it well and excel in it.

"Disneyland is a phony and commercial place, according to my mother. They put short people in animal costumes and tell children these little animals are real. 'They're not real, Sarah, nothing is real in Disneyland,'" Sarah said imitating her mother in a harsh tone.

Alison asked Sarah if her courses brought her any pleasure. They had not. Up to now all of her college classes had been extensions of high-school sciences, preparatory classes which were nowhere near related to what she would eventually be doing in medicine. She would have to go back to high school to remember any pleasure from a class; there was an art history class she enjoyed, and then an elective architecture class in which she built elaborate, imaginative models of two houses and an office building. She was proud of these creations, and she confessed to both interest and ability in art and in architecture.

"I changed my major many times in college," I told Sarah. "I had many interests and few abilities. Have you thought about changing your major?"

"From biology?" she asked. "It doesn't matter what my major is, I still have to take the same pre-med classes."

"Pre-med is your mother's major, isn't it?" I asked.

"I am my mother, or she is me."

"College is that wonderful time when you get to separate from your mother," I said.

"Nobody separates from my mother," she said.

If truth be told, and Sarah literally whispered out the truth as if her mother was not far away and could hear her, she had been thinking ever since her entry into Berkeley of pursuing architecture as her life's work, but her path was inflexibly paved. She did not want to even imagine how her parents would feel if she "turned her back" on medicine. The point of college for many is growth and separation from parents, and separation spurs on growth and growth spurs on separation. It is a rare time, blessed with more freedom than young adults may ever have again, freedom to become acquainted and comfortable with who they are, freedom to embrace the qualities they have and to forgive themselves for the qualities they do not have, a time to pursue their passionate interests. I wanted for Sarah, as I envisioned her future, the opportunity for her to realize that she was unique from birth, separate and different from her parents. It was important for her to discover for herself her value and place in life, that nobody could become a better Sarah than Sarah, certainly not her parents. To do this she needed to turn the coach around and go the other way, but the resistance for changing course was mighty and came from forces outside of her and from forces within.

"I wonder if you are right, Sarah," I said. "It seems like nobody has separated from your mother. Not your sister, and not you."

"At least I moved farther away than my sister," she said. "I got all the way to Northern California."

"Moving away from your parents is not separating from your parents," I suggested. "You have a parent that lives inside you. You have to move away from that parent. You could live in an underground research bunker in Antarctica, but that parent is still going to be right there next to you, and that inside parent is the harshest of all. Willing to kill you."

At Sarah's request, Jason joined us in our talk, having arrived with all of Sarah's study materials. Sarah, Jason, Alison and I engaged in a talk of pure fantasy, a talk that was a "waste of time." It involved many "what if's." What if you change your major? How would you feel, what classes would you take? What if every day of your life was not ruled by the need to get into medical school? What would you do this summer if you could do anything you wanted to do?

Sarah explained that her mother had already gone to great lengths, using the father's connections, to get Sarah an unpaid, but very valuable research position in the Department of Orthopedics at UC San Francisco Medical Center, an "opportunity of a lifetime" for a prospective medical student. Sarah had accepted this proposal, albeit unhappily. This did not prevent Sarah from engaging in her fantasy world and laughing at herself as she changed her major, set her sights on architecture, took art history classes, and took a summer job in Berkeley teaching kids to dance at the ballet studio where she took lessons. In actual fact, the owner of the studio had asked her if she would be willing to take a summer job at the studio because Sarah was observed to be very good at instilling the joy of dance into young children.

Then there was the fantasy magnum opus: a trip with Jason to Disney World in Florida this summer, the most magical, most happy place on Earth.

"Like my parents would ever go for this," she said.

"Is it what you want?" Alison asked.

"It doesn't do any good to think about it."

That is when the three of us, in unison, unplanned, two therapists and a boyfriend, voiced the same question, a little too firmly: "Is it what you want?"

"Yes," she said, barely audible.

Alison and I took a break. We had been talking for two hours and it was time to leave Sarah and Jason alone to study and think, to plan the next day, the day after that, and maybe the summer. We would be back to talk more about Sarah's suicidal thoughts, her depression, and a treatment plan for her as well as a life plan. Her medical attending told me that Sarah could eat now, and she was soon to be medically cleared.

. . . .

There is a rainbow of colors to depression, and it would be helpful if we could pick our shade, but we are forced to accept an unwanted gift. There are types of depression that stand as living

94

proof of the genius of anti-depressant medication, yet some moods are impervious to all medications. Some low moods kick your ass, send you to bed and keep you there, while other states of sadness are not so debilitating, like drifting clouds of melancholia prompting the sufferer to embrace a good blues album. Depression can be severe and lethal, or mild and mystical. It can come out of nowhere, or out of bleak and sunless seasons, out of anniversaries, or out of trauma, change, and loss. Some people, racked with guilt, blame themselves for their pain, as it confirms what they have always suspected, that they are worthless, undeserving, and broken. Other people are mad at the world for the perceived injustices piled upon them.

There are sufferers who cannot eat when they are sad, cannot sleep, and will not walk to the bathroom because they cannot get out of bed, while others are restless, agitated, and ready to fight. Sometimes depression comes and goes like an unwanted relative and sometimes it burrows in to stay.

In the Emergency Department I see all kinds of depression, patients who are having reasonable reactions to loss and change, and those who slip into a dark hole of bad chemicals and vulnerable biology. Some people I see are depressed because it is embedded in their core personalities and they become familiar with this stalking friend, but other confused and frightened patients feel their depression as an invasion from a foreign terrorist.

Any type of depression can provoke suicidal thoughts, or not, and every suicidal thought or attempt has its own motivation and risk. A critical task in a psychiatric assessment is to know that risk, to research it thoroughly, and to guess well.

Not every therapist is good at this and all therapists can make mistakes. I am aware that I can miss things that I should have seen, but I also know that people and circumstances change after they walk out of the hospital, and I have no control over those changes. I have assessed many suicidal patients, thought they were a low risk for hurting themselves, and let them go, only to doubt myself immediately after and for days later until they were concretely and safely secured in another therapy or treatment program. I have also second-guessed myself after admitting patients to a psychiatric hospital on a psychiatric hold, wondering if I was sacrificing their freedom for my peace of mind.

I saw a Latino man, a student from University of Southern California attending college on a swimming scholarship, who was living with his family during the summer, who came to the ED and told me a story he had never told his parents or anyone else. He said he had been suicidal since early childhood, that suicidal thoughts were always with him, that he thought they were normal and that everyone else had them, too. He chronically had obsessive, intrusive thoughts about killing himself, vivid pictures in his mind of specific attempts provoked by the props around him, like a rope hanging on a tree, a knife in the kitchen drawer, a car in a closed garage, or a bottle of pills in the medicine cabinet.

By his early teens he was regularly engaging in creative fantasies of how he could kill himself. As he progressed in his teenage years, his intrusive thoughts became more detailed, and he began to slowly move toward action, like holding and staring at a knife, or tying a knot with a rope, or holding pills in his hand. He said he had never made a suicide attempt, but there was one time, in his apartment near USC, that he put dozens of capsules of Tylenol into his mouth to see how it would feel, before he spat them out. I asked him if he had been rehearsing for suicide, but he said that he did not think so. "I only wanted to see how they felt in my mouth."

In late high school he took to cutting himself when he was angry or frustrated, but he was a year-round swimmer, and in a Speedo bathing suit scars could not be hidden, so he limited this way of releasing his emotions. He went to high school in the San Joaquin Valley where his parents, originally from Mexico, were farmers. The parents did well, retired early, and enjoyed life with a large extended family in Sacramento.

"I thought about killing myself by drowning," he said. "My culture is not known for its great swimmers. My culture is known for drowning in the canals in the summers trying to cool off in the hot valley. But for me drowning is a little far-fetched. I'm a good swimmer."

This patient came to me because he was having disturbing, intrusive thoughts while driving, thoughts about turning his steering wheel and the car directly into a tree or over a cliff. Trees and cliffs called out to him. What frightened him the most was his practice maneuvers; he was swerving the car slightly here or there to see how it felt.

He described himself as episodically depressed, with good times and bad times, the bad times invisible to friends and family. For most of his life he believed his intrusive thoughts were normal, that his suicidal musings were harmless preoccupations, but he was not so sure about this now, and he wanted to talk this out before he went back to USC. He said this was the first time he had ever talked to anyone about these thoughts. He carried this burden alone all of his life, and he wondered if his parents, who were always kind and supportive to him, could be his allies now.

I have talked to many people, normal to dangerous, who have intrusive thoughts about hurting themselves or hurting someone else: the hiker who has an impulse to jump when standing at the edge of a cliff, the new mother who suffers a momentary alien thought of stabbing her newborn child while she is handling a kitchen knife, the freeway driver who visualizes swerving into oncoming traffic. These thoughts are common, but acting on the thoughts is rare. Many normal people have intrusive thoughts that are frightening to them, but they will never act on them. But this young man was practicing for suicide in secret and he was worried about it. He had never asked for help and never thought he needed it until the day he walked into the emergency room.

He was right and courageous to ask for help, and he made a smart move in widening the circle of people who knew his thoughts from one to two. I had a productive conversation with him that day, and then we both had an emotional talk with his confused but supportive parents. He cried, they cried, I teared up. We arranged for him to see a psychiatrist in private practice the next day.

I thought there was a low risk in discharging him. He had a long-standing problem with no true suicide attempts, he had caring and involved parents, he was motivated to get help and help was readily available to him, and he made the decision not to drive for a little while. These were all good indications of diminished risk, but I would never say that my decision was without risk.

. . . .

Depression can be the darkest and most powerful cloud, virulent chemicals too strong to control, a force of biological nature rendering victims helpless, a tidal wave of destruction. It can compel a caring man to hang himself in his family's home or it can force a sweet, gay teen to jump off a high bridge onto rocks below. Dark moods, deep sadness, and self-disgust are potent. Many patients I see judge themselves harshly. Imagine how deadly it can be when family and friends judge them harshly also and cast them out.

There is a big difference in outcomes when parents are loving, accepting, and supportive of their children as opposed to parents who reject their children outright. Some of those differences can be measured in the child's self-esteem, self-destructiveness, self-hatred, drug and alcohol abuse, academic success, relationships with peers, teachers, and other adults, and severity of suicidal thoughts.

A very kind and concerned Sacramento City Police Officer, a young woman, brought to the Emergency Department a 19-year-old gay man, Paul, who was sleeping under a bridge. When she confronted him, he broke down and cried and told her he did not want to live anymore. He was tired—tired of running, tired of being homeless, tired of being alone. My first impression of him was that he was, indeed, tired of living. He was rejected by his parents, condemned by his church, scorned by his peers, beaten by his father, and living on his own since the age of 14. His crime was being gay, although he tried furiously not to be.

After being ejected from his house by his disgusted mother and his angry father, he traveled from Sacramento on his own as far south as San Diego and as far north as Seattle, sometimes living in teen shelters, but often living on the streets. He stole small things

98

and panhandled and learned from more experienced homeless men to collect cans to recycle for money. He did what he had to do to survive but survival was no longer his goal. Paul had recently been to San Francisco, and he twice walked out to the middle of the Golden Gate Bridge with the intent to jump. He hated himself for being too frightened to follow through.

The day before he was brought to the emergency room he stood on a freeway overpass waiting for a large semi to approach so he could jump off the bridge into the oncoming truck. He did not want to just kill himself; he wanted to obliterate every single sinful cell of his body. He hated himself and he hated his life, and he truly believed that he had no one to blame but himself. He was evil, demonic even, and he was going to hell, and he was motivated to accelerate that trip.

With Paul's permission, I talked to his mother who told me, "We did everything we could for him but he was an odd kid to begin with." The parents were long-standing members of an evangelical church, and in their house it was unacceptable and unforgivable to "choose" the sin of homosexuality. The mother said that the father, who had recently separated from her, always blamed her for her son's sins. Growing up, his father forced Paul to participate in sports in which he had no interest, and he took him duck hunting hoping to make a man out of him. The father soon gave up on Paul and turned his rage on his wife for her part in encouraging Paul's obvious "girlish" qualities.

Neither parent encouraged Paul's artistic talents which were considerable. Paul had virtually no possessions when he arrived in the emergency room except a folder of his drawings which were remarkable for many reasons. Some of his drawings and paintings were striking self-portraits depicting distorted images of ugliness and illness. In his artwork I could see Paul, the leper. Paul's mother ended her self-imposed short conversation with me by saying that Paul was not welcome back at home. Paul was welcomed into and was grateful for a psychiatric hospital that day.

I taught a class in human sexuality at Sacramento State for many years, and, predictably, the most controversial part of the semester was the week we talked about gays, lesbians, bisexuals, and transgender people. All these young students in the class tolerated pretty well the idea that old people could have enjoyable sex, that disabled people enjoyed sex, that ill people had sex, and, especially, that young college students had exciting, athletic, magnificent sex. But when it came around to two men having sex there was trouble. Invariably, some young men in the class, while having few objections to two beautiful "straight-looking" women having sex with each other, thought two men together was unnatural and repulsive.

Each semester I had a gay man, an exquisitely handsome young man who had studied for the priesthood but changed his mind, and a successful lesbian businesswoman, come to my class to talk about the subject of gays and lesbians, and to talk about themselves. Women in the class flocked to this gay man, crowded around him to meet him after class, sometimes asking him to autograph the assigned book that the lesbian speaker actually wrote. Some women confided to me that they wanted to convert him from gay to straight, that they were confident they could, and that they looked forward to the challenge.

Most women, and many men, too, were attracted to his gentle, kind, non-defensive, humorous, and articulate presentation. He was an ambassador of acceptance and tolerance to those who were neither accepting nor tolerant of him. He was an expert on the Bible having studied it all his life, and he patiently addressed ignorance with knowledge.

All the intelligent studies on the cause of sexual orientation and sexual identity say the same thing: we are born who we are, and no type of parent, no experience or trauma, no enticement or rebellion is going to change that. Our sexual orientation is somewhere on that continuum between gay and straight, and we are not going to move much from that birthing point. That point will determine with whom we fall in love. Men in the class who knew they were straight, who knew they were 100 percent straight, the absolute outer edge of the continuum, also knew that nothing could change them into being gay. What made some of them think that the opposite could be true, that a gay man could be or should be converted to being straight? Developing crushes, falling in love, having sexual feelings are all quite automatic and natural emotions, unaltered by our attempts to control them. All the rewards in the world are not going to change a person's deepest feelings and instincts, nor will the most severe punishments. People can change their behavior in a forced, tragic way, but never their inner yearnings.

The American Psychiatric Association, the American Psychological Association, and the National Association of Social Workers have all said the same thing for many years: same-sex orientation is a normal variation and expression of love and affection. It is not a mental illness, it is not a moral weakness. To attempt to psychologically treat gays and lesbians with the goal of coaxing them, coercing them, or shaming them into being straight is to take healthy people and make them ill. There still may be a few therapists trying to give it a go, self-righteous people with scripture in hand prepared to do God's work, to which I would say this: God's work is done at birth, stupid.

There is work to be done, however, for some young gays, lesbians, bisexuals and transgender people; self-loathing, depression, and suicidal thoughts can be common in vulnerable people who are abandoned by family, friends, church and community, left to stand alone. Suicide can be a high risk for these rejected children who are surrounded by powerful influences, the army of ignorance who will force dark brown contact lenses over their beautiful blue eyes because blue is different and bad and the Bible says it is so.

So to parents I see who are placing their children at suicide risk, I say step back, let go. You are not responsible for your child's sexual orientation, but you are at fault for the judgments and condemnations you hurl at your child, and you will lose your child and possibly your soul if you do not help your child love himself and embrace whomever he loves.

. . . .

101

I did not think that Sarah was a high risk for suicide. Jason was giving her strength by the minute and so was Alison. Alison, herself, was a social work intern who became a social worker rather than the attorney that her mother wanted her to be, so this was personal for Alison. Alison told me she was an argumentative child, the product of two attorneys, and during our healthy disagreements I understood her mother's disappointment; Alison could argue very well and I had no question as to her advocacy skills. Alison was not going to stand by and let Sarah pursue a profession that was not Sarah's choice and was not meant to be.

Alison asked if we should try to initiate a "suicide contract," an agreement between patient and therapist where the patient agrees or promises not to try to kill herself until the next meeting with a therapist. I have always thought that contracts against suicide with patients were a little gimmicky, favored by some professors in graduate programs who teach theory but do not see patients. These theoretical safety strategies may seem like they provide an extra precaution and can therefore be promoted by professors to students, but students live in the real world of seeing patients, and that is a much different world than the theoretical one.

A bargain of this type is certainly not binding and it is presumptuous. It presumes that I am so powerful as a person of influence in this patient's life that I can make a successful solemn agreement with him or her when all of the important people in this patient's life were not able to. Before suicidal people are physically sitting in an emergency room, they have broken a lot promises and told numerous lies to many people already. Many unspoken or clearly delineated contracts have already been broken. A safety contract against suicide also assumes that people are more powerful than depression and that the contract will act as a shield against deep sadness. That has not been my experience.

I felt safe without contracts anyway since we had so many good signs: involved parents and a helpful sister, all willing to fly to the rescue at a moment's notice, a healthy, strong patient who overdosed impulsively and regretted it immediately, a forward-thinking student who could hardly stop studying for her chemistry final, an awakening young woman who was approaching the dawn of redefining herself, and a boyfriend who genuinely cared for Sarah and who hoped for a long future in their relationship. Sarah is not someone I would place on a psychiatric hold, but I would make recommendations for the next days, and for the summer, that would embolden Sarah, support her, and enable her to "follow her passion." It would be important to have her parents on board with the same plan.

An insightful patient who wants to live and has much to live for, who has loving and supportive parents, is not guaranteed success in changing or bettering her life course. People do not change rapidly, not patients, and not their parents. Life values and inherent personality qualities are stubbornly rooted and slow to change. The minimum requirement for Sarah to break away and to set a new course for herself was to have ongoing support and encouragement. Her change in course would be naturally resisted, not only by her parents, who genuinely believed they had set the right course for her, but also by Sarah, who lived with her parents' values inside her. But sometimes a crisis of this gravity can loosen up everyone, break living patterns up, reshuffle the deck, and create a small opening for change, and this was the moment that Alison and I were attempting to seize.

As a candidate for ongoing psychotherapy, Sarah had the raw materials that any psychotherapist would love to work with. She had a promising road ahead, much like her sister, and possibly a budding will to forge her own path. With a little help, Sarah might be able to choose her own profession based on her own passion, joy, and abilities. A therapist could give Sarah a little push and then watch as Sarah's go-cart raced down the hill while the therapist sat back and took credit for the progress and speed. Sarah would do well in psychotherapy with a therapist like Alison, who would not allow Sarah to live life with a rigid script.

. . . .

Psychotherapy is not easy work for anybody but some people

103

need only a light touch on the shoulder while others need heavy equipment to move them. It is common to have patients, especially in an emergency room, whose feet are cemented to the floor. They will not move. They prefer to have the therapist change the cruel world around them.

In a very different case than Sarah's, with a seemingly similar story, I saw a 28-year-old man who had overdosed on six tablets of low-dose Ativan, an anti-anxiety medication, to persuade his girlfriend not to break up with him. Like Jason, he was not favored with his girlfriend's parents' praise.

He had led an uneventful life, at best, since high school graduation, and his high school years, while being his best, were not notable either. He signed up for some college classes after high school but dropped out of them before he expended any real work or effort. After his short college experiment, he tried various jobs out and generally did not like them, and so he lost them or was fired from them soon after he started. He smoked marijuana daily and drank heavily whenever he had the money, whenever his girlfriend would give him some money. His girlfriend, on the other hand, had finished college and was working full-time as an analyst for the state of California. Of course, her parents wanted better for her than this boyfriend.

His suicide risk was relatively weak and not prompted by his desire to die, but provoked by a need for attention, affection, and commitment from his girlfriend whom he believed was drifting away from him. I gave him the best strategy for keeping his girlfriend that I could think of, the only strategy I thought would work because his gamey suicide attempt was serving him poorly. I told him that his girlfriend's parents were right and so was she in their belief that she deserved a better boyfriend. He only had one choice—be a better boyfriend. Nobody likes a lecture, but after gathering history from his girlfriend, who was surprisingly sympathetic to him, I thought he needed one. In an ED we have little time and much to do.

"This is how it seems to me you show your love to your girlfriend," I said to him. "You control her, envy her, are jealous of her, get angry with her, think little about her needs, and ask everything of her while giving her nothing. She's going places in her life, you are going nowhere. She's trying to lift you up, you're trying to drag her down."

"I know," he said.

"Why would her parents or your girlfriend want someone for her who is broken and needs to be made whole, when she could easily be with someone who is already whole. Why would they want someone who sits at home drinking and smoking marijuana when she could have someone who is drug-free and alcohol-free like she is, and, for that matter, why would they want someone who sits at home doing nothing when she could have someone who is out working and contributing something?"

"Yeah," he said.

"Why stay with someone who is not making it when she could have someone who has already made it, and why somebody who is not even trying to get better when she could have someone who is already better? She doesn't need a sad, troubled question-mark of a person; she deserves a happy, fulfilled, exclamation point."

My lecture was winding down. There was not one word of sarcasm in it; it was delivered strictly to give him one desperate chance of holding on to what was dear to him. I told him not to resent her parents but to listen to them and take his cue from them. "They want you to be better. Don't just try to be better. Be better."

I let him know that he possibly had one advantage: everybody loves an underdog and he was a big underdog.

"She is with you for a reason or at least she was, but she won't be for long, not if she's smart, and she is. So start today. You don't have much time," I told him.

When we finished he knew what he had to do, but he would need help, encouragement and advocacy from a better therapist than me to do it. He needed to be chemical-free, back in school, focused on a job, thoughtful to his girlfriend, and contributing to the relationship. Simple as that. But not so simple at all because most people who have lived the life he had, lived off the good will and mercy of another, are not champing at the bit to shake this up. Bad habits die hard and most underdogs do not win. I was concerned that he was too passive and complacent to take even the first step, that of following up with outpatient psychotherapy.

I have seen many passive patients who want the riches of life to come to them. They tell me they have no control over their lives. Yes, they have sails, but they are stalled on a dead sea. They are not the author of the script of their life—they live with cruel uncertainty and place the blame of their failures on others.

They take cover, hide, and play defense. They do not know they can rewrite their own script, give themselves a more powerful role, enter their movie as a reinvented character. They do not know they can do this because they have not done it before and doing something different in life is a leap of faith, a risk. Risk-takers are generally not people who stay at home drinking, smoking marijuana, and overdosing; they are the ones out there falling down and getting back up, eventually creating a better life for themselves and the people they live with.

So before he left the clinic I tried to penetrate his passivity; "Don't argue with your girlfriend or her parents. Don't get angry. Don't try to convince your girlfriend that you are a worthy boyfriend—Clarence Darrow couldn't make that argument right now. Decide to be a good catch in a relationship and be one, period."

"OK," he said.

It was a weak "OK." I am not sure that he fully embraced all my metaphors: start your own movie, write your own script, cast your own characters, assign yourself the role you want. The next therapist he saw, if he saw one, might want to skip the poetry and stick with plain English, "Stop drugs, get a job, don't be a loser."

. . . .

Sarah's parents and her sister provided more help than we could

106

have hoped for. They were not worried about the chemistry final; they were completely focused on Sarah's well-being. News of a suicide attempt is sobering for parents, provoking fears that they are at fault. But it can also create an opening for reflection and change, support and love. I have worked with some parents who are frustrated with their child and blame that child for the suicide attempt. Sometimes these parents have gone through this process many times before and are angry, hopeless, and discouraged. They no longer have faith in the mental health system, and they no longer have faith in their child; the bridges to hope have collapsed. So it is very, very helpful when a loving family comes together for the single purpose of making things better—no more tearing down, all building up.

While I talked further with Sarah's parents about different alternatives for follow-up plans and about follow-up therapy, they were flexible and open to all ideas. Sarah's sister joined Sarah, Jason, and Alison in a warm, emotional, tearful reunion that helped prepare Sarah to face her parents. Alison's job was to bolster Sarah, and my job was to prepare and soften Sarah's parents before they met the new, "improved" Sarah, the one with her own ideas. My job was easy—Sarah's parents were pretty soft already.

Our large group gathering was a beautiful thing to see, and I appreciated every moment of it because it was a minority experience: Sarah was able to talk to her parents and her parents were able to listen with interest and approval. Her parents went beyond my expectations of helpfulness, especially after I had heard so much about their strong values, opinions, and goals for Sarah. The more her parents listened with acceptance, the more Sarah was able to freely express her own desires. Sometimes I can see a person melt right in front of me. Sarah's mother melted, and it was her love for Sarah and her deep concern for her that provided the heat.

Sarah decided that she was going to take her chemistry final after all, which was one day away, but she was worried that her apartment was full of festive bedlam making it difficult to study. Sarah and her parents had once stayed at an iconic hotel in Berkeley, the

Claremont Hotel, when Sarah first toured the campus, and Sarah loved its elegance and atmosphere. So the first step of the treatment plan was for the family to book two rooms at the Claremont Hotel for that night and several days after, one for the parents and one for Sarah and Rebecca. Step two was to take the chemistry exam the next day and face her two other final exams the day after. Then she could commiserate or celebrate with her family.

Step three was the biggest step and Sarah approached it hesitantly. Sarah wanted to change her major and steer toward architecture. Berkeley had one of the best architecture schools in the nation. Sarah's sister, Rebecca, was eloquent and persuasive, reasonable yet firm, in her advocacy of Sarah's desires, and as I looked at her parents I could see the evidence again of two hearts softening. When Sarah took her own turn verbalizing the words that she did not want to go to medical school, the words came out slowly, each word interrupted with tears. Her parents were also tearful in their love and sympathy, and so was Rebecca and so was Jason. And in that moment there was a flash of connection and affection between Sarah's parents and Jason as Jason comforted Sarah with his arm around her and with his own tears. Architecture it would be, the vote in the room was unanimous.

The arranged summer job as a research assistant at UC San Francisco was cancelled and replaced by the prospect of a job tutoring children in ballet. Mrs. Headley started with a small protest, "But don't you...," but she quickly pulled herself back and laughed.

Alison and I waited for the one glitch in the plan, the icing on the cake. Sarah asked to take a vacation in the summer with Jason to Disney World in Florida to celebrate the halfway point of their college careers. Rebecca and Sarah argued that this would be a consolation prize for not getting an "A" in organic chemistry. It would soften the psychological blow to Sarah. I believe in rewarding low grades with valuable prizes to high-performance students. It takes the edge off of competitive perfectionism. Her parents thought briefly about this proposal, as they would be the ones financing Sarah, and they accepted: "Disney World for a low grade.

Who would have thought?" said Mrs. Headley.

I took Dr. and Mrs. Headley aside and quietly asked them, "And what happens if Sara gets an A in organic chemistry?"

Mrs. Headley did not hesitate: "We send her to Disney World anyway."

"Great parents," I said.

. . . .

I heard from Sarah that summer in an email accompanied by dozens of pictures of her hugging Disney characters: Mickey, Minnie, Donald, Goofy, Pluto, Snow White, both Chip and Dale, Peter Pan, Captain Hook—even Captain Jack Sparrow.

"They're real," she announced.

Sarah got a B in organic chemistry. True to their word and a bit more, Dr. and Mrs. Headley paid for a one-week trip to Disney World for Sarah, and offered to pay for Jason, but Jason wanted to pick up his own part. They stayed at a Disney resort hotel, the New Orleans French Quarter, and lived life to the fullest from early morning to late at night. They partied hard and made lots of noise.

Sarah wrote to me, "It is hellishly hot here, the crowds are staggering, it rains every day, there is terrifying lightning, and I'm having the most fun of my life."

The Declaration of Independence

A little narcissism is a good thing. After all, why shouldn't I see myself as important, good-looking, excellent at my job, the envy of my coworkers, and deserving of all those awards I should have received but didn't, awards that were unjustly handed out to others. I like to keep my self-esteem on full throttle, a moving target always dodging the arrows of enemies, those who do not appreciate my exalted status. I refuse to let the negative opinions of others humble me or sober me up from my intoxication of self-love. Oh, it is good to be me.

Of course, this delusional giddiness has its downside; it blinds me to me, and if I cannot see me but others can, then I am proudly walking in the parade of life as the emperor with no clothes. My only way of protecting my royal grandiosity is to surround myself with doting devotees or frightened ones, and hope they will never burst my bubble.

Narcissism is hard to hide. It is out there, big time, self-advertised, self-promoted, self-inflated, full of super adjectives, self-congratulatory phrases, big words like "big," the best words, the most intelligent words. It is uncomfortable for the other humble occupants when a bigger-than-life narcissist enters a room; he fills it up, no more room, no option but to clear out. The narcissist has a feel, a smell, a slime if you will, giving the exposed a sudden demotion from person in the room to insignificant person in the room.

I do not think that most people see themselves clearly; certainly I do not. And unfortunately, those of us who work in the field of mental health, and who have logged in years of psychotherapy, do not necessarily improve our introspective sensitivities. We have our blind spots, many of them. And we have some extreme narcissists practicing in the field, too many of them.

One of the Chairs of our Department of Psychiatry, many years ago, was a megalomaniac, an empire builder with an enormous ego and wicked rage. His skills at inflicting humiliation were legendary and his charisma followed him like a great spotlight. His vainglorious self-trumpeting announced his presence, and he was near-comically followed about by his posse of disciples. He was genuinely talented and brought fame and fortune to the Department of Psychiatry, expanding programs, promoting ambitious community mental health teams throughout Sacramento, and wrestling funds from the county for innovative projects. He was an accomplished man and he was a tyrant, not quite like Caligula, but like his mellow cousin, still capable of inflicting much pain.

His life was about winning—the small battles, the big battles, all battles. He was a take-no-prisoners leader interested in crushing his opponents and humiliating them. He was, in his mind, the leader of his empire, a substantial empire at that, and his accomplishments served to reinforce his emperor status. If he could not be the chosen one, leader of the world, he would have preferred to destroy it. It was not the world he was concerned about, it was his place in it. Loyalty was the First Commandment in his kingdom and betrayal of that loyalty meant death.

This giant of a man, who stood tall on his history of good works and even taller on his exaggeration of those good works, once fired me from my job, which was a compliment to me. For one brief moment in time I came to this superior man's attention, and he acknowledged me, a peasant addressed by his emperor. I do not think he ever registered my name, perhaps it floated by the many important things he was thinking about at the time, but he could not ignore the fact that I was sitting in a chair in his office, the subject of a complaint against me by a resident in psychiatry with whom I had argued.

The argument with the resident concerned just who was in charge of the patient dispositions, the final treatment plans, in the Psychiatric Emergency Services during the evening shift: was it me,

111

the supervisor of the evening shift, as I argued, or was it the resident? In my view, the most experienced clinicians should decide treatment dispositions for the most fragile and high-risk patients. The resident argued that only a medical doctor, an M.D., should have that position of responsibility. The Chair, this larger-than-life man, both physically and symbolically, whose office I meekly sat in, sided with the resident, and he admonished me by giving me a harsh, intimidating scolding.

Due to the fact, through no fault of my own, that I have a life-long, neurotic conflict with authority, I was forced to defend myself with a second try at convincing him of the logic of my position: patient safety and hospital liability would be best served if the most experienced clinicians made the critical dispositional decisions. He responded by making his opinion clear: "You're fired," he said to me.

I was accompanied at this meeting by our medical director of Psychiatric Emergency Services, a kind and gentle psychiatrist who said to me as we walked away from the Chair's office, "Don't worry about this. Come to work tomorrow. He'll forget all about it. He won't remember you were here. He yells at me like this every week." This prescient man was absolutely right. I kept coming to work with no consequence and my paychecks kept coming to my house. Many months later the Chairman of the Department of Psychiatry left UC Davis Medical Center to become the chair at another university, a well-deserved promotion, I'm sure. And our clinic returned to the old way of doing things: experienced clinicians, not residents-in-training, deciding patient dispositions.

The egomaniac listens to himself, the only audience he cares about. He seeks the recognition he knows he deserves, and he demands the position commensurate with his talents—King of the World. Narcissists can be found in high places because they are so practiced—nearly perfect—at self-deception, and they can fool others by their glitter and glamour. If they happen to be therapists, they think they are the best therapists, to the exclusion of all other therapists, the weak and stupid ones, although they do like to keep a

112

small party of loyalists close to them, devotees who hang onto them seeking scraps of approval. These grander-than-all therapists charge the highest prices, wear the most refined and tasteful clothes, have the most elegant cars, and the finest office furniture. They are a perfect picture on the outside of how they wish to be seen, all-powerful and beautiful to boot. Lies and misinformation, distortions and exaggerations, are conjured up and released into an alternative world that is created to prop them up.

As students, residents, and interns-in-training, they are not open to supervision. Although they may appear to be listening, the only voice in the room worth listening to is their own. They have much grander ideas than the supervisor could ever have, but it is not yet time for them to reveal their greatness. They sit and wait until their time arrives, and they attribute their holiness to no one but themselves.

It is easy to be fooled and seduced by the obsequious charm which they employ as they step over others on their way up the ladder to power and success. Starting out, as we all do, on a low rung of that ladder, they are the first to cheat, steal, subvert, and rig the game of life in their desperate attempts to make it to the top, and they are the first to cry foul and claim innocence as they accuse others of their own sins. If you catch them lying, they will call you a liar, if you catch them stealing, they will say you stole. Like a boomerang, they bounce back to the giver the accusations given to them.

I knew a licensed clinical social worker, an L.C.S.W., a proud man, proud of himself, who left graduate school and dove right into private practice in a beautiful coastal town in California. I had a nice conversation with him years ago at a Christmas party where he sincerely, with a humble tone, told me he was the most successful psychotherapist in that town with a long waiting list of beautiful, wealthy women.

"I've always found countertransference, that sticky attachment so many women have to me, to be a nuisance," he said to me. He bowed his head sadly in recognition that this

113

burden would likely always be the case for him. He asked me how I handled this problem, and I told him that I did not have to.

"It is an overwhelming position to be in when you have obvious skills and you practice in a town that is not known for good therapists," he said. I thought how wonderful it must be to have so much wisdom right out of school, and I wondered if this man, so confident, so inflated and bloated, had problems with chronic flatulence.

He said to me, "Why don't you move and practice in this town, too? I could set you up with a ton of referrals." Such a generous offer, referrals of those patients who only made his second tier, but I declined. The gift from a narcissist is never given, it is loaned, always ready to be taken back, always offered with invisible strings, a loan given with exorbitant interest and hidden fees. Whatever they appear to be giving they are keeping; it is a clever worm that controls the fish. Here, look how the diamond sparkles, yours for the small price of devotion and obedience.

It is dangerous to give power to the self-inflated, but if the malignant narcissist already possesses power, legitimate power, then dreadful things will befall all under his influence. My coastal acquaintance, this "super-smart" therapist, the popular healer who attributed his success to being able to "blow other therapists out of the water," this P.T. Barnum blowhard, was arrested and charged with inappropriate sexual contact with multiple female patients. He was enraged by these charges. He told friends and community colleagues, most of whom scattered away from him quickly, and he told his wife, a loyal subject, that he was the innocent victim of ungrateful patients who, in fact, tried to seduce him. The District Attorney was not treating him fairly, and he suspected that his own attorney was not smart enough to understand or appreciate him. The women were liars, strictly after his money.

He claimed to anyone who would listen, and many who would not, that he was only doing some "necessary handholding" with these women. The very few men he had in his practice apparently did not need handholding. He never comprehended the gravity of

114

his predicament, and so he was shocked at the injustice of losing his license and infuriated by the lawsuits that followed. He never accepted responsibility, he never apologized. Why should he, he had not done anything wrong. Narcissists never apologize, they double down and attack. And even if they are trapped and exposed, apology is a sign of weakness, and above all else, they are not weak.

Not all egotistical therapists necessarily cause great harm. Many are simply annoying and transparent, and are the subject of cathartic conversations between coworkers who are exhausted by the narcissists' excessive demands, drama, and needs. There are likely narcissists in every department of psychiatry, and all of the staff know who they are, all of the staff except the narcissists themselves who wander in the dark.

I once interviewed a psychologist who applied for a position with Psychiatric Emergency Services. At the time we had a standard, 12-question interview which generally took about 40 minutes to complete. The first item was, "Tell me about your experience that qualifies you for this position." I learned that day that it is unwise to ask an extreme narcissist that particular question unless you bring a sack lunch and a change of underwear to the interview. I only had one hour to give him, ample time for this interview. After nearly two hours he was still talking about himself and his extraordinary experiences that qualified him for this position. His speech was enthusiastic and pressured and not amenable to interruption. I never asked him the second question on the interview list; I was an hour late for a patient, and I had to pee. I also felt dead inside.

. . . .

We all need our own court jester, a trusted appointee who can laugh at us and reveal our failings with impunity. Medieval kings were right in appointing trusted clowns to show them qualities about themselves that others could so clearly see, but hidden to the kings themselves. I have appointed my son to be my court jester. He met the qualifications: kind, trustworthy, bright, insightful, non-punitive, objective, without anger and with no harmful intent or hidden motive.

He can reveal to me qualities in myself that I am unable to see, habits or behaviors I need to know about myself, problems I have that I cannot correct because I do not know what they are. He can do this because I asked him to, I trust him to, and I am confident that no one can do it better. He can tell me how I am embarrassing myself and how and when I am driving other people crazy. He recently told me to stop ordering "expressos" and start asking for "espressos." Twenty years of ordering a drink that had no "x."

. . . .

So, I repeat, a little narcissism is a good thing, but a little too much and the lights to your inner workings go dark and your desire to look inward evaporates. Full-bore narcissism defends itself viciously from the annihilation of self-reflection.

It takes constant vigilance, and tireless defenses to hide from all others the fragile broken self that is so carefully disguised with deceptive bells and whistles. Narcissistic rage is the consequence of a break in the dike, a weakness in the defensive system that could bring a flood of exposure. The great tragedy of a defensive shield is that when it is penetrated, the broken pieces are scattered and the flesh is visible to all. As Abraham Lincoln said, "You can fool all the people some of the time and some of the people all the time, but you cannot fool all the people all the time." Eventually, the narcissist is going to be exposed.

. . . .

Having a narcissistic boss is tough, much like hell is tough. But having a narcissistic parent is a special incarceration for the child, an undeserved sentence to the hottest corner of hell.

I first met Collin Sanders when his 66-year-old father, William Sanders, died in the Emergency Department after suffering a stroke. I was the first to inform Collin and his mother, Louise Sanders, that William had died. Collin was deeply affected, visibly shaken, and unprepared for his father's death. His father was a healthy, active, relatively young man with no history of cardiovascular disease, who

116

was his son's frequent hiking partner in the Muir Woods area of Marin County. William's wife, Louise, whom I recall only vaguely, was late to arrive after her husband's death, an hour later than Collin, although they came from the same house. She stayed in the ED only briefly, leaving Collin there by himself, and she chose not to view William's body or spend a last few minutes with her husband before he was moved to the morgue.

Two weeks after his father's death, Collin contacted me and asked if it would be possible to talk with me in person. He told me that he found the support I had given him the day his father died was helpful, but he had since been overwhelmed by emotion. Ordinarily, I do not have much contact with family members after the day of the death, but there are few hard-and-fast rules in the ED. Time and again I found I could do almost anything in the ED I wanted to as long as it was the right thing to do and I did not tell anybody about it.

Naturally, we do not charge grieving families for the counsel and support they receive after the death of a loved one, so I would not be registering or charging Collin as a patient. I offered him a time to come in to see me for normal grieving and support, not for psychiatric assessment or treatment.

Collin opened the conversation by apologizing for being vague over the phone. It was not his grief over the loss of his father that had prompted his call, although the loss was very significant for him; it was the rage he felt toward his mother. She had not shed a tear since her husband's death, and she became impatient and irritated with Collin when he did. She left the hospital quickly after William's death, and went straight to a hair appointment and beauty treatment. Collin said she left her hair appointment and drove directly to meet with the minister from the Methodist church they attended, but the conversation between Louise and the minister was about a party planning committee. She never told their minister about William's death; Collin told him about it a day later when he ran into the minister.

"She must have been terribly confused and upset after such an unexpected and shocking event," the minister said to Collin. Collin did not think so.

Collin planned a memorial service because Louise would not. William was an elder in the Methodist church, a beloved member and a tireless worker for the church. He sang in the choir, he organized the youth and teen ministries, and he worked enthusiastically on church-related community projects and international projects.

No one ever did because no one ever could say a bad word about William, except for Louise. Louise was his self-proclaimed superior by all of her measures, and she had a long litany of complaints ready to recite on every occasion: William was a "dumbass" who never went to college as she had, he never read a good book, never had a clever thought. In her mind and constant report, so many handsome men would have loved to converse with such a fascinating and intelligent woman as she was, but she was stuck with dumbass. Louise said she knew so many bright, ambitious men in college who were successful, respected, and wealthy now, and she could have married any of them, but she chose dumbass who had never had a decent job. Collin said the truth was that his father worked his way up to being a regional manager in a large Bay Area electronics firm and retired from that company after 46 years of steadfast, dedicated work. In his 46 years, he won work-attendance awards for going a year without a day of sick leave for 37 of those years. "He was a good, steady man and he always provided well for us," said Collin, but Collin explained in detail that his mother had a different opinion.

Louise thought William was a plain man with pasty skin, a bulbous nose, and thick, short legs. She described all the men she went to college with as tall, athletic, and gorgeous, and, "Boy, did they have eyes for me." She was aggravated that William was "too dumb to make wise investments," and that he completely missed the rise of the tech stocks. He put money in the bank because he knew where it was, in downtown Oakland. "Even a dimwit made money on stocks, but not dumbass."

Louise was uncensored when she talked to Collin about so many things that he did not want to know about. William was a terrible lover. "Oh, the lovers I could have had," she would say. Collin said there were times when she did have affairs, often with younger men, and she was proud of her ability to attract these younger men. On the day of her husband's death she came home to Collin and said, "I'm as beautiful as I was in college. My hairdresser told me that today."

Her sexual affairs were short-lived; they tired of her, she tired of them. She bragged to Collin about the men who fell in love with her, and she hardly kept her conquests secret from her husband. William was a good and decent man who forgave his wife and considered it to be his mission, his trial and burden in life, to live with and support the woman whom Collin referred to as Lucifer's daughter.

"I have hatred for her, Dr. Farrell," Collin said. "I wish she was the one who died. At the memorial service she was drunk and loud and openly calling my father a dumbass. She was so ugly, flirting with other men in the presence of their wives, hanging onto them, kissing them. I tried to lead her away but she turned on me and viciously slapped me in the face."

Louise did not stop there. She publicly shamed Collin at the service, calling him a loser, like his father, 31 years old and not married, living at home, a second-grade teacher. "Not even smart enough to teach the third grade," she yelled out.

"Cruel, childish behaviors. I have children in my class more mature than she is," said Collin. "But she is an adult and she continues these behaviors. Other people look aghast at her immaturity, her drama, her ranting and raving. For days after the memorial service I didn't talk to her. She never said she was sorry. When I think about it, I've never heard her say she was sorry in her whole life. Instead of an apology at the memorial service she told me to shut up and stop acting like a baby."

"You certainly have every right to be angry with your mother," I said.

"I'm not just angry," he said. "My mother was standing at the

119

top of the stairs in the house yesterday and the thought came to me of pushing her down the stairs."

Unbeknownst to Collin, that push would be the ultimate, final victory for his mother, destroying her son with the manner of her death. Much of his life he had witnessed the horrific abuse of the father he loved by the mother he loathed, only to be punished again by one triumphant push at the top of the stairway.

Collin's childhood was one embarrassment and humiliation after another, often in front of his friends. His mother was not more contained in the company of his friends; she actually seemed to revel in having an audience. She screamed at Collin, called him names, slapped him in the face and head, threw objects at him, smashed plates in front of him, and after she broke him down and squashed his spirit, she might turn to his friends, wild with a crazy smile, and say, "look at the little crybaby."

Collin had few happy childhood memories, and they were all associated with his father with whom he fished, camped, and enjoyed the silence and solace of nature. Like his father, he enjoyed activities at the church, and, like his father, he sang in the choir. Louise also attended church weekly, volunteered her time generously, and lived, she thought, a faultless Christian life.

The Sanders family contributed to the bedrock of the Methodist church community, and the minister often wished he had more families like them. Of course, the minister was not present in the Sanders home that year on Christmas Eve when Louise mercilessly and repeatedly kicked William in the legs and buttocks, booted him out the front door of their house, and then locked the door behind him. She walked straight to Collin, eight years old, nose to nose, and said, "now open your goddamn presents."

The minister was not there when nine-year-old Collin won the only thing he had ever won in his life—a colorful, mystical, remarkable fortune-telling machine with a magic genie inside who had a deep, kind voice, and who was able to answer life's most important questions. Collin won the prize by sitting in the right seat at a special movie theater presentation, and he fell in love with that

120

genie instantly.

His irate mother, late to pick him up from the theater by an hour and a half, yelled at him to get in the car. She was late to her manicure appointment, and she blamed the heavy traffic on Collin. Collin did not care; he played happily with his enchanted fortune-telling machine with the comforting voice of the magical genie. Happily, that is, until his mother slammed her hand down on the top of the toy, crushing it, breaking it forever. "Shut that fucking thing up, I'm trying to drive," she said.

She broke a fingernail crushing the life out of that genie and Collin got punished for it. One sacred rule in the Sanders family was that you did not interfere with Louise's schedule of personal grooming and beauty care. Collin learned well to avoid his mother, but William did not have that option. Louise's husband was at fault for everything that went wrong in the Sanders family, and everything did go wrong; this poor man was responsible for all the misfortunes that befell them, including slow traffic and bad weather. Louise always had William drive their car because driving made Louise nervous and infuriated, but William's slow, cautious driving made Louise so exasperated that she repeatedly slapped his right arm hard as a reminder to him to go faster. He took to wearing long-sleeve jackets on their drives to reduce bruising.

As a family they could not eat at a restaurant without tension and confrontation with waiters and waitresses over the food, the bills, the service, and many, many other things. Louise was convinced that the people waiting on her were cheating her, and she painstakingly sought to discover just how. She never left a tip, so William became skilled at sneaking back to the table after they had apparently left, to leave a tip without her knowledge.

"I cannot eat in a restaurant today without stomach pain," said Collin.

What Collin needed from a mother was love; what he got was incessant demands. His mother could be charming when she needed something, a favor, a back rub, a quick walk to the neighborhood store for her sugarless gum. Sugarless gum made her teeth white, and

121

she liked showing Collin how white they were—"whiter than anyone's." And it was not just her bright teeth she crowed about to Collin, it was her slender legs, thin waist, ample breasts and smooth skin. When Collin was in high school his mother would joke to him about how his friends were a little too interested in her firm breasts and tight butt. The fact was, Collin's friends were afraid to enter his house.

....

"You've made a good case for pushing her down the stairs," I said. "What held you back?"

"I wish I had pushed her. Now I'll never be rid of her."

"What's keeping you in the house?" I asked.

Collin explained that he had too much guilt to leave. "Whenever I thought about moving out, she sobbed and begged me to stay, and pleaded with me not to leave her with her dumbass husband. She would threaten me, tell me I'm out of the will. Say it's all going to the SPCA. 'I'd rather give my money to a dog than you,' she told me."

"Is it the money that keeps you there?" I asked.

"No, it was my father. I thought he'd die without me there. Now he died with me there. And she killed him, I know that. Never gave him a day of peace. My mother would plot and plan the downfall and humiliation of anyone who got in her way, and she sent many innocent people to the guillotine with no remorse, but she had a special vicious streak saved for my father."

Louise accused everyone in her life of being stupid, liars, cheats, ugly, crooked, fat, and boring, all things she feared she was, all things she shrieked at others to attack them before she was attacked by them. In her fantasy she was the smartest and most attractive young woman in the world, more like 26 than 66, and it bothered her every day that people did not always recognize that. She could have been somebody great, she said so many times, and she deserved to be with someone great, but instead she spent her life with a dumbass who never made anything of his life, who prevented her from making something of hers, and who died without even thinking about her

122

needs.

"I cannot meet my mother's incessant needs," Collin said. "I wake up on my days off to a long list of errands she has prepared for me, all personal needs of hers, a certain lipstick, her favorite bar of soap. If I don't hop out of bed to serve her she becomes enraged. She demands constant attention, and she has insatiable cravings for praise, love, time, affection, and recognition. God forbid I forget to thank her for a gift; she'll slap me right in the face."

. . . .

I have always thought that if you want a great bargain in life, if you need to make the perfect deal, if you are standing toe to toe with a used-car salesman or a Moroccan rug hawker, hire a narcissist to do your bidding. They never give an inch while the humanist might hand over your wallet. A great narcissist never gives up anything. Even their gift to you, all pretty and wrapped, is a disguised loan. If something is given, something better is expected in return. What Mrs. Sanders expected from her child was not only blood, sweat, and tears, but also his soul, ready at her command, responsive to her every need. Collin might entertain some faraway fantasy of the house he would one day inherit or the car that would be passed on to him, but he would pay a high price. And Louise's house and car and money did not belong to him, she would make that clear, and he might never see any of it, not one penny if he disappointed her, which he would. As I talked to Collin, a fine man who had suffered mightily, I too wished his mother had died first.

. . . .

"I don't suppose your mother has ever talked to a therapist?" I asked. I did not suppose it, I knew it would never be the case. Who goes to therapy after all: people who think they have a problem. Find me a narcissist who thinks he or she has a problem. They do not have problems; the world has problems, and they are the only ones who can fix them.

"Counseling for my parents was meekly suggested once by our

minister after my mother was witnessed kicking my father as they sat in the pew listening to the Sunday service," Collin said. "They attended one meeting with the church counselor. My mother said it was like sitting in a room with stereo dumbasses—two dumbasses instead of one."

....

Narcissists proclaim they are too intelligent to go to therapy; they already know more than any therapist possibly could, and they could give the therapist a pointer or two about how to live. They have a lot at stake when confronted by a therapist, more than they know, and they have much to hide from a therapist, more than they realize. Exposure is annihilation for them. So they declare they are smarter than the therapist, richer than the therapist, better-looking than the therapist, and clearly in no need of the therapist.

Here is an example of a very, very short-term psychotherapy session with the perfect patient, the patient who has no need for a therapist.

"What brings you in today?"

"Sadness."

"Why are you sad?"

"My cat died."

"I'm so sorry. What do you think will help?"

"I'm going to cry for three months and then get a new cat."

"I think we've made good progress here. Good luck to you."

Most of my psychotherapy sessions are not this short and never this successful, but some patients do work quickly. Here is a short session with a narcissistic patient:

"What brings you in today?"

"My husband."

"Why did your husband bring you in?"

"Because he's a dumbass."

"I'm so sorry. What do you think will help?"

"Obviously, a different husband, you dumbass."

The first patient has a problem, she recognizes the problem,

124

she locates it, it is inside her, she has a plan, she executes the plan, and it helps. The second patient has a problem, she is blind to the problem, she cannot locate it inside her, so obviously it is outside her, she has a plan, the plan is to blame someone else, she executes the plan, it does not help, the therapist must be an idiot.

Narcissists come to couples psychotherapy for one reason: to have their spouses fixed. They may be tapping their feet, glancing at their watches, facing the windows, gazing at birds outside, as they wait for the big fix. They have no real part in the therapy because they have no real problem, and it was foolish of the therapist to insist on their presence. The hidden agenda of the narcissist is to be proven right. The therapist's agenda is more complex. First, it is difficult to change anybody who sees no reason to change. Second, the narcissist in the room who the therapist might like to change, is absent from the room, mentally and emotionally absent. So the narcissist is ultimately correct: psychotherapy is a waste of time.

The sad truth in psychotherapy is that people change slowly, if at all. Every once in a long while I witness a patient's flight into health, an epiphany, a flash of lightning, like Moses and the burning bush, an apparent true transformation with genuine and permanent change. But most often quick change in patients turns out to be a charade, motivated by a hidden agenda, like the alcoholic or the battering husband or the man with serial sexual affairs, all sorry for their behavior, all quickly cured by psychotherapy, in a single session sometimes, and ready to come home to forgiving families. For the most part psychotherapy is a long, hard, slow process with little steps forward and little steps backwards, and each step forward is measured in inches, not feet. I could not see Mrs. Sanders as a promising psychotherapy candidate.

. . . .

"Maybe I should be grateful. I had one good parent," Collin said. "But I hate myself for hating my mother. She is so full of herself—all pumped up, ordering me about, strutting around like a queen. I can practically see her crown. She does not give a shit about me and it's

125

finally come to this: I don't give a shit about her."

"I have to tell you," I said. "I'm not feeling too good about her either. Why are you so slow to leave her?"

"I'm getting faster."

"It sounds to me like it's time to pick up your poker chips, hold onto your memories of your father, and quit this game with your mother. Leave the table."

Collin was ready to make that move, and he knew better than anyone that even a symbolic gesture toward independence from his mother would cause fury. But a concrete move out of the house would be a declaration of war. He had one foot out the door stretching for freedom and one foot planted in the reality of the familiar, glued there by guilt. He was stretched so far now it felt like the splits, and he was not a limber man. His urgency to leave battled his guilt and his lifelong sense of responsibility for his mother. Against his will and good judgment, he felt deeply that he wanted to have a relationship with his only remaining parent.

"Do you think she will ever change?" he asked.

"No, I don't," I said, "but I think you will. I think she will come to need you even more as she gets older and that may change some things for the better and some things for the worse. But there is no medication that will change your mother's core personality."

"I am doomed, aren't I?"

"Not at all," I said. "Her needs will always be great, her demands unreasonable, her threats cruel, but how that affects you can change dramatically."

"How?" he asked.

"Today, you are a prisoner in her home, tomorrow a free man in yours. But even a prisoner doesn't immediately feel free when he walks out from behind bars. It takes time to adjust to freedom. Time and a plan."

Collin and I worked on that plan like generals with toy soldiers, a plan of anticipation and execution, with thoughtful preparation for the likely psychological impact on both mother and son. We developed a long chronological list of steps to be taken.

126

These are some facts he anticipated: he had to be prepared for the reality, not just the threat, that everything his mother possessed, everything she could potentially give him, would be taken away and would likely be squandered on people or projects deliberately offensive to him. He had to be prepared for the certainty that his mother would berate and chastise him, would blame him and make up untrue, offensive stories about him, and would share those stories with everyone they mutually knew. She would scold him, manipulate him, and beg him to come back where he belonged. She would feign illnesses, have sudden falls, call 911 for self-diagnosed strokes and heart attacks, lock herself out of the house, drive her car into the garage door, and cry out to the neighbors for help, neighbors who would come to see Collin as neglectful and cold. Collin had a long, and I am sure, accurate list of the many manifestations of his mother's impending narcissistic rage.

Collin was an ethical man unaccustomed to warfare, an amateur, but his mother was a professional with lifelong experience in managing her needs for attention, affection, and praise through schemes, manipulations, and her natural ability to ignore the needs of others. It was not a fair fight, nor one Colin would win without a consistent strategy.

The most provocative step in the master plan—the firing of the first cannonball, the declaration of independence—was the physical move away from the house. His choice of an apartment had to be a generous distance away, and it had to be comfortable, better yet, luxurious. There is a reason why generals' quarters are plush: wartime is stressful. Collin must furnish and move into his new apartment without his mother's knowledge, knowing that all the possessions he left behind would be taken prisoner. He knew this step would be startling and abrupt, but he could not engage in prolonged, hand-to-hand combat. He had to rip off the Band-Aid.

In my office, Collin went about methodically preparing a brief, kind, but firm separation speech, and he practiced it on me. He was a skilled teacher who could write a good speech. He planned to deliver that speech in person to his mother, armed with an exit plan and high-quality running shoes. He would follow up with a phone call to her that night which would delineate, for the first of many, many times, the limits Collin would set on the contact he would have with his mother. Being a soft man, loathe to cut off his mother entirely, he would employ the low-contact rather than the no-contact limits and rules to surviving a narcissistic parent. No contact at all was certainly better for some children as they attempted to separate from their narcissistic parent, but Collin could not pull that trigger. He would answer calls, but only so many. He would listen attentively, but only for so long. He would schedule visits, and he would stick to that schedule, and he would abort a visit whenever his mother erupted.

Setting limits on a narcissist is like housebreaking a six-week-old puppy—that dog is going to shit on your floor. And as they say in counseling, "The narcissistic parent is always there when they need you."

I talked to Collin for two and a half hours and the pleasure was mine. I enjoyed the occasional freedom and flexibility of the Emergency Department where appointments were not rigidly scheduled, where 50-minute hours were not the norm, where time could be taken and the job could be done at the pace I required. I entered this profession because I almost always enjoyed listening to people's stories, stories that might last 10 minutes or 10 hours. I enjoyed time with patients who were not paying by the minute. I was free to do what I needed to do, and free to take the time I needed to do it.

Colin asked me, apologetically—as he was not a registered patient, not paying for services—if he could see me one more time following his declaration of independence. He thought he might need one booster shot in about two months, and I agreed with him.

. . . .

Two months is a lifetime after you poke a tiger with a stick. The reactions he anticipated came to pass, but there were many more offensive moves played and relentless shots fired by his mother that he did not and could not have anticipated. Perhaps the most valuable and immediate consequence of his moving out of his mother's house was not foreseen; he was able to grieve for the loss of his father. It took time and distance away from his mother to feel the pain of losing his father.

He cried and laughed over memories, talked to friends, talked to other teachers, talked to strangers, and talked to himself about his love and admiration for his father. He took long walks and thought about the frustration he had felt over his father not standing up for himself, not fighting back, and he saw his father's weaknesses in himself and was steadier and determined not to surrender to his mother. I believed that the man who sat across from me this one last time was not the man I had seen two months before, but was a stronger one, moving closer to being a free man of independence.

Louise fired her biggest guns, used all of her experience and talent, rose to the occasion with surprisingly creative and destructive maneuvers, including calling up Adult Protective Services, APS, to say that her son was abusing her by stealing from her. Collin was able to gather the story of this accusation from a variety of sources, including the APS worker who was very forthcoming to him, and Collin told me about it with a remarkable attitude of humor.

The APS worker was a handsome young man who came to Louise's house to take a report on the allegations presented to him. He waited patiently in Louise's living room as Louise delightfully changed into more revealing clothes after she saw him. She re-did her make-up, and walked through a mist of perfume. The APS worker, Mr. Pine, was a matter-of-fact investigator, inattentive to information other than the relevant facts, and altogether immune to Louise's overt advances.

Mr. Pine did not seem to care about Louise's carefully coiffed hair or her many fine features or her inflated musings about herself. He constantly interrupted her so he could focus on just what it was her son was doing to her.

"He took everything," she said. "One day he was here, next day he was gone. No warning to a mother who loved him all his life. I doubt very much that you would do that to your mother, Mr. Pine. Of course, your mother is probably quite a bit older than I am. I had my child when I was very, very young."

"Can you tell me what he actually stole of yours?" asked Mr. Pine.

"He stole my heart," she said.

Collin was contacted by Mr. Pine and told the story of his mother's peculiar accusations, and he was informed that the case was closed. "She seems angry with you for moving out," Mr. Pine said to Collin. "That seems to be the gist of it."

Louise removed Collin from her will, she said, and she informed him that all her property and wealth would go to Collin's school district with the specific stipulation that his school would get none of it. She told him that she put all that down in writing. It turned out that Louise had stashed away a lot of money that she had hidden from her husband. She handled all the money in the family because, as she said, her husband was a dumbass.

One day Collin was out of the will, the next day he was back in if he would just do her this one favor which always led to another and another, a trail of favors leading back to prison. He owned the family house one day, the next it was wiped away. His mother suddenly developed night blindness so she could not drive herself any longer, and she was sick and weak and could not shop, and ill and could not get to the doctor, and she was frightened at night and certain of a break-in. However, on her own, she did make it on time, every time, to her weekly appointment at the beauty parlor.

Four weeks into his separation from his mother, Collin dropped the nuclear bomb. He told his mother about the woman he was dating. Collin had long been attracted to another teacher, one from his church who was, for over a year, recovering from a painful divorce. Collin had been supportive, caring, and patient with this woman he described as the opposite of his mother; she was kind, selfless, and giving. Louise knew her from church, vaguely remembered who she was, and hated her instantly.

Louise let her opinion fly to Collin: "This woman is a whore,

130

only interested in your money, desperate for any man, having already proved she cannot keep one. She will never set foot in my house and will never get one penny of my money.

Collin took to wondering just how much longer his mother could live; she was an old 66, but people were frequently living 30 years longer than that, especially if you did not want them to. That was a long time for a couple to avoid a mother.

For the time-being, both Collin and his new girlfriend stopped going to church, the only place they were likely to encounter his mother when together. The day before Collin came back to see me, a donnybrook occurred.

"She's not a whore for Christ sake, she's a Methodist," Collin yelled at his mother.

"She doesn't give a damn about you. She's just trying to get to me," she yelled back.

"Every single thing in life is not about you."

"You're the same dumbass your father was. If you don't stop seeing her you're out of my life. I'll never see you again."

"If that's a promise, I'll marry her tomorrow."

"If you marry that woman you'll be digging my grave," she said.

"Great. Hand me the shovel."

This last statement was followed by cat-like reflexes as Louise gave Collin a powerful slap to the face.

The morning that Collin came back to see me, his mother had left a message on his deliberately unanswered cell phone and he played it for me: "Honey, I made your favorite cherry pie. What time will you be over for dinner?"

Collin laughed a hearty laugh, something he could not have done two months before. He would not lose his dignity, respond to bribery, fear threats, or be conned by his mother's constant barrage of immediate, emergency needs. And he would not push his mother down the stairs. He held liberty in one hand and independence in the other, willing to be scarred but not defeated.

Days of Thunder

Hospitals are a place of birth and death, healing and decay. There is more sadness than joy in a hospital and few people embrace their stay. It is a bad vacation: drama in the transportation and arrival, disappointing accommodations, unwanted roommates, limited menu options, no ocean view, unpleasant non-optional excursions, and exorbitant prices. Life is precious but death is frequent, and fear permeates every corner of every room like a poisonous gas. It is the fear that life will never be the same.

The Emergency Department is an exaggeration of the larger hospital, a breeding ground for fear. It is a fortress of security precautions, in preparation for security breaches, with the built-in protection of keys, badges, codes, and two branches of law enforcement officers: hospital security to address ordinary eruptions, and the UC Davis Police Department, DPD, for the heavy lifting. In the ED there can be a few dull moments—pleasant breaks in the constant flow of incoming patients—but there are also days of thunder, bad days, with multiple deaths, irreparable traumas, psychosis, and violence all culminating in a tragic circus of chaos.

I was first hired by UC Davis Medical Center for Psychiatric Emergency Services in the ED, and I worked side-by-side with critical care social workers who served the trauma patients and their families. At the time, the 24-hour Psychiatric Emergency Services was a group of 30 or so psychiatrists, psychologists, social workers and nurses assigned to assess all psychiatric patients in the ED, while the critical care social workers attended to the seriously ill or injured patients and their families, which included doing death notifications, grief counseling to family and friends of patients, child abuse assessments, and elder and dependent adult abuse assessments. The critical care social workers initiated and completed most of the reporting to Child Protective Services and to Adult Protective Services, and they counseled and provided referrals and safety plans to patients injured by domestic violence.

As time went on, upper administrative managers, eager to streamline and collapse services, integrated Psychiatric Emergency Services with the critical care social workers creating one unhappy family. I did not want to do death notifications, donning the grim reaper outfit, and the critical care social workers had no desire to do psychiatric assessments.

Mental health and critical care were two different concentrations of study in graduate schools of social work, two different professions as practiced, and two different areas of interest for the practitioners. But the two services were collapsed and combined by the blind decisions of powerful administrative nurses, who did not know and did not care about us as individuals, and had no knowledge of our interests, training, or abilities. They condensed all the mental health workers and all the critical care social workers into one service called the Crisis Team.

This is how I came to be the angel of death in the ED, a decision not of my making, but by the edict of an administrative nurse not of my profession, acting in a manager's role not to my liking, performing her function of changing things for better or worse. Why not combine ophthalmology and neurology and call it the Department of the Nervous Eye? I was resentful, resistive, and passive-aggressive; many of us were.

As it turned out, it was a good idea, which I never admitted to anyone. It was a good idea because it meant less repetition and a broader scope to our jobs making the work more varied, enjoyable, and fulfilling. It created the new social worker, the super social worker, capable of juggling death and psychosis, child and adult abuse, domestic violence, and community disasters all at one time. That is not to say we did not drop a lot of balls in the juggling act; we did during the days of thunder. But it was a good idea because super social workers felt super as they distanced themselves even further from the layman's misinterpretation of a social worker as someone who hands out food stamps, signs people up for general assistance, figures out

133

medical insurances, or takes babies away. Super social workers appeared only in the most severe crises, very much like Batman, and we called ourselves the Crisis Team. All we lacked were the capes and the Batmobile.

One problem I had at the time of the merge, and a problem that never went away, was that I could be working at any given time by myself, at which time I would be overwhelmed and cursing our managers for never, and I mean never in my many years with the Crisis Team, providing adequate staff to do the job. My complaints made no headway, forever falling flat, never reaching sympathetic ears. Mercifully, on a better staffing day, I would be working with one or two super social workers. One of us would carry the Psychiatric Emergency Services pager and another would carry the Critical Care pager, one staff member devoting the day to psychiatric assessments, and the other assigned to the sick, injured, and dying.

When we traded off pagers, day by day or week by week, we traded off jobs, and I do admit this made each job a little fresher. Whenever I was active on one job, I was taking a vacation from the other. However, single coverage called for double pagers, guns on each hip, but with no time to draw and shoot. The onslaught of incoming patients was unpredictable and would occur irrespective of our inadequate coverage, and, as I always suspected, because of it, like bad magic in the air.

. . . .

Single coverage on a bad day, a day that rained death and psychosis, could be simply stressful, or it could be disastrous and dangerous. A few years ago I had a single coverage shift, 4 AM to 4 PM, that started with the death of an 84-year-old man, Mr. David Washington, who woke up in the middle of the night to go to the bathroom and died on the toilet. The "wake up and die" phenomenon is well known to the ED because the stress of getting up or having a bowel movement in the early hours of the morning can be lethal to the fragile.

"He is a good man," said his wife, not yet knowing of his death. "An elder in the Baptist Church, a hard worker, a fine and kind father of four children. Please do everything you can to save him." She told me he had many friends, many who loved him, many who would be arriving soon at the Medical Center.

Mr. Washington was a universally beloved husband, father, and friend, a true pillar of his church and his community, and his church and community were eager to come to his aid and support his family. He was a tall, African-American man, very good-looking, much younger-looking than his 84 years. He was declared dead at 4:27 in the morning in the ED resuscitation room after aggressive attempts to restart his heart with CPR and medications. He had a history of high blood pressure and congestive heart failure, and the normally weak pump of blood to his heart failed him on his trip to the bathroom that morning. His heart stopped beating at home, it was not beating when paramedics arrived, CPR en route to the ED was unsuccessful, and he was not revived in the ED.

Death is the common conclusion to a presentation of this kind, and it is a rude awakening in the early morning to family members who are in the home, confused, unprepared, immobilized, and terrified. The physicians attending to Mr. Washington were called away to a serious motor vehicle accident, one of many that morning, and I prepared to notify Mrs. Washington that her husband had died. It works out best when a broad clinical team, or at least the lead physician and a member of the Crisis Team, is able to meet with the family after a death; the team approach can provide the most comprehensive medical information and the best support. But our ED, being the largest level I trauma center in the area, could be uncontrollably busy so that available medical staff were often called upon to move quickly from one trauma or illness to another. During days of thunder, the Crisis Team was generally left with the responsibility of death notification to family and friends.

Nobody grows up aspiring to do death notifications. Nobody who does them would mind if another staff member stepped in for them on a day of multiple deaths. There are predictable and understandable reactions to the death of a loved one like shock, confusion, terrible grief, anger, fear, and there are unpredictable and unappreciated reactions including blame and violence: violence of family members against family members, violence by family members against themselves, and sometimes violence by family or friends against the medical staff. I have seen many instances of destructive finger-pointing, fault-finding, and wild accusations.

No one wants to hear news of death, news that the person you love the most and need the most is gone. Many people have to be told the truth simply, slowly, and repeatedly before they can hear it at all. The stunned appearance, confused look, and disassociated state after a clear explanation of death can sometimes be followed by questions like, "But is he awake now? Can I talk to him?" I have had family or friends of expired patients fall to the floor, run out of the ED, punch their faces with their fists, charge the walls with their heads, throw chairs, phones, books around the room, kick off their shoes, rip off their clothes, punch a friend, punch a brother or sister, and threaten to punch me.

I might have to do one death notification for one person, like Mrs. Washington, and then repeat that notification to each new family member who arrives and each new friend who comes to support them. At a time of death, people get on their phones to call people who then make more calls creating a problem with crowd control as more and more people arrive at the hospital.

Mrs. Washington, who was the only family member at home when her husband's heart stopped, was the first to arrive, and she was my highest priority for support. Her three children and her grandchildren would soon follow, as would the pastor of her church, then Mrs. Washington's sister, Mr. Washington's two younger brothers, and an assortment of more distant family members. Friends came next, followed by members of the church, and then many other people who were, well, we did not know who they were.

It is almost always helpful, when a church is at the center of a patient's life, to have the pastor of that church present. This man or woman often provides much needed support and a calm presence, and a wise Crisis Team worker will immediately bestow a special role on that pastor to help de-escalate any impending calamity. The family pastor is likely to be heard and respected, but if the family pastor is unavailable we do have our own chaplaincy service in the hospital and they, too, can be very helpful when family is receptive to them.

When a young man from Afghanistan died in our ED and his inconsolable mother was banging her fists on the floor begging to die herself, an extraordinary Iman from her mosque spent six long, hard hours on the floor with her providing comfort and warmth. This bereft family was able to take the mother home, and the Iman went to the home with them. The Iman did what I never could have done, had no time to do, and was poorly equipped to do.

Mormon bishops, Jewish rabbis, Hindu priests, Buddhist monks, Catholic priests, and the leaders of all faiths have given time and compassion to come to the aid of their congregation members when they are in the hospital. The quality of their services is irreplaceable, and they are not on time-and-a-half pay during the long sieges like I am. They are there, often for many hours, staying strong for the family after the time when I am antsy to pass off my pagers, get out of the hospital, and go home. So, I do believe in organized religions; I believe in how organized they are, how generously they extend themselves, and what good work they do when they come to the hospital. I believe they rally support around the sick and they comfort the afflicted. I use them and I sometimes abuse them, but they are forgiving by nature and by philosophy.

There is, according to research and literature, a science to death notification, a right way to do it, but having read the literature, the right way still escapes me. The theoretical right way goes something like this: ask the family member what they know already, whether they were at the scene, what they saw, what they did, who called for help. Ask about the paramedics: how quickly did they get there, what did they do, what did they tell you. Find out what the family understands about the facts: are they aware their loved one stopped breathing, that his or her heart stopped, that paramedics started

CPR, and continued with CPR, and paramedics were not able to get his heart to beat. And then proceed slowly with the truth: the heart was stopped for over a half-hour by the time the patient arrived at the hospital, we continued CPR in the ED, we gave medications and we tried to shock the heart to start it. And the conclusion: I'm so sorry, but we were not able to get his heart started.

This is a typical flow, a slow progression allowing family members to recall what happened, to remember how serious it was, to digest the gravity of the illness or injury, and to realize the high probability or the actuality of death. This allows for a slow understanding, a dawning realization of the death of their loved one. But even the perfect explanation, clearly given, can be followed by the question, "Is he going to be OK?" The mind cannot hear what the heart refuses to accept.

I brought Mrs. Washington into a small office, the Crisis Team's designated death notification office, near the ED waiting room. The office is large enough for only four medium-sized people, at best, not nearly large enough for the crowds sometimes drawn to an event like this. We had no other space. Space in the hospital is more valuable than real estate on New York City's Fifth Avenue, and like New York City real estate, it goes to the rich and powerful, not to the poor and weak, like the Crisis Team. What little space we have is repeatedly coveted by other services, keeping us constantly alarmed and vigilant. We will sometimes steal the space we need from other services, space like the large, peaceful, meditation room, but we do not own these other spaces and we are likely to be removed from them. The Chaplaincy Service owns the meditation room, and they are understandably protective of it. It is too beautiful and valuable a room for agitated or violent families.

Even before we sat down, Mrs. Washington asked me calmly, with tears in her eyes, "David is gone, isn't he?" I told her he was, that the doctors had tried very hard to get his heart started, but they were not able to. She heard this news clearly and realized quickly her husband was dead. The perfect delivery of a death notification is rarely perfect because the reception of the news of death varies from person to person and family to family. Each death notification, and each reaction to it, is unique, but most loved ones are calm and poignant, as they receive information with grace and dignity and deep sadness. Most often family members support one another, and are kind to the poor soul, the Crisis Team worker, who is giving them information that will change their lives.

It is a sacred position to hold, the bearer of permanent bad news. I often experience a poignant, sweet moment of calm, being in the presence of the family when their lives are altered. There can be a feeling of beauty, love, and meaning during catastrophic changes in a family's life, and that mood can infect everyone in the room. It certainly does affect me. While I admit I do not run enthusiastically toward the next death notification, I do not fear them either, because women like Mrs. Washington remind me of the value and depth of a loving relationship.

We moved Mr. Washington to a private room, I called the coroner's office to get his permission for Mrs. Washington to view her husband, the coroner gave permission as coroners tend to do in unsuspicious deaths, and I accompanied Mrs. Washington into the room to be with her husband. As in many similar deaths, it was sad and sweet to see her talk to her husband as if he was there. Perhaps he was. At her request, I left her alone with her husband, and I gave her a phone that had reception within the hospital so she could call out and reach her children.

. . . .

The coroner's job is to investigate or determine the cause of death, and in many cases that determination can be made quickly and easily by reviewing the patient's medical history and the current emergency department medical report. In unknown or suspicious causes of death, the body belongs to the coroner before it is released to the family or, specifically, to the mortuary service representing the family. The coroner has the right to refuse viewing by the family or to set strict conditions on the viewing, conditions such as no touching of the body.

I worked with the family of a young Pacific Islander man who was pronounced dead in our ED, and the cause of his death was unknown. He was a large man, tall and wide, probably in his 20's, and very peaceful-looking. He was discovered by family members, likely already dead, in his bed, with a headset on with music playing. He might have been lying there a long time, face up and wearing a smile, according to paramedics.

The coroner put the strictest limit on viewing—no viewing at all—but this large family of Pacific Islanders refused to abide. They demanded to see their loved one. This young man's mother was distraught, repeatedly falling to the floor, crying out to God, and running at and ramming the door where she thought her son lay, not knowing it was the door to a utility closet. She was quickly seen medically, given Ativan to calm her, and allowed to lie on a gurney in the hallway close to the utility closet where she thought her son rested. Her many family members, having turned their attention from the patient to the mother, were able to assist the medication we gave her in settling the mother down.

The family members refused to surrender to the coroner's rules, and they demanded to talk to the coroner. The coroner was unyielding at first, as this was a completely unknown cause of death in an otherwise young, healthy male with no medical history. This case required investigation and any touching of the body could contaminate that investigation. The family assured the coroner that no one would touch the body, and so the coroner asked to speak with me. The coroner set these conditions on the viewing: First, I had to be confident that all viewing family members were in control of themselves, capable of seeing but not touching the body. Second, it would be a short viewing, 10 to 15 minutes, with me in the room at all times. Third, the body would be transferred to the coroner's morgue within 30 minutes.

I talked to every family member, each one of whom assured me that he or she would not touch the body. I spent a few of the precious moments we had left before transferring the body, carefully and repeatedly extracting a promise from the formerly emotional mother to view but not touch the body. She calmly promised she would follow this rule, so I brought the family in to view this young man.

Within seconds this large woman was making a double fist with her hands together and was repeatedly pounding on the chest of her dead son shouting, "Get up! You're coming home right now! You get up! You're not dead, you get up!" Before anyone could stop her—and family members tried—she pulled her 250-plus pound son off the gurney, and we all witnessed a thunderous explosion when his cold body hit the hard floor.

No one or two people could have dragged that mother away from her son, but five family members eventually did. The medical staff looked at me and at the ugly scene that had unfolded with some disapproval as they helped me lift the big body back up onto the gurney, all staff wondering what I had done and why I had done it so poorly.

I had a difficult story to tell the coroner, but damn it, I cannot always predict behavior and neither can anyone else. Most medical staff do want family members to be able to spend time with loved ones who die in the ED, talking to them, holding their hands, kissing their foreheads, and saying goodbye, but the coroner has a job to do, and that job is in conflict with our human instincts. After hearing my story, that coroner, on that day and for each day thereafter, would be stricter about his decisions whether to let families view their loved ones in the ED. I, personally, created a little change in that coroner, closing his heart, making him a little more rule-oriented. That was my bad. I learned later that the cause of death for this Pacific Islander man was a drug overdose and not related to any trauma, but that coroner still learned a lesson, a bad lesson, he would never forget.

. . . .

Mrs. Washington soon had many brothers and sisters, children and grandchildren, and her pastor and church friends, at the hospital, possibly 30 in number, many of whom rotated, several at a time, into the room where Mrs. Washington sat in vigil beside her husband. Family and friends were doing what they needed to do, love each other and express their grief, so they could start down the slow road to living life differently. My job was to give to the family that which I did not have to give—time, space, and privacy to grieve. Contrary to what is right and what is needed, the hospital had no available space at that time, and short-staffed workers, me in particular, had little time to give, and there was no privacy in the crowded ED, not on that morning. Multiple motor vehicle collisions filled the emergency room with patients, and another CPR was about to arrive in the ED, an older woman found down and unconscious at her home by her family. There was an unmanageable backlog of ED patients in the waiting room, registered and eager to be seen, the least critical of whom might not be seen for 24 hours or more. There was a patient in every room and in every hallway space, and there was a line of ambulances backed up in the ambulance bay.

We had no space for a dead body because we had no space for a live one, and many more patients were coming in during these early hours, normally the slow hours of the day. Mrs. Washington understood, said goodbye to her husband who was transported to the morgue, and gathered with her family in the quiet, serene meditation room which I momentarily commandeered for her. She had other friends still to come, and she would patiently wait for them at the hospital. Of course, Mrs. Washington's time with her husband at the hospital was not her last opportunity to sit with him, and any friends and family who came late to the hospital would also be able to view Mr. Washington's body at a later point in time. After a death in the hospital, after the coroner releases the case and the body is picked up by the family's mortuary service, the mortuary staff is happy to offer a host of services to the family: viewing, burial, cremation, ceremony—all manner of expensive things.

....

When a serious trauma or grave illness presents in the ED, the critical care social worker is assigned to locate the family, support them, and be their information source during this scary time. In the more serious traumas and illnesses patients cannot talk and creative measures need to be taken to find family—nosy procedures like going through wallets, finding contact lists on phones, or searching the internet. Talking patients often do not know the phone numbers of their wives, children, parents, or workplaces; these numbers are in their phones, left at home, left at the scene of the car collision, left with the police or the paramedics.

Sometimes I get excited because the cell phone of an unconscious patient is available to me, only to realize that the phone is protected by a code. There are times when the Crisis worker has to go through elaborate, convoluted pathways just to call the patient's home. This is why I try to remember my wife's phone number, and I carry it in my wallet, but I am of a generation that remembers phone numbers, a generation that did not always have the world's knowledge in their pocket, a generation that was required to carry much information in their burdened brains.

There were many patients from motor vehicle collisions in the ED that morning, not all critical, but many needing family contacts. Finding family can take a long time and I had no time. My priorities became death and severe psychosis, and all other patients were at least temporarily ignored. In Crisis Services, during single coverage, there can be a tipping point where the numerous urgent pages beeping at me can prevent me from completing any task. I become immobilized; all I can do is write down a long list of immediate and necessary things I have to do which I have no time to do. The longer the list, the higher my anxiety level, the greater the frustration from patients, and the more severe the disapproval by managers.

The ED charge nurse repeatedly paged me because the Washington family, many of them, were in the meditation room and the Chaplaincy Service needed it. "There are too many

Washingtons," she said. "It's time for them to go home."

At the same time I received three pages from the nurse manager of one of the pediatric inpatient floors telling me they needed me to instantly come to their unit to manage an irate parent. Normally there is a separate group of pediatric social workers who cover all the pediatric inpatient floors, but they cover only during normal business hours, Monday through Friday. There would be no available pediatric social worker until 8 AM, and I was the sole Crisis and social work coverage for the whole hospital until then. I put this request on my long, long list realizing that I would never get to the pediatric floor before 8 AM.

I did apologize to the nurse manager, assured her that I was not ignoring her urgent need, and gave her a brief summary of my very bad morning so far. After the third page, the pediatric nurse manager told me that I needed to come to the floor immediately, her situation up there was intolerable, and that I was responsible for resolving it. She also told me she was reporting this incident to the hospital administrative nurse, "a regrettable but necessary act," smugly warning me that the administrative nurse would compel me to come to the floor. "I don't care what you're doing down there," she said to me. "Nothing takes precedence over the safety of a child." I applauded but ignored her fine advocacy, albeit her childish, threatening advocacy, for her patient and her unit.

I did try to explain to the pediatric charge nurse that I was the sole coverage, dealing with a death, multiple traumas, crowd control problems, and another CPR about to arrive. And as I was on the phone defending myself, a naked, manic-looking, middle-aged female walked past me saying, "If you can't get me French fries, I'll get them myself." As I had phone in hand, the ED charge nurse passed me, heading to the naked woman, and said to me with irritation, "You have to put that one on a 5150 hold now or she'll walk out of here." I was receiving stereo commands from the two charge nurses at that very moment when both my pagers sounded their alert again.

I thought to myself I had no more time to give to pediatrics, and

144

I responded to the two new pages—the CPR had arrived and another serious trauma, an explosion and a patient with burns, was on the way. I did place a quick 5150 on the woman heading for French fries. Some 5150 evaluations are quicker than others and a manic state, a nude body, and an unabashed public march to the cafeteria for French fries gave this patient's grave disability away. I did tell her, as I wrapped her in a hospital blanket, that the cafeteria was closed—it was still too early in the morning—but I promised her I would get her French fries for lunch, a promise I would try to keep if I survived the day until lunch.

The CPR went south quickly so I turned my attention to it and ignored all the other traumas and all the nurses who were demanding things of me. Instead, I listened to the CPR paramedics who gave me a rapid-fire report of the chaotic scene they had encountered in the field: a large Latino family, mostly Spanish-speaking, hard to get information from, patient went down, sharp headache, slurred speech, possible chest pain prior to losing consciousness, lots of people out there, including husband, headed this way. "Good luck," said one of the paramedics.

Mrs. Washington was still waiting for a few more members of her church to arrive at the hospital. She would have preferred to go home, as exhausted and emotionally spent as she was, but she was a kind woman who wanted to greet all of her supportive guests. All of her entourage stayed with her and they now gathered wherever they could, many outside the hospital but some in the ED waiting room, much to the annoyance of the ED charge nurse. In deference to the charge nurse, it was a hellish morning in the waiting room with many angry, demanding patients, in pain or with serious illness, suffering, with no relief. She had faced a relentless barrage of, "Am I next?" These patients had no idea that "next" meant a mini-trip from the waiting room to the ED hallways—not a room, not a doctor, not treatment yet or relief. One exasperated person in agony cried out, "How can you do this to people?" Personally, I do not know how we can do this to people; we never should, we just do. Like a war zone, we attend to the worst of the very bad and some days the very bad keep coming in. ED coverage is staffed for the average flow but the average flow never happens on a specific day. How did I get to be sole coverage on that day? I do not know: sick coworker, poor staffing, sloppy management, feeble funding, full moon. Shit happens.

....

The ED physicians were not able to revive Elizabeth Garcia, our second CPR of the morning, and her family and friends had begun arriving. I took three years of Spanish in high school and a little in college, and I have taken many trips to Mexico. I have a wife and daughter who speak Spanish so I have plenty of opportunity to practice, and I live in a state with a large population of Spanish-speaking people, making it invaluable for me to speak Spanish. None of this explains why I cannot speak Spanish.

Juan Garcia, Elizabeth's husband, was under the impression that his wife had a cold, maybe some difficulty breathing, maybe a headache. He asked, through our interpreter, if he could take his wife home now. He said he had some medicine at home that helped her. She was in good health, a strong woman, 73 years old, a good cook, a hard worker in the fields and in the kitchen. Like Mrs. Washington, Mr. Garcia came with support: brothers, sisters, children, grandchildren, cousins, cousins of cousins. One of our chaplaincy interns spoke Spanish, and he contacted a Catholic priest who also spoke Spanish, and I was relieved to have the assistance of the two of them.

I took Mr. Garcia, three of his children, and his sister, along with the chaplaincy intern, and packed them into our small death-notification office. I started out slowly, talking about what Mr. Garcia knew, and ended up carefully talking about what he did not know: his wife expired after all attempts to resuscitate her failed. He could not believe it, nor could his children or his sister. The air in this room became thick with sadness and confusion, and loud pleading voices begged me in Spanish for things I was sure I could not provide.

146

"We don't want you to give up. Keep trying to save her," Mr. Garcia said through the pastor's interpretation. I told Mr. Garcia that we had tried everything and explained to him each and every step we had taken with intubation and medications and chest compressions to try to save her.

"We have insurance. We can pay. Keep trying," he said. He was crying uncontrollably.

I waited and gave him some time. "The doctors here treat everyone with everything they have," I said. "Absolutely everything was done that could have been done."

"She is a citizen. We are citizens."

"The doctors here cared for her like she was their own family member," I said. "They tried very hard. It is so sad, I know. But they could not save her. I am so sorry."

One daughter left the room crying and was met by other family and friends who received the hard blow of death news suddenly, without preparation. I could hear the wailing from my office and was told, by the charge nurse who came quickly from the waiting room to my door, that people were crying and falling to the ground out here and it was upsetting an already explosive waiting room. I had no good answer for the charge nurse. I had no place to put anybody. The meditation room was taken from me, the hallways by the waiting room where filled, partly by the Washington group and partly by the Garcias, and I did not have the pediatric waiting room, sometimes saved for large grieving groups, because it was full of patients with their parents waiting to be seen. What people need most in times of extreme distress, exposed to terrible loss, is time and space to feel feelings and express them uninhibitedly. I had no time and no space to give anyone.

The chaplaincy intern and the priest were both very helpful attending to as many people as they could, but large emotions in small spaces were beating down my best efforts to lend helpful support to grieving family members. Crowd control was becoming worrisome and more people were coming in than people were leaving. After obtaining the coroner's consent, I solicited help from

147

hospital security and from two hospital volunteers—yellow-shirted young men and women giving time to the hospital to gain experience—to rotate family members into Mrs. Garcia's room. Mr. Garcia's son, Roberto, who spoke English fluently, and who was sad but composed and capable, took a leadership role in allowing various friends and family to join Mr. Garcia and his brothers, sisters, and children, in the room where Mrs. Garcia peacefully lay. As is common in patients who have died after CPR, Mrs. Garcia still had her intubation tube inserted and taped to her mouth, so family needed to be cautioned not to touch or remove the tube as it could contain information for the coroner.

The rotation through Mrs. Garcia's temporary resting place was orderly, but the sheer number of sad people in the ED waiting room areas was overwhelming, and more Garcia family members continued to arrive, unaware of the death. One family friend, who was also an employee of our hospital, who was working the day of Mrs. Garcia's death, identified herself as Mrs. Garcia's sister, but Roberto told me she was not related to the family. She was the girlfriend of a cousin. Her name was Lucia, and she found me as I was supporting Roberto outside the hospital as he told newly arrived friends of the death of his mother.

Like a volcano, Lucia suddenly and unexpectedly erupted, scolded me bitterly, and berated me for not giving her family and friends a private room in which to grieve. She threatened me with HIPPA violations—violations of rules and codes for hospitals—for what she viewed as a disrespectful, wide-open, public corralling of her family. She demanded a conference room, told me she was an important person in the hospital, and said that another of her family members had been treated disrespectfully like this only a month before. She was not going to stand for this and she would be talking to the CEO of the hospital that afternoon. She was certain that the hospital was treating her family "like dirt" because they were from Mexico. She was literally spitting words out at me in her nose-to-nose verbal assault of invectives. She stomped away from me several times, but always charged back, her face close to my face, to yell at me again, calling me stupid and ignorant, and blaming me for killing her sister, Mrs. Garcia. Roberto had to stop helping his own friends to rescue me. He told Lucia to go away and to not come back—she was making things worse—and he told me not to pay any attention to her.

"She always stirs up trouble in our family," he said.

. . . .

Occasionally, one person in the crowd, having received a death notification, takes it upon himself or herself to be the defender of the family, the one who acts out the family pain, the person who carries the mantle of everyone's agony. Many times this histrionic person is the least stable member of the family or no family member at all, but is there to do battle with the perceived forces of evil, especially the messenger of bad news—me. The self-appointed pain-bearers, in their very special role of demonstrating their own unbearable suffering and the suffering of the family, can go wild with accusations in order to demonstrate their misery. They are tormented, they are afflicted, they are suffering: they are the family martyr. They lay claim to any audience willing to listen that they, themselves, are in the worst pain of anyone because they cared the most for the one who died.

This inconsolable dance, this theatrical play, acted out for the benefit of the family, often backfires, as family members are exhausted by those who add drama to an already devastating event. The flag bearers will strut around, confront staff, argue with rules, and bully anyone in their way. They take the spectacle of death away from the dead and place the attention onto themselves. They often care less and mean less to the dead patient than most anyone else present, but you could not tell that from the control they steal from the family, the attention they demand, the privileges they require, or the anger they express. They do not understand, as most of the family does, that a hurricane does not blow away an earthquake.

149

....

I saw a woman in her late 90s who died in our ED after three previous trips to other emergency rooms that week. The family had already come to terms with the woman's terminal illness and had placed her in hospice the day before arriving at our hospital. No family could have been more prepared for a death; they expected it any day, any hour. The patient was supposed to be allowed to die at home, but paramedics, called by a confused caregiver, mistakenly brought her to our hospital unaware that she was a hospice patient. The whole family was appreciative of our efforts and they were relieved by the passing of the patient—all except one, her grandson, in his 20's, who was once arrested for slapping his grandmother, who never visited his grandmother, and who once stole his grandmother's Vicodin. The grandson became incensed when a young, kind, gentle ED resident softly told the family of the woman's expiration. This was one of the first death notifications that this resident had ever delivered, a death notification that would ordinarily come and go without incident, but the grandson stood up after the death pronouncement, pushed the resident, spit in her face, and yelled, "Fuck you, bitch, you killed her."

I was in the room when this shocked, young physician was assaulted, and I removed her from the room as quickly as I could because I could see she was too stunned to move. By the time I returned to the grandson, he had destroyed our office, smashing holes in the walls with a chair and ripping down the acoustic tile ceiling of the room.

His mother was aghast and made an attempt at excusing his behavior by saying he had been going through a lot lately, and then she corrected herself and said, "He's always going through a lot." In a worst-case scenario, there is more than one person vying for attention, needing to carry the "I-care-the-most" trophy. Such a coveted title provokes a surprisingly intense competition among the chronically volatile, and for them instability in daily life becomes nuclear during a crisis.

150

....

When I looked for Mrs. Washington and Mr. Garcia to give them our Grief Packet, a folder of information about referrals and resources after a death, I found them outside, and I saw that many of Mrs. Washington's family members were talking to, hugging, and caring for Mr. Garcia's family and vice versa. They were all coming to the aid of each other, all doing the job I was supposed to do but continued to find no time to do. I approached Mrs. Washington as she was holding Mr. Garcia's sobbing daughter and telling her, "I know honey, I lost someone, too, today." The Washingtons and the Garcias were sharing grief and soothing grief. Language was not an issue; loss and sadness was their common language.

I had been at work for less than four hours, four hours that seemed like 40, and it was closing in on 8 AM. I assured the hospital administrative nurse, who paged me 911, our pager code for "call me right now or else," that our pediatric social worker would respond to the pediatric floor very shortly, that I would immediately send the social worker directly to the trouble spot as soon as she came to work, only 15 or 20 minutes from now. The administrative nurse expressed grave concerns about the lack of coverage that Crisis Services provided to the pediatric floors, and she accused me of not giving priority to pediatric services during the off hours. She told me she was exceedingly disappointed in me, personally, and she informed me she would be writing me up in an incident report and passing this on to my supervisor. I think I said, "I'm sorry." There was much to do, I had to go, and her phone call was taking up too much of my time already. I had the impression before I let go of the call that she had other disapproving things to say to me, dissatisfactions long felt and now rehearsed and ready to deliver, but I simply had to excuse myself.

The charge nurse in the ED, not rich with natural patience or tact under the best of circumstances, now had none at all, and told me I must remove the Washingtons and the Garcias from the Emergency Department and the surrounding areas. Both dead bodies were gone and transferred to the morgue and, "Now the families are just loitering. They can loiter at home." She also said, casually, that another CPR was en route, eight minutes out, that a man with multiple stab wounds was just one minute out, and that an agitated patient—drugs, alcohol, psychosis, who knows what— was in triage and needed a psychiatric hold. Then this charge nurse abruptly changed her tone and did something unexpected. She hugged me and said, "Love you, babe."

At 8 AM the cavalry, a very small cavalry, came to the rescue: pediatric social workers for the hospital floors and a social work intern to shadow me. The intern was not exactly a seasoned staff member but any fresh horse would do. The teaching steps for a social work intern or any student in training is standard in the ED. The process is slightly more elaborate than "see one, do one," but that is the general idea. The trainee will start by shadowing a clinician, following unobtrusively and observing without much participation. As comfort level dictates, the student will participate increasingly with staff until the she reaches a point of true co- participation. Finally, the trainee is cut loose to see cases independently with a report back to the supervisor for approval and final disposition.

When life is unmanageable in the ED, I pay no attention to this age-old, low-risk, time-tested, step-by-step process. I suddenly draft and promote interns into roles they have not assumed before, functions they have never performed, and tasks with which they are neither comfortable nor familiar. On solo coverage days, it is either them or nobody to the rescue, and I choose them. Fuck shadowing. Don't just stand in back of me, pick up a weapon and charge.

Most students do remarkably well when asked to sink or swim, so well that I cannot remember being burned by using students beyond their self-perceived abilities. On the contrary, I find students of all types in mental health to be brave, to boldly move past their anxiety, to deftly employ intelligence and intuition over experience and repetition. They consistently do a great job with little hesitation under stressful circumstances, and I am inevitably proud of them and grateful for their help. I notice, too, that they have a little more swagger, a useful swagger, after the experience. Yes, I have had a student or two develop mild post-traumatic stress disorder after throwing them into the ring, and I take full responsibility for that. They seemed to recover very well, however, and I am sure they are excelling in their chosen profession outside of an Emergency Department.

Our social work intern's name was Jill, and she found me interviewing the newly-arrived, agitated man who ostensibly needed a psychiatric hold, and who was being held down by paramedics in internal triage as he was fighting staff's attempts to secure him in cloth restraints. He was combative with paramedics on the way in, actively violent with staff, smelled of alcohol, looked drunk, and had a lot of fight left in him. There was no need to place him on a psychiatric hold because a psychiatric hold is for psychiatric disorders, not for intoxication. Physicians can hold someone who is intoxicated on drugs or alcohol without a psychiatric hold, just like they can hold a combative, head-injured patient without a psychiatric hold. Doctors can hold them on the basis of incompetence: they lack the capacity to adequately understand the benefits of care or the consequences of not receiving care, and so we can hold them in the hospital until they do understand. This man was headed for a long rest before we attempted a psychiatric assessment, and I could see the anti-combat, sedative medications coming his way.

Jill was technically still in the shadowing stage of learning, still new to the ED, but shadowing was an abandoned luxury today, and Jill was a game intern. I asked her to see the man coming in with the stab wounds. She saw him all too clearly, saw him as he rolled past us on a gurney on his way to a treatment room. He was a prisoner in the custody of two prison guards, and he was stripped down to his waist, lying on his stomach with a knife stuck in his back as a result of a prison assault. It was a long knife and a gruesome scene.

I did not see this patient as his gurney rolled past me, and I did not see Jill fall into that surprised prison officer's arms as she fainted upon seeing the patient. Jill saw all too vividly that knife

153

planted in the back of a heavily tattooed man; it was her last memory before fading out. Most of us, when we are first hired in the ED, spend our first few months reacting strongly and involuntarily to certain traumas. For example, I do not like compound fractures, the look of bones protruding outward where they should not be. I worked in the ED a long time, but I never did adapt to seeing compound fractures. To this day they make me queasy. For some staff it was blood, for some burns, for some amputations. Horses, bicycles, skateboards, skis, motorcycles, and especially cars cause all sorts of terrible traumas to the body. It is remarkable that ED workers are able to leave their houses every day let alone ride their motorcycles, bicycles, or skateboards to work. I did not see Jill's reaction coming because I did not see the patient coming, and Jill did not anticipate her reaction having never seen a person with a big knife stuck in his back.

Quality supervisors try to ease trainees into the ED so they develop confidence and a sense of standing on solid ground. I was not a quality supervisor that day, and Jill was not standing on solid ground. Thanks to the prison guard, Jill had a soft landing, and then she awoke quickly, apologized unnecessarily, and asked to go back to work.

"You sure you're OK?" I asked.

"Completely OK," she said.

"I'm so sorry."

"Don't be sorry. My bad completely," I said. Do you need more time?"

"No, I'm good. I'm so sorry."

"Happens all the time," I said.

"Sorry."

"You have to stop saying that," I said.

"Right. Sorry."

The new CPR was a man from a motorcycle collision, motorcycle versus mattress, apparently an inadequately secured mattress from a truck which took flight on the freeway ramming one motorcycle rider and barely avoiding others. There were 15 or

20 motorcycle riders in close formation, and one rider was unable to dodge the monolithic missile coming at him. Flying off his motorcycle, landing hard on concrete, he took a damaging blow to the head, according to paramedics, and he had fixed, dilated pupils and decorticate posturing, signs of a grave prognosis due to a brain injury. CPR began in the field and continued in the ED. The paramedics warned us, saying they thought the patient was a member of an "outlaw" motorcycle gang—they did not know which one—and we should be prepared for an invasion of potentially agitated gang members.

When they came, they came in numbers, coasting in on the impressive roar of raw power. They arrived shortly after the patient. Some people think that if they get to the hospital quickly, they can help, and this is why some people never get to the hospital, other than by ambulance after their own collision while racing to the hospital.

Our motorcycle patient was likely dead on arrival but CPR was continued in the ED, and the time of death was called by the ED attending shortly after the patient's arrival. This patient was death number three, and the first two required multiple death notifications, in my first four hours of work, 4 to 8 in the morning, a calamity for a solo coverage day. The Washington and Garcia groups still lingered at the hospital bound by family members on phones calling more family members, creating a slow but steady current of more mourners arriving at the hospital. Now I would have to tell many beefy, leather-clad, outlaw rebels, and the women who loved them, that one of their tribe was lost, likely defeated by a massive head injury.

. . . .

I tried to quickly sum up for Jill, my rapidly recovered and enthusiastic partner, not shadower, the anticipated problems we might face and the preparations we should take to prepare for this perilous death notification. First, when someone is killed, someone might be at fault. The person at fault might also be a patient coming

155

to us. The person who died might have family or friends seeking revenge on the person at fault. In our ED we have, on more than one occasion, unknowingly placed two injured patients who are mortal enemies in close proximity to one another, and then had family and friends visiting, all standing side-by-side. Some people place revenge at the top of the to-do list after a tragedy, and this declaration of war does not respect the rules of a ceasefire just because everyone is in a hospital. There is nothing sacrosanct about a hospital. So, when a death has occurred, and someone is to blame, and the people blaming look ominous, then the hospital and law-enforcement must take safety precautions. When the police are investigating a possible crime that resulted in injury, law enforcement might choose to place a "blackout" on the patient, a formal status of absolute secrecy in which the patient is secluded while police stand guard and the hospital strictly denies the existence of the patient. "We have no idea what or who you are talking about," is our official response to inquiring family members or friends.

This blackout is awkward at best, an enforced lie by law enforcement. Often relatives know their family member is at the hospital, they may have come in with them, so the conversations might go like this:

"My son was shot. I was at the house with him. They brought him here. I have to see him."

"What is your son's name?"

"Michael Brown, he's here in the emergency room."

"I'm sorry, we don't have anybody by that name."

"Yes, you do. I just saw him come in. I'm his mother. I gave birth to him. I know what he looks like. I saw him just go through those sliding doors by the ambulance."

"I'm sorry. We do not have your son."

"Why are you lying to me?"

Why indeed. This is the point where I want to stop this charade and tell this poor mother that of course I am lying to her. I am lying because the police told me to, it is my job to lie to her, I am only

156

following orders, I could get into trouble for telling her the truth, I have no spine at all, common sense and decency have eluded me all my life, she is not crazy, naturally her son is here, he is right over there, but I will die with that knowledge, so go home lady, I am a vault, a paid vault.

What I actually do, in fact, is apologetically explain to confused and angry family members the intent of a blackout, which is to protect their loved ones from harm by anyone who might be looking to cause them harm. If a patient is here and a blackout has been declared by law enforcement, it is only an active blackout until the police can sort out the potential good guys from the bad guys, the helpful visitors from the dangerous ones. This explanation is little comfort to a mother whose son's life hangs in the balance, and who needs updated information and physical contact with her son, but it is the best we can do while the blackout is in place.

It is shocking and terrifying to have someone you love die. It is also dreadful to kill someone accidentally or to feel at fault for another person's death. I have said this sentence, "There is nothing you could have done," hundreds of times to family or friends of a dead patient and most often this sentence is true. But occasionally it is not true, even though I may verbalize it anyway, but it is not convincing because it is not true.

A four-year-old Asian boy died in our ED when his 14-year-old brother, in whose care he was placed, got distracted and did not notice as the four-year-old stepped into traffic. The young child was killed instantly and when the older brother was told by his family of the death, he wanted to die, too. We had to restrain him from seriously hurting himself. I know I can count up many, many times when I have been careless or inattentive, and this could have resulted in a disaster to someone I love. I do not think the words, "There's nothing you could have done," would have comforted me.

It is not unusual for a person who causes a death, for example, the man who did not adequately secure that mattress to that car on that fateful day, to rush to the hospital, juggling guilt and concern, to inquire about the injured patient. I cannot give him information and I cannot comfort him because he is in the wrong place at the wrong time. Most people are not hit-and-run and forget-about-it people. Most people care.

Everybody cares when a child dies. No one dares rush the body off to the coroner, no one dares take the baby out of the firm grip of the mother. Some parents want to stay for many hours, even days before they let go of their still, silent baby. There is nothing more savagely sad, nothing more inexplicably wrong, nothing more religiously baffling, and nothing more permanently excruciating than the death of a child. A thick wave of darkness permeates the emergency room and staff crumble right alongside the family.

The second thing I told Jill is that we had to get our medical information straight—we were the communicators. She and I are not physicians, but we are the preliminary mouthpieces of physicians. This is why we stand in the resuscitation room, trying not to get in the way, listening unobtrusively to paramedics, doctors, and nurses give the details of what happened in the field, during the transport, and in the ED. We take notes, ask questions when time permits, review injuries with doctors, and try to understand the prognosis. We try to get it right because we sound foolish and create confusion and unnecessary pain when we don't: "I'm sorry, Mr. Jones, your wife has a broken neck, oh, wait, no, I'm sorry, that's a broken thumb, she has a broken thumb. Well now, that's better, isn't it?"

Third, I reviewed with Jill the strategy I have for delivering bad news, starting from the slow warm-up to initiate a dawning awareness and ending with the plain, clear truth. I told her how we try to avoid, but sometimes cannot avoid, the, "I'm sorry, he's dead," approach. I once had the wife of a patient tell me she was a nurse, a critical care nurse unfazed by trauma and grave illness. She knew her husband had a long history of heart disease, she was at their home with him when his heart stopped, and she was the one who started CPR at the home before paramedics arrived. She knew paramedics continued CPR as they transported him to the hospital and had not been able to get a pulse. She asked me to just tell her straight out, "Is he dead?" I said, "I'm sorry, he is." She cried out, "Oh God, oh God, I can't take this," and she ran out of the hospital, and I did not see her again. I tried all available phone numbers but there was no answer and, eventually, her husband's body was sent to the coroner's office so the coroner could follow through by finding the wife. The irritated coroner thought I had done a sloppy job of death notification, and I suppose he was right as I did create much more work for him.

One potential conflict and confrontation that I was relieved did not present itself in all three deaths that morning, was any decision about withdrawing life-support. All three of our deaths that morning were quick and certain. When a patient does not die, but is going to die, or is as good as dead, the family has to struggle with the decision about starting or continuing with intubation and chest compressions. Physicians can guide families but families often make the final decision about when to let their loved ones go. Not all family members agree on this painful decision; some in the family might be rational and scientific while others are waiting for a religious miracle.

Some family members claim a higher authority in the decision-making chain, and they believe that their voice should be respected above all others. The chain of command is sometimes confusing. For example, who has the say in a conflict between a 10-year, live-in girlfriend and the long-separated but never-divorced wife. The hospital ideally seeks agreement, a consensus among family members.

Some people like to be in control and others prefer to yield it, but when two opposing forces need to be in control, then bitterness can reign, ambiguity rules, and no one knows who calls the shots. Naturally, it is best for the medical staff if a prepared, thoughtful patient has an assigned Durable Power of Attorney for Healthcare and an Advanced Directive clearly delineating the preferred health decisions of the patient. But who plans for death when life is moving forward? Well I do, I plan for death, because I work in an emergency room and I know when I walk out my door I am going to be hit by a bus. I have a Durable Power of Attorney for Health Care because I

159

do not want my evangelical third cousin, who I have not seen in years, screaming "lawsuit" if medical staff take my lifeless body and dead brain off life support.

....

UC Davis police officers were prepared for outbursts and the hospital security officers were ready as Jill and I set out to deliver bad news to big tattooed men in leather. Once again we had no available space to deliver that news and no privacy. I did not want to isolate us in some faraway corner of the hospital, lone therapists fending for themselves, because I feared a confrontation, but I could not carry out a private and intimate conversation in a crowded ED waiting room. The chaplaincy service declined our request for the meditation room because the room was sacred, with walls of glass, stained glass art works, and a fragile waterfall fountain with decorative river rocks unattached and available as weapons. The room has a quiet and respectful vibe, but not all in need of solace are welcome.

Jill and I introduced ourselves and took the chance of spilling the truth to this huddled group of 20 or so motorcycle riders in the ED parking lot where they all had congregated by their motorcycles, like cowboys by their horses. They were all close friends and one was the girlfriend of Patrick Dooley, our deceased patient, a 54-year-old man, divorced, with a son, no living parents, and no contact with siblings. "We are the only family he has," said his girlfriend. "His son must be 30 now, but I think he lives with his mother in Florida."

One of the motorcycle riders, Randy, a very articulate man and the spokesman for this group, said he was riding right next to Patrick when that mattress shot out from nowhere. There was no avoiding it, no braking, no dodging, no laying down the bike; it all happened too fast.

"I saw the collision and the force of Patrick's flight into the air. I saw him hit the road." Randy said. "I sat next to him, on the road, on the freeway, before the ambulance came. Nobody could have survived that."

"I do have bad news for you, hard news to hear," I said.

160

"We know what you have to say. Man, you must have picked the short straw today," Randy said to me.

"I think we've both had better days, but your day is the worst," I said. "Patrick didn't make it. They were doing CPR, doing everything they could, but the physicians said the head injury was too severe."

There was silence. Several big men, long beards, long grey hair, hugged Patrick's girlfriend, hugged each other, and then they hugged me, and then Jill. With great respect, calm, and dignity they rotated in to pay their respects and say good-bye to Patrick. Everyone shared loving and humorous stories about Patrick, and Jill and I were emotionally moved as we got to know him. The setting seemed perfect, an intimate circle of motorcycles, a sacred place of respect every bit as beautiful as our meditation room. His girlfriend told me she usually rode with Patrick, but they had had an argument that day, and she chose to ride with a woman friend. Randy said that there was not a soul alive gentler than Patrick, although Randy seemed like a close second to me.

"You have a helluva job there," Randy said to me. "They got the right guy."

And they rode off. I do not remember a compliment that affected me so much. It lifted me from a low place.

A full staff of Crisis Team workers came in at 10 AM and, once again, I was part of a team, not the whole damn team. The administrative nurse for the hospital reported to my supervisor that I was repeatedly unresponsive to the urgent needs of the pediatric floor. Lucia, the Medical Center employee and the girlfriend of a cousin of Mrs. Garcia, complained to my supervisor that I was wrong and thoughtless to her family by denying them privacy and confidentiality during my discussions of Mr. Garcia's death. My supervisor emailed me saying she was "very concerned" and wanted to talk with me. I have learned to accept praise with suspicion and criticism with peaceful surrender at the Medical Center because I think I do my best work when I appear to be doing my worst work.

Men Behaving Badly

Laura Owens looked like an Olympic athlete—young, tall, slender, the long legs of a sprinter—and her athleticism may have saved her life as she escaped through a window on the second story of her house, fell hard onto the dirt below, rolled, jumped up, and ran. She had been beaten with fists to her face, chest, and abdomen, but she felt no pain, just fear; fear that propelled her legs in a race against death. She was chased for over two miles by the man who loved her, he had said so many times. Strong legs and fear kept her going long after Rodney, her live-in boyfriend, collapsed, exhausted from the beating he had delivered and the chase that ensued. She did not understand how he could profess to love her so much and then hurt her so badly, and she did not understand him when he said that his only problem was that he loved her too much.

Rodney returned to Laura's small, old, weathered, two-story, one-bedroom house, her rural home outside the small town of Winters, California, that sat on an acre of land with a pond, a few unhealthy oak trees, and not much else. He searched for the keys to her Volkswagen Bug without success and took off on his motorcycle to pursue her. There was no place to run, nowhere to hide; she had few roads to choose from out in the country, in the dark, alone, on foot, no friends, few neighbors, no help. He would find her.

Laura did have one friend, unbeknownst to Rodney because Rodney did not allow her to have friends. Dorothy Mitchell was a husky woman in her 70s, strong and independent, a neighbor three miles away who lived on a ranch with beautiful horses. Laura had a dream to be like Dorothy one day, a single woman, no man for miles, living on a ranch with horses.

Laura had met Dorothy months before in the parking lot of a small market in Winters when Dorothy's car would not start and Laura drove Dorothy home, just three miles away from her own home. That one encounter would have been the extent of Laura's friendship with Dorothy had Rodney not been hospitalized after a fall from Laura's roof. He was three days in the hospital after sustaining complicated elbow and wrist fractures and a significant blow to his head. It was a rare time when Rodney was unable to monitor and control Laura's activity. Laura took this opportunity to visit Dorothy three evenings in a row after her work when visiting hours were over at the hospital, and before she returned home.

After Rodney's discharge from the hospital, Laura apologized to Dorothy telling her she would not be able to see her again because her boyfriend had "special needs," which required her constant attention. Dorothy imagined a severely disabled man and asked if she could bake a pie and bring it over for the two of them. Laura told her that Rodney did not do well with visitors.

Rodney raced down one road after another searching for Laura, confused when he did not find her. It was after midnight and very dark, the country streets were not lit, there was no sound of other cars, no sirens, no activity in the town. Winters was a tomb that night, a tomb every night, and Rodney kept riding the streets, his roaring engine the only noise in a silent world. He assumed Laura must be hiding off the road, in the dirt, by some brush, on someone's land.

It was a fear-driven, three-mile sprint to Dorothy's house and Laura made it long before she started hearing the sound of a motorcycle cruising the area. She pounded on Dorothy's door and was met by an angry woman with a shotgun whose expression changed quickly to shock and then to heartfelt concern for Laura. Dorothy was looking at a friend she could barely recognize: two darkened, swollen eyes, a crooked, bleeding nose, and a face streaming tears and blood.

Laura could not talk, could only cry, but she did gesture to Dorothy to keep the lights off. They sat in a back room with a single candle lit while Laura cried out her troubled story—two years of living in a relationship with a violent man.

. . . .

Laura had poor luck with men. She was a pretty, blonde

163

woman, naturally beautiful without make-up, and she was a magnet for bad men; they were drawn to her and she to them. In high school, boys wanted her for sex, and in adulthood they wanted more: sex and comfort, a place to live, and a woman with a steady salary. Laura had inherited her mother's broken-down house, which sat slouched on an acre of land, when Laura was 23 years old, after her mother died of breast cancer. Her father was murdered at a drug deal gone bad when Laura was 16 years old. She had a steady job right out of community college with a large insurance firm in Sacramento, a 30-mile commute from her home.

When Laura met Rodney she was sure he was different from the men she had chosen before him, the ones who drank heavily, spent all her money, demanded sex when they wanted it, had sex with other women when they wanted to, and beat her without provocation. Rodney was nice to her. He worked in a motorcycle repair shop and had striking good looks that turned the heads of many women, and he was a gentleman who did not cheat on her. In fact, he was very loyal to her and protective of her, accompanied her everywhere she went, and taught her to trust no one but him because no one but him could ever love her like he did.

And love her he did, in his own special way, by controlling everything she did and everything she said, slowly at first, changing one thing about her at a time, adding one prohibition after another to limit her life. There were the halcyon days, several months of riding tandem on his motorcycle, cruising down country roads together, no one else in the world. That is how Rodney preferred his world, Laura and him, and no one else. He had moved into Laura's house after three months.

The motorcycle repair shop did not do well so he lost his job. He told Laura he was running his own repair business out of her home, but she never saw a stray motorcycle at the house. He had no money of his own, no friends, no contact with his family, no property, and no life outside of her. She was his whole life and he defined her whole life as him. He was the rightful ruler of the home, her home but his divine right. He set the rules for who entered the house, and the rule was no one did.

Laura was aware that Rodney spied on her at work. She worked in a large office building on the first floor with many of the cubicles open to window viewing. Rodney revealed to Laura his peeping of her one day when he was in a rage, by confronting Laura about a man who sat in her cubicle talking to her for nearly 20 minutes. Rodney said he was picking up motorcycle parts in Sacramento and was close to her office so he rode by to see her; he literally stared into her window, into her cubicle, to see her. From that day forward Laura automatically and nervously looked outside from her office cubicle many times a day to see if Rodney was looking in, and sometimes he was, out there poorly hidden, peering into the windows of her building.

Laura did not have close friends when she met Rodney, but after she met Rodney she was not allowed to have any friends. He demanded she go straight to work and demanded she come straight home. Any deviation, to a store, to a coffee shop, would be witnessed by him because he secretly followed her route to and from her work. His tailing her was no secret to her, it was an obvious daily occurrence. When Laura objected to any of the strict rules imposed on her, there was a fight. When there was a fight things got broken. When there was a bad fight she got broken, pushed down or struck by him.

His first response after hitting her was often, "Why do you make me do this to you?" Several days after an assault, days of silence and sadness, he would apologize, cry, and promise he would never hit her again. He would repeat his mantra: his problem was that he loved her too much. She would forgive him. All men were like this she thought, and all the men she knew were, but he could change, she was sure of it.

There was one occasion early in their relationship when Rodney and Laura were at a bar and one of Rodney's ex-girlfriends confronted him with a baseball bat to his back, a swing and a glancing blow that knocked him off his barstool.

"That's for all the times you beat me up, you fucker!" she

165

shrieked. "How does it feel?"

Before Rodney could rush Laura out of the bar, this determined woman, with a good handle on her bat, shouted out to Laura a brief history of all the times Rodney had beaten her up and all the other women he had also beaten. Rodney was in his mid-thirties and had logged in many relationship years developing bad and violent habits. But Laura believed she was nothing like this terrible woman, and she believed that Rodney would surely be different for her.

During his early, unsuccessful relationship years, Rodney had grown to understand that women could not be trusted, and he developed some tricks to control them. He installed small cameras in each of the rooms of Laura's house and a recording device in her car. Laura suspected he was planting something similar, a viewing device, onto the roof of her house when he fell. He told Laura these cameras were installed to keep her safe from intruders, but she knew he was the only intruder. With his laptop he could observe and hear everything in every room as it was happening. Rodney had lost too many women, women who never understood him, never understood his love, and he was not going to take any chances with Laura.

. . . .

Dorothy wanted to call the police and an ambulance, but Laura begged her not to. Laura was too frightened to think, too terrified to plan. The two women huddled in the dark, occasionally hearing the distant sounds of a motorcycle, as Laura told Dorothy the truth of her life with Rodney and the details of that night.

He was insane like she had never seen him before. It was Laura's birthday that day, and it was a normal workday for her. Before she left her workplace for home, her coworkers presented her with an elaborately decorated cake, a bouquet of blooming flowers, and a voluminous, floating balloon that said, "Happy birthday. We love you." It was a gesture that so touched her, it made her cry, and her surprised coworkers, including several men, comforted her, hugged her and celebrated with her. Rodney saw the whole thing, standing behind a short tree, his head topping the tree, looking into her

166

cubicle window.

The fight started immediately as she walked through the front door of her house: accusations of betrayal, seductiveness with male coworkers, secret liaisons behind his back, office affairs. Disgust and rage permeated Rodney. Now he was able to put it all together: those three nights when he was in the hospital, she was having sex with other men. His indictments went on for hours, an incessant prosecution uninterrupted by her whimpering. The violence started slowly—he threw a box of Pillsbury cake mix at her, the cake he said he was going to make for her birthday before she brought her "work boyfriends" cake home. Then he threw the whole pan with the cake from work at her. He grabbed a kitchen knife and cut to pieces the birthday balloon. He was a predatory animal, pacing the house, ready to pounce, and she was terrified.

She asked him to leave and he scowled at her. She asked if she could leave and he accused her of running to her boyfriend. She lost control and called him a monster, and he snapped, repeatedly punching her in the face and body, stopping only when he was exhausted and his fists hurt. It infuriated him when she put up her hands to protect her face because he had only one good arm with which to punch her, the other was still recovering from the fall off the roof.

It surprised Rodney when Laura sprang up so quickly from the upstairs bedroom floor, jumped out the window, and fled from the house. It surprised him when she ran so far so fast, and it enraged him that he could not catch up to her even though he ran hard and long. He could not keep pace, but he could and would hunt her down.

The sound of the motorcycle would come and go, and then come and go again and again.

"We have to get you to a hospital," said Dorothy.

Laura began to feel intense pain in her face, her head, her chest, and her stomach. She vomited on Dorothy's floor, apologized, and vomited again.

"Oh honey, I'm so worried about you. I'm going to take you to

167

the hospital."

Laura could not object. She was barely conscious and in terrible pain. She said to Dorothy, "He'll see us, he'll follow us, he'll kill us."

"I have a shotgun and a handgun and I'm bringing them both," Dorothy said. "His little motorcycle is no match for my truck. I'll start out with no lights and you can lie down on the back seat of the cab. We'll be fine, sweetheart."

Dorothy rolled the truck out to the road slowly, engine nearly silent, lights off, and she started down the road driving in the black night for a few hundred yards before she turned on her headlights. She drove straight to U.C. Davis Medical Center where her daughter worked as an intensive care nurse. They arrived at the Emergency Department about 4:30 in the morning, just a half hour after I started my shift.

It was a wonderfully slow early morning in the ED, like many early mornings, and Laura was quickly triaged and brought immediately back to a treatment room. One of the ED residents took a preliminary look at her and was alarmed by the extent of her injuries and by her inability to speak through her tears, and so she requested that Crisis Services get involved. The resident told me that Laura had severe cuts or bruising on her face, hips, abdomen, chest, and arms, and that she had swelling and possible fractures to her face consistent with multiple blows to the face. And the physician was right, Laura could not form words through her tears.

I was told that the person who drove Laura to the ED was waiting in the waiting room wanting to speak with someone. Dorothy Mitchell and I introduced ourselves and Dorothy began to tell me the story of what had happened. She was a few words into her explanation, "He beat her up," when she started to sob.

"Please excuse me. I'm not like this. I'm a tough wrangler, ask anyone who knows me. That son-of-a-bitch should be shot."

One reason I listened to Dorothy carefully and took her a little extra seriously is that while she was sitting talking to me I could see part of a handgun tucked into her belt underneath her jacket. I thought it was a bad idea, even if she thought some son-of-a-bitch

168

should be shot, for her to do the shooting. Also, it was not legal for her to have a handgun in the hospital. I asked Dorothy if she would tell me the whole story from the beginning, everything she knew about what happened and everything she did for Laura, as we walked out together to her car and deposited her gun in it.

"Oh my God," she blurted out. "I had no idea I was carrying my gun." And then she laughed and laughed. "I've had quite a night," she said. "I live on a ranch in the country because it's quiet, nothing like tonight. Me and my horses, two dogs, and a pig. A friend gave me the pig but I didn't want it. But he's like one of the dogs now."

I admired the fire in Dorothy's soul, her escape to the hospital, her race to save her friend, and I was alarmed when she told me she thought Rodney had followed her to the hospital.

"I can't be sure. I didn't want to tell Laura, she was so scared, but I think a motorcycle followed us here," Dorothy said.

With Laura's permission and her encouragement, I brought Dorothy into the locked inner sanctum of the hospital and into Laura's treatment room. Having only the briefest relationship, the two seemed to me to be like mother and daughter, and Dorothy was there for the long haul to protect her friend, albeit without the benefit of a gun for the moment.

I worked quickly to take steps to protect Laura, first by initiating a blackout on her, and then by informing the front desk, the hospital security, and the UC Davis Police about a possible hostile visitor. I prepared the external triage nurses and the registration staff for what might come their way, and I alerted Laura's treatment team, her attending, residents and nurses, about the steps I was taking. It was imperative that every staff member involved with Laura's care know that Laura was on a blackout—to the public she did not exist in the hospital. I was in the middle of my preparations when the front desk informed me that a man who identified himself as Laura Owen's husband was here to visit Laura.

One of our hospital volunteers, unaware of the situation, came up to me and said, "This man says he is the husband of a patient here, a patient named Laura Owens. Do we have this patient in the hospital?"

I told the volunteer I would take care of this, and I asked the man standing before me who he was and how I might be able to help him. He said he was Laura Owen's husband and that he was here to see her.

I once again engaged in the odd "blackout" conversation in which two men lie to each other, and both know the other is lying, but they both are still steadfastly invested in their lies.

"We do not have anyone by that name in the hospital," I told this man.

"I think you are wrong. You must have my wife, Laura, here. She called me to tell me she was here."

"No, I'm sorry," I said. "We have no patient here by that name."

"I am her husband, damn it. She needs me back there with her."

"You are welcome to try other emergency rooms," I said. "She is not here. Why don't you give me your cell phone number in case she does come here, or maybe I can make some calls for you." The call I intended to make was not a call but a short walk to our U.C. Davis Police stationed in the ED, after a brief exchange with Laura confirming Rodney's assault.

"This is bullshit," said Rodney. "I know she's back there. Maybe the name is mixed up. Let me go in and check. I'll find her."

"We have 100 patients back there, all in private rooms. None of them are Laura Owens. Give me your cell number and if I find out anything I will call you." We actually had 27 patients back there. It was a slow morning.

"God damn it, I'm her husband. You have no right to keep me out. Let me in to see her." And Rodney pushed past my shoulder, grazing me, and walked straight at the main double-door entrance to the emergency room, but the doors would not yield. A security guard appeared immediately and glanced at me for advice. I firmly told Rodney, in the presence of a uniformed security officer, that he could not enter the ED, and one more attempt to do so would result in his ejection from the hospital. I told Rodney to wait with the security guard while I checked for Laura one more time. Now my plan was to involve U.C. Davis Police immediately and have Rodney detained. That was my intent, but Rodney swiftly exited the hospital, well aware that I was working against him.

....

It was time to interview Laura, create a bubble of safety around her, and plot out a step-by-step course for her future. I needed to know where she could safely go and to whom I could confidently discharge her. Law enforcement needed to be involved, and Laura and I had to work on both immediate measures and long-term plans for her protection and survival. I often work with battered women who have no friends, no family, no money, no place to stay, and serious injuries from the violence they were subjected to. Many women have to flee, live in hiding, fearful of their husband's or boyfriend's rage and revenge. The complexity of the treatment plans and the safety plans are magnified many times if children are involved since many more resources need to be tapped.

Some women are ready to leave the man who beats them, ready because the last beating was too severe, or ready because the last beating was one too many. Other women are stalled, out of fear, imagined love, loneliness and isolation, or hopelessness; they will not turn on their assailants, will not testify against them, will make up convincing excuses for them, will tell alternative stories about how they became bloodied and broken, and will forgive the repentant man hoping he will change, knowing he never has. Dependent women, terrified of being alone, believing they possess no value, accepting of the devil they know, living in their own reality of one brutal man after another, aware that there is no better life to be had, choose to stay in a relationship of endless torment. Some women do escape from one violent man only to be captured by another. A broken woman finds another broken man and asks herself what the point is in leaving. There is a point. The very act of leaving is one step away from being broken, one small step toward becoming whole.

It is an important turning point when a woman is ready to leave, and it is understandable that many women, having had so few loving encounters in life and so many hateful ones, need a few practice attempts, or many practice attempts, before they truly walk out the door, literally and emotionally. When a woman is ready she puts on an unfamiliar coat of courage and she grasps at a chance, not always a good chance, of leaving the relationship. Her problems do not end there because her desperate mate, every bit as dependent as she is, is threatened by the loss of the woman he owns and the comfort of the home she provides. He might have nothing without her and he might be nothing without her.

I have seen many false starts to the act of leaving: a woman who is enraged by a beating and tells all to the police, and then faces her remorseful boyfriend who promises it will never happen again, who pleads for her to come home, and she does. She remembers she loves him. She then recalls to the police that she was confused, never beaten by her boyfriend, must have fallen down the stairs. It is all a blur to her now, very foggy. A bang on the head will do that, she tells the police.

The only two times I have ever testified in court in over 43 years of seeing hundreds and hundreds of patients a year, including suicidal, homicidal, psychotic, drug and alcohol abuse, child abuse, and elder abuse patients, have both been in cases of domestic violence, each time testifying against an assailant whose girlfriend or wife returned to the relationship and changed her story about what happened. The men were being prosecuted anyway, without the testimony or cooperation of the women who were loyal and obedient to them.

The best time for me to talk to a patient who has been beaten by her partner, if I am seeking the whole truth, is when that patient first arrives at the hospital. The state of shock, the state of fear and rage, is raw, and the truth pours out freely. The beaten woman will tell the facts of the assault to the nurses, the doctors, the police, and me. We all write down the facts exactly as they are told to us, using quotes generously, and writing exact details. Physicians will document the injuries in pictorial detail using representative drawings of the human body, and CSI, from the investigating police department, will take pictures. There is a small universe of information which we collect and document, information given to us by the patient herself, and so our collective documentation of facts about the assault is usually in perfect agreement. Just because the patient falls back "in love," just because it is not her time to break away, just because she changes her story, does not mean that our body of documented information changes. When the district attorney calls the nurse, the doctor, the police, and the Crisis worker to court, we all have the same story to tell.

I am not saying, by the way, that all domestic violence cases involve men assaulting women. I would guess that 90% of the domestic violence cases that I see are, in fact, men assaulting women, but the argument has been made that relationships in which men are beating men, women are beating women, or women are beating men, are reported less frequently. I had the odd distinction of seeing a couple in the emergency room two years in a row, each time on Thanksgiving night, because the woman attacked her husband with their turkey-carving knife after he criticized the dinner. That woman should not carry a knife during the holidays. That man should sit quietly, eat the dinner, and give thanks for being alive.

. . . .

Laura was calm when I entered the room, owing to Dorothy's maternal kindness and Laura's inherent strength. She was in pain, all-over pain and multiple points of specific pain, and she had an extensive medical work-up to look forward to: X-rays, CT scans, and multiple trauma consultations. My own Crisis consultation would weave its way through the other more pressing medical procedures and consultations and, if all went well, would end with the arrest of the assailant and a safe discharge for the patient. All does not always go well.

"Good morning, Ms. Owens. I'm John Farrell, one of the Crisis workers. I noticed from your registration sheet that yesterday was your birthday. I would wish you a happy birthday but it doesn't look promising."

Laura tried to laugh a little but it hurt too much. "Please call me Laura. It was a nice birthday, really sweet. So many people at work said such nice things to me. And then it was a nightmare."

"I'm here to help you in whatever way I can," I said to Laura, "and while I can't undo this birthday, I am determined to see you safe today, tomorrow, and with any luck, safe for your next birthday. It would help me if you told me what happened last night."

....

If I am in the process of doing a psychiatric evaluation, not a domestic violence assessment, I talk with a patient without taking notes because note-taking, at least at first, appears distant and clinical, and it interferes with the intimacy of the contact. I do not really need to memorize all of the small details about a psychiatric patient during my initial contact, so I do not need to take copious, meticulous notes to reference that interaction. I am in an emergency room, less restricted by time and contact, so I can get the details I need on the second or third pass with a patient.

I am interested in hearing the unique life story of patients when I initially sit down with them: who are they, who were they, what happened in between, what was helpful for them in the past, what was not, who are the major players in their lives, who is still actively involved in their lives, how does love, school, work, and family play itself out in these patients' lives? I want to collect impressions of how someone thinks, how they feel, how they act, react, or don't act, and I want our conversation to be truthful and comfortable, rich and unguarded. I need every advantage I can get in keeping the river of thoughts and feelings flowing. I can pick up the facts later and then write down the information I cannot remember, details like medications, previous hospitalizations, former and present doctors and therapists, treatment dates, or phone numbers of significant people.

On the other hand, domestic violence evaluations, child and elder abuse assessments, and critical care evaluations require more immediate, fact-oriented documentation. These assessments pose different problems and require a different therapist role, which may or may not resemble the role of a psychotherapist. The facts come first when hunting for the family of a seriously injured patient, when exploring suspicions of child abuse or elder abuse, or when detailing the events of domestic violence. In all of these cases facts drive the assessment, and faulty information has serious consequences. The safety of children and adults is at stake, as is the successful joining of family members to their ill and injured loved ones. The accuracy of my documentation of facts can be the difference between helping someone or placing them at further risk, so I take careful notes from the beginning.

With a domestic violence patient, I want to know who did what to whom, when and why they did it, whether drugs and alcohol were involved, whether children were present, and who the supportive, safe people are in the life of the beaten patient. I need the names of everyone involved, possibly their dates of birth, their addresses, a description of the alleged assailant, with his contact numbers and likely location, and any other relevant information helpful to the patient, to me, or to the police. However, I do have to be careful not to approach a fragile patient with a clipboard and a cold, just-the-facts attitude, or I may get no information at all. Cooperation is about trust and trust is about relationship. I try to strike a balance, with every domestic violence case I see, between supportive, nonjudgmental therapist and accurate recorder of detailed information.

. . . .

Laura and I had a comfortable first exchange and she was completely forthcoming in telling me the whole story. As physically painful as it was for her to actually talk, she did remarkably well, interrupted only by an announcement from her nurse that she would soon be taken to X-ray and then to CT scan.

"Laura, I must tell you that Rodney was here, looking for you, saying he was your husband," I said. "He knows you are here, although we denied that you were, and he was angry and persistent in wanting to see you. We need to involve law enforcement."

"I don't want to get him into trouble," she said. "I only want him out of my life."

"Laura, honey, he almost killed you," said Dorothy. "He won't stop until he does kill you. I know men like him."

I told Laura, sensitive to the fact that I was taking away even more of her control over her life, that medical staff in the hospital are legally bound to report an assault like this to law enforcement. Upon hearing a statement like that, some women will immediately backtrack, will stop the conversation, will deny the very details they just exposed, and will inform me that they will not talk to the police. Some women are fearful they will lose the relationship, in spite of the obvious and graphic example of how bad the relationship is. Other women are terrified they will provoke a violent man into a murderous one.

Most men who beat their girlfriends and wives are broken themselves, extremely dependent, paranoid with jealousy, and unable to control their rage. Many of these men, oddly enough, quickly zero in on another victim soon after their current partner escapes from them or discards them. When the victim no longer chooses to be a victim and the man is cast aside, it is impressive how charming and attractive this same man can be to a new recruit.

The more dangerous pattern is the man who feels he loves too much, claims his present mate is his true soulmate, believes he is mystically bound to her for life in this one relationship, and never surrenders the pursuit of her. He is determined that as a couple they will live together or they will die together, and she will never be separated from him and never be with someone else. These are men for whom police reports, threats of incarceration, restraining orders, and threats by family and friends of the woman, mean nothing. They are men who have nothing without the woman they own, and so they have nothing to lose.

Faced with the knowledge of an impending police report, Laura did not stop the conversation; she resigned herself to her new reality,

176

and she freely gave the information that would set the police on a hunt for Rodney. There was still a piece of her holding onto the fantasy of having a relationship with a changed, gentler Rodney, the man who would love her but not hurt her, and she asked me if I thought couples counseling could turn things around for them. I told her I could not predict Rodney's future, but I was certain he was a danger to her now, and all our efforts had to focus on making her safe, secluded from Rodney. I told her a clever, desperate man would search tirelessly for the woman he needs, so she had to be smart and cautious.

. . . .

Couples therapy works best for couples who do not need couples therapy. In such cases, everyone leaves therapy happy, much like they came in, and therapists are quite proud of their work.

I once did couples therapy with a young, engaged couple, in love and darling, who came to me because their church minister said that he thought all young couples should have premarital counseling before the solemn commitment. I had a happy session with this charming couple. I looked at their engagement pictures, heard all about the wedding plans, was told the story of how they met and how they celebrated each month anniversary of their three-year relationship. This couple was lucky to have the support and love of both sets of parents. They spoke to each other respectfully and listened to each other attentively. They had good educations and good jobs. They loved each other coming into therapy and loved each other when therapy was over, one hour later. All that needed to be done—nothing—was skillfully completed in one session.

I had little to say in the way of advice, just a few axioms of a good relationship, axioms they did not need but were still delighted to discuss. First, no one person ever wins an argument, there are two losers or two winners, you get to choose. Second, flexibility trumps certainty every time. Third, you have it all wrong if you have to be right. Fourth, you will not be heard any better if you talk longer and louder than your partner. It is possible that all four of these relationship truths say the same thing, but nobody wants to pay big bucks for a single axiom.

This young couple thanked me graciously and told me how helpful I was, and they said they were going to refer their friends to me. I wished them all the happiness in the world. They reminded me how fun it is for me to work with people who do not need my services. I was working in the outpatient department at the time and we had two categories for billing: brief psychotherapy (30 minutes), and regular psychotherapy (50 minutes). I did not check either category, nor did I fill out a billing sheet. I discreetly and appropriately made up my own billing category, "unnecessary psychotherapy," which is free, as it should be.

Some predominately healthy couples can benefit with a brief intervention by a good couples therapist. They can come to see more clearly their partner's love and motivations, they can better understand the origin of their partner's frustrations and sorrows, and they can learn to adopt new and expanded abilities in expressing love and intimacy. A motivated couple, each person loving the other, can remove some obstacles to the flow of their love by understanding and appreciating their differences, and embracing and celebrating those differences. Two people rarely think alike, feel alike, or act alike, thank God, and our differences do not need to provoke our demise.

A broken couple, with great needs and little capacity for unselfish love, both starting out with a fantasy vision of the perfect partner who would make them whole, each disappointed by the partner who fell so short of that fantasy, does not do well in couples therapy. I have repeatedly failed to remold one person into the fantasy figure of the other, nor have I ever created love where none exists. I have no interest in being the referee of endless fights, no skills in proving that one person is right or wrong, the winner or loser. I probably break up more couples than I piece back together. I should carry a sign, "Enter Couples Therapy at Your Own Risk."

My own thought was that Laura and Rodney had no chance in couples therapy, that Laura, in spite of her traumatic injuries, might be underestimating the danger she was in from Rodney, and that making Laura safe was not going to be easy. My first step was to call the Winters Police Department, as they were the law enforcement agency with jurisdiction, and report this incident. They told me they would send an officer to the hospital to begin the investigation. I gave the dispatch officer all the information that might be immediately relevant to the case including Rodney's name, date of birth, description, address, motorcycle license number, and a brief history of what happened as it was reported to me by Laura. I also told them my story of Rodney's attempt to barge into the ED without permission to see Laura at the hospital. Our U.C. Davis Police were also alerted to the details of the case and were prepared to arrest Rodney if he showed up again at the hospital.

As they rolled Laura off to X-ray, she thanked Dorothy heartily for all of her help, both out at Dorothy's house and at the hospital, and she apologized for the terrible storm she had brought into Dorothy's life. Laura told Dorothy she should feel free to take care of herself now, to leave whenever she wanted to.

"I'm not going anywhere, honey," said Dorothy. And Dorothy did stay right in that room waiting for Laura's return from X-ray.

I asked Dorothy what she would order if she were at Starbucks right now, and she said a venti chai latte with soy milk. "Regular milk gives me gas," she said. I walked across the street to the hospital-sponsored Marriott hotel, a hotel on hospital grounds for the convenience of patients' families, went to the Starbucks café within, ordered a venti chai latte with soy milk, and brought it back for Dorothy.

"Aren't you an angel," she said.

"I think you've seen enough of the devil today," I said.

Laura had a ways to go before we knew the full extent of her injuries and whether those injuries would require hospitalization. I

179

let her nurse, resident, and attending know I was working on a plan for Laura's safety and that an officer from the Winters Police Department would be arriving to take a report from Laura. The resident told me she would be filling out the "Suspected Violent Injury" report used to document the injuries in cases of domestic violence.

. . . .

While it was a slow morning in the ED, it was not a dead morning, and both my coworkers were busy with cases. I picked up the newest case of a walk-in patient who told the triage nurse that it was important he speak to a psychiatrist. He had an event coming up and needed to talk with someone about it today.

"You need to speak to a psychiatrist, sir?" I asked this well-dressed man in his 40s.

"Yes, it's very confidential. I see from your badge you are a Ph.D. What do you do?" He paused as he looked at my name tag.

"The Ph.D. is in psychology," I said.

"And an L.C.S.W.?" he asked.

"A licensed clinical social worker," I said.

"That will do," he said.

Sometimes that will do, other times not. Sometimes people only want to see a psychiatrist because psychiatrists are thought to be smarter and they can prescribe medications, but sometimes a psychologist or a clinical social worker will do. We are less expensive and we try harder.

Mr. Michael Foster had no medical complaints and was not requesting to see a medical doctor. He had asked his primary care physician for a referral to a psychiatrist because he had a problem to discuss, and he needed to discuss it quickly, before the weekend in fact, just several days away. His physician tried but failed to secure a quick psychiatry appointment for him, and so his doctor suggested that he go to an emergency room. It is not typical for our Crisis Service to see patients who are not in a severe crisis, who are more appropriate for outpatient services, nor is it our habit to see patients who are in treatment with a private physician but cannot get an urgent appointment with a psychiatrist. But I never make any assumptions about people coming through our ED doors until I hear their story. Maybe I can help, maybe I will refer them elsewhere. I need to know more.

Since Mr. Foster was not a medical patient and had no need for a gurney, we talked in the small interview office the Crisis Team used for death notifications. He was a friendly man who thanked me enthusiastically for seeing him, and we agreed on first names. He said he urgently needed my opinion on a decision he was about to make, and he gave me some history of the showdown he faced.

Michael was 48 years old but looked younger, a man of average height made taller in appearance by a very powerful build undisguised by his elegant gray suit. He was an attractive man, chiseled in face and probably in body, and he was an articulate man who appeared ready to start this day in a professional work office, not here in the emergency room.

Michael started quickly and had a lot to say. He spoke directly to the point; he was not a meanderer who drifted down irrelevant tangents never to return upstream, and he was not withholding, waiting for me to pull out information like a heavy weight. He was focused, ready, and organized—valued commodities in a busy ED.

"I'm about to encounter a man I hate, a man who taunted me, and I need your advice."

"Tell me about this man," I said.

"He is a bully. The most hateful man I have ever met. Countless times he went out of his way to humiliate me. He is ruthless, heartless, and god-damn mean to everybody, but he saved his worst venom for me."

"When are you going to see him?" I asked.

"This weekend."

"And you are fearful about seeing him?" I asked.

"No, I'm not fearful about seeing him. I'm no longer afraid of him. I am worried about what I might do to him."

Michael owned his own business detailing very expensive, high-performance cars. He was an artist whose work was appreciated and rewarded by wealthy patrons, and he had been devotedly married to his college sweetheart for 25 years and counting. He showed me pictures of the beautiful woman he was proud to call his wife and of his two sons, one in college and one in graduate school. He also showed me a picture of a wall with shelves full of taekwondo trophies, dozens and dozens of them. That is what Michael carried in his wallet, pictures of his wife and children, and pictures of his taekwondo trophies. He valued those trophies and, in fact, he had had a relationship with the sport of taekwondo for slightly longer than his relationship with his wife, having met the sport in his first week of college and his wife in the second week. Thirty years in the sport he loved and 30 years knowing a, "beautiful, sweet woman, kindest woman on earth."

"My two boys are smart, smarter than me, thank God," he said. "Good boys, real good to other kids. I taught them to always stick up for the underdog."

Michael was a man who had made much of his life, so he had much to lose. Everyone knew him as a good man, a good husband and father, generous with friends and with strangers, a capable man to have around in a crisis. He had many good friends and over 100 of them had recently surprised him at his 48th birthday party planned by his wife. He really was surprised, too. There was nothing special about 48, so that was a surprise. His wife joked with him about what she was going to do for the next really big milestone when he hit 53. His sons and their girlfriends were in attendance at the party and his sons each made a speech that brought tears to his eyes.

"I am a lucky man, John," Michael said. "But I don't deserve this wonderful life. I have a demon living inside me ready to leap out at the slightest provocation. Not many people have seen that demon, maybe my wife once or twice, and me."

"What does that demon look like?" I asked.

"I was in a restaurant once with my wife when a man, drunk and stupid, was being ejected from the bar area. He was being a complete asshole. As they escorted him out he hoisted the remaining beer in his glass over his shoulder and it soaked my wife's hair and dress. I went berserk. When he was outside the restaurant I ran straight at him with a full body slam smashing him into a car and onto the ground. He started to get up and I pushed him down again, full force. He kept getting up, stumbling around, drunk, maybe injured, and I kept body slamming him to the ground. My wife had to pull me off. I felt like killing him."

Michael was not only a man to come to the aid of his wife, he was a man who had to be pulled away from coming to her aid. He accepted within himself that anger, even rage, was understandable when provoked by a drunken man insulting his wife, but he had gone too far. There were other times he thought he overreacted when there was less cause; his stop button was defective once his start button was pushed.

"I exploded at a bat-shit-crazy, homeless woman who followed me down the street cursing at me because she thought I was following her. She slapped me, or tried to, and missed, and I went nuts, screamed in her face, scared the shit out of her, made her fall down and beg me not to hurt her. I apologized and gave her 20 dollars and got the hell out of there."

"Is your anger getting worse?" I asked. "Why the emergency visit?"

"No," he said. "I've always been like this and I've never hurt anyone badly, but I'm worried I could get worse. A stranger might elbow me in a crowded shopping center and I'll turn around and look for the guy. I don't act, but I am angry. This weekend I might act."

Michael said his violent outbursts started after college, nothing similar to it in his childhood. He was a small, weak child and a fragile adolescent, shy and passive, described by his teachers as a sweet kid, never in any trouble, never gave anybody any trouble. While he did have some friends, he was not popular and was not a great athlete, although he had tried to make the basketball team. He was not one of the cool kids. He had exactly two dates in high

183

school, both with the same girl, a nice girl, an academic girl. They went to one movie and one high school dance.

"I should tell you, John, I know where my anger comes from."

"High school?" I asked.

"Why do you think that?"

"High school seems to be a breeding ground for anger," I said. Middle school, too. Was it for you?"

"Yes, it was. Worst time in my life," he said.

Michael Foster, the small kid, the weak kid, the sweet kid, was ashamed of himself all through high school. He attended a large high school on Long Island in the state of New York, and he majored in survival. Michael said the kids were mean and tough, and he was small enough for kids to shove him into a locker and slam it shut, an assault that happened to him three times. As he told me about each assaultive incident, his face became a darker shade of red, his teeth became more clenched, and his sweat more profuse. The heat of his rage was immediately available to him as was the terror of his claustrophobia. As he spoke he realized that the small, windowless office where we talked was closing in on him and he could not tolerate it. I suggested we continue talking outside, and I led us to a grassy area with picnic benches, much to his relief. He told me he could barely get on an airplane and could never sit in a middle seat. He always flew first class, not for the luxury, just for the space.

"My humiliation and panic were my classmates' source of mild amusement," Michael said. "One guy in particular, Tommy Rosa, took an exceptionally cruel interest in me. He sought me out. He never missed an opportunity to ram his shoulder into my side when he passed me in the hall. He slapped my books and papers out of my hands, and he always shoved me or hit me in front of his friends. He was in my same grade and he made my life hell for four years. I thought about getting a gun and killing him, I seriously did."

Michael referred to the name Tommy Rosa as if it was one word, never Tommy.

"What did you do?" I asked.

"Nothing. I did nothing. One day when I was a senior I was

with my friends, including the girl I really liked who I dated twice, and he walked straight to me and he pushed me down and said, 'You and I are going to fight by the football field right after school.' Apparently, he had told everyone in the school about the fight because a crowd of people showed up waiting for it. I had a choice in life: get beat up, maybe killed, or get on my school bus and go home."

"An ugly choice," I said.

"Ugly is right. You can't imagine."

"I think I can," I said. "I went to high school, too. What did you do?"

"Nothing. I did nothing again. I got on the bus. I think about that decision every week of my life. No shit. Every week."

"I think it was a good decision," I said. "The only sane decision. You were fearful in high school and you got mad in high school, and you had every right to be fearful and mad, but you never got violent, is that right?"

"I had nothing to get violent with. Not a weapon in the world and a gut full of fear. I was a coward. I was a fucking coward," he said, and he surprised me by breaking into tears. "I was terrified of being hurt. Terrified."

"You were a child," I said. "Fear was your best defense. It is for almost all of us in high school. Even the bravest of boys and men would not risk death needlessly. Tommy Rosa was a bully, a professional bully, trained to hurt people, and he would have hurt you badly. I would have done the same thing you did."

I have rarely seen someone punish themselves so much for so long for making a rational decision, a decision to choose life over death, a decision to get on the bus. Michael had punished himself for 30 years for getting on that bus. He had obviously developed size and strength over his nearly 30 post-high-school years, and transformed himself into a skilled and fearless fighter, a man of superior fighting ability, a readied warrior poised for combat, anxious to stomp out the coward he accused of living inside him. Just one more fight and that coward might vacate him; only one more, or maybe one more after that. But after each contest, after each taekwondo victory, the memory of the coward remained. Each time he encountered an accidental bump to the shoulder, the rude ranting of a psychotic, homeless woman, the foul act of a drunken idiot, the deliberate insult of a thoughtless stranger, he relived the story of the small, fragile, weak coward, abused and humiliated by his high school classmate.

The memory of that boy, Tommy Rosa, the memory of that day, the day he got on the bus, and that old feeling of humiliation were alive in the current life of Michael Foster. He could not outrun or outlast those memories, could not hide from them, and could not defeat them on any battlefield.

"I will never be a passive punching bag again," said Michael. "I will never back down from another fight. I have learned from my discipline of taekwondo to feel no fear and to ignore pain, which is to say I no longer fear pain. I have participated in a lot of full-contact sparring in the last 30 years, and I have been hit and kicked many times by powerful opponents. I have the scars and injuries to prove it: broken ribs, a broken wrist, lots of hard body blows, tons of blows to the face. I am not afraid of pain anymore and I am not afraid to fight."

"You are not the person you used to be," I said.

"Not at all."

"But you are not the person you want to be," I said.

"Not yet."

"What will it take to forgive yourself?" I asked.

"One more fight," he said.

"Truthfully, you think you can fight your way out of this?" I asked.

"I do. If it's the right fight."

"What fight would that be?" I asked.

"The fight with Tommy Rosa."

"High-school Tommy Rosa?" I asked a little surprised.

"Yes, high-school Tommy Rosa."

And so I realized why Michael Foster had come to the

186

emergency room, why he could not wait for a regular outpatient appointment. He was flying back to Long Island that weekend, just days away, to attend his 30th high-school reunion where Tommy Rosa would be in attendance, the reunion roster said. Tommy Rosa had no idea he was in for the fight of his life with an opponent who possessed unlimited motivation. I would not have wanted to be Tommy Rosa.

"I think this will finally subdue my demons," said Michael.

"I don't think so," I said.

"Return to the original source. Undo the past," he said. "Elegant, don't you think?"

"No, I don't think so," I said.

Michael was sure he could destroy the parasite within by killing the source of the torment without, the original source, Tommy Rosa. Michael was also certain that a reasonable therapist would see his point and agree with his plan. It was the warrior's rendition of psychoanalysis, a return to the past, to the origin, to the primary cause. He wanted my stamp of approval for his plan, my assurance it would work, my appreciation for its brilliance.

"How will life be different for you after you beat up Tommy Rosa?" I asked. Maybe he deserves it, I give you that, but will life be better for you?"

"Yes," he said.

"I don't think so," I said.

"You keep saying that," he said to me a little irritated. "I'm not going to kill Tommy Rosa you know."

"I'm not sure I know that," I said. "I thought you said you wanted to, at least at one time."

"That was a long time ago. I had no control then, no options. I have plenty of options now, and better control."

"Do you have better control?" I asked. "I worry for you. The matchstick becomes more dangerous as it is approaches the flame."

"You know I really thought you would encourage me here. I don't think you appreciate the perfection of closing this loop."

"If you thought this plan was perfect, if you thought this plan would resolve all of your anger, I don't think you would be here right now talking to me. You must have some reservations. I am trying to give a voice to those reservations."

Michael continued to try to talk me into this plan and I continued to try to talk him out of it. Michael's idea was to confront Tommy Rosa, call him out for the bully he was, the torment and torture he had inflicted, the cowardice of his evil soul. Michael figured that Tommy Rosa would be frightened and would back away, too scared to fight. Michael had a fantasy of throwing a glass of wine in Tommy Rosa's face, but he was able to surrender that piece of the plan. If Tommy Rosa fought, then they would fight—Tommy Rosa's choice. If Tommy Rosa did not fight, Michael would openly demand that Tommy Rosa leave the reunion, humiliating him as Tommy Rosa fearfully got into his car and drove away, the emotional equivalence of Michael having to leave school and get on the bus 30 years ago.

Michael had been indirectly and vaguely planning for an opportunity like this all of his adult life. He had rehearsed beating up Tommy Rosa thousands of times. He had seen the face of Tommy Rosa on every opponent with whom he had sparred. He was ferocious in life, compliments of Tommy Rosa.

"This is what I think will help," I said to Michael. "Let go of Tommy Rosa in your life. Not by fighting him. He has a death grip on you, a hold so tight that escape is impossible, not even by the best of fighters, like you. He has controlled your life long enough and I completely agree with your goal, but not your methods. The goal is to put Tommy Rosa away, but fighting him won't make him disappear. Tommy Rosa has become bigger than the man to you, he is a force in your life and it is that force you need to defeat, not Tommy Rosa."

Michael thoughtfully pondered what I said, and then he said, "No, I disagree. The act is symbolic. To defeat the man is to conquer the force."

"Too much to lose, Michael. Too little to gain. You can't predict what will happen, but you will be responsible for what happens. You have a great life, a great wife, family, fantastic job. Tommy Rosa, by no design of his own, has given you a life-long quest for excellence, excellence in taekwondo, and excellence in life. You can't deny he's motivated you to do great things. Let him go. Otherwise you are a prisoner of his world. You are now, you will be after this weekend. There are ways to let go of Tommy Rosa. Therapy is one of them. I can help you with that. Others can too."

"I can't let go," Michael said.

"You can," I said.

But he could not. He had prepared too long for this one moment in time, a moment now rushing toward him like a fast train. Generally speaking, I have a poor record of talking someone out of anything they really want to do, or talking them into anything they do not want to do—just ask my children. Michael had made his own plan, set his own course, launched himself, and was ignoring the danger signs. Changing course meant openly looking at alternatives to confronting Tommy Rosa and Michael was way past looking at any alternatives. The recollection of cowardice, no matter how ancient the act itself, lives clearly in a man and grows like a weed, and it can empower a man to hurt others. Many horrific acts of violence have been committed by a once bullied boy, and a bully should be aware that those he has bullied have long memories.

In treating Michael, I faced the profession's worst legal, ethical, safety, confidentiality, and therapy dilemma: my legal obligation to warn an intended victim of a serious threat of physical violence against him by one of my patients. If I believed that Michael was actually going to attack Tommy Rosa, I would have the duty to warn Tommy Rosa and to notify law enforcement. The Tarasoff law requires me to break the normal rules of confidentiality in order to protect an intended victim from physical harm. When patients are a danger to others as a result of a mental disorder, I have the option of placing them on involuntary psychiatric holds and admitting them to psychiatric hospitals, but Michael Foster was not mentally ill, and he did not meet the criteria for an involuntary psychiatric hold. However, I would not want to be Tommy Rosa at his 30th high school reunion, and so I was concerned about the outcome.

The Tarasoff law, like many laws, is written vaguely and it is confusing and aggravating to therapists, while also giving them freedom and flexibility to exercise their judgment. The law does not clearly state how serious the threat has to be, how violent the act must be, or how likely the confrontation is to occur, in order to trigger a Tarasoff warning. Many people say things like, "I'm going to kill that guy," yet so few people mean to do it. Some of my patients have made all sorts of threats without any intention or likelihood of carrying out those threats. Each case of potential violence demands a therapist's judgment and each therapist has judgment that is a little different than that of the next therapist. I am certain I have placed more than 100 psychiatric holds on patients every year, but I doubt I initiate a Tarasoff warning more than two or three times a year. For me there has to be a strong likelihood of serious physical harm to someone, not just wild tirades of frustration, before I initiate a Tarasoff warning.

. . . .

Predicting violence in men is easy; so many men, normal men and not so normal men, have problems with violence. Rage gone haywire plagues many men and some seek help from God while others go it alone. But predicting the likelihood of a specific man being violent on a specific occasion is not so easy. Studies can guide me on this: a young, poor, uneducated, unemployed, mentally ill, drug-abusing, alcohol-addicted, personality disordered, previously imprisoned, male with a long history of violence, who is the victim of family violence, who tolerates frustration poorly and is under significant stress, who physically fights as a lifestyle and ignores the consequences, who could not care less if he lives or dies but wants to take others down with him, might pose a danger. But a man with none of these qualities might also pose a danger.

Sports parents can lose control when a bad call by a referee jeopardizes the outcome of their child's game. Fine men, good men, can be homicidal when cut off in traffic. Football defeats, political losses, or a boss's insult at work can turn peaceful men into violent animals. Shame and humiliation are diseases that turn placid men deadly.

Violence is not the exclusive playground of the seriously disturbed; it is all-too-familiar to the undisturbed male who feels provoked. I am concerned about a normal man with a gun, the law-abiding man, the one who knows about gun safety. Perfectly normal men might think about shooting out the tires of the car that almost killed them if they have a gun in their glove compartment.

As a country, how do we keep our citizens safe when so many of our men are so heavily armed? There has been much talk about restricting guns to only those who would use them safely. In my mind, that would be mainly women. Women, with exceptions of course, have a much lower incidence of violence, and of sexual assault for that matter. As a group they are much less likely to shoot somebody and much less likely to kill out of rage; on the whole they have less craving for power and less desire to overpower. Men kill for all sorts of reasons—honor, justice, self-righteousness, jealousy, fear, hatred, greed, pleasure—while women are not so easily poisoned. In a theoretical society where only women had guns, I imagine that women would mainly be using those guns to protect themselves from men with sharp knives.

I am not saying that no man in our theoretical society should ever own a gun. To make it fair I think some select men could possess a gun, men with a proven track record of no gun violence, like Amish men. I know I would feel safe in a society where women and a handful of Amish men controlled all the guns.

In the service of honesty and fairness, I must confess that women are not harmless all the time. For example, I have reported just as many women as men for child abuse and elder abuse, though possibly because more women are involved with the care of their children and elderly parents. The cacophony of a child screaming or the incessant, repetitious questions of a parent with dementia can make a good caregiver have very bad thoughts. The job of a parent to a young child, or a caregiving adult to an elder parent, can be challenging and thankless, especially if the same person has both jobs.

I personally know as friends some good people who have never hurt anyone in their lives, but who have sometimes reached a boiling point with their children or elderly parents. They would defend their children or parents to the death and would never allow others to chastise them as they do. This is common, and it is forgivable. However, there are men and women who cross severe lines in their abuse of children and old parents, and these caregivers need help, sometimes forced interventions, up to and including the loss of custody of their children or restricted access to their elderly parents.

In the Emergency Department we see many cases of the possible violent abuse of children and elders, where fractures are suspicious, where a baby may have been shaken, or where an apparent SIDS death may not be SIDS. And there are many nonviolent cases of child and elder abuse that present themselves, such as the neglect of a child or the fiduciary abuse of an elder parent. Suspecting abuse and reporting abuse is the job of many hospital professionals and, as always, no two professionals think alike, no two professionals have the same judgment, no two professionals have the same criteria or standards for child and elder abuse.

This contributes to the inconsistencies in the practice of reporting. Generally speaking, and vaguely speaking, my job is to report suspicion of abuse. It is not my job to actually prove abuse; that is the job of Child Protective Services, Adult Protective Services, and law enforcement. However, my suspicion may not be someone else's suspicion. For example, does a three-year-old child who breaks through a window screen and falls two stories to the ground mean that a parent neglected that child? Sometimes, sometimes not.

Some pediatricians, psychologists, or social workers believe there are few accidents and many cases of poor supervision while others believe there are many accidents and fewer cases of neglect. My recommendation to my patients for avoiding pain, shame, and reports of abuse is to raise a child or care for a parent with an army of compassionate part-time soldiers rotating shifts, providing breaks, helping with rest and recovery, easing exhaustion, and listening to frustrations. Few caregivers have a small army to count on and many caregivers have no one, like the single mother of multiple children or the adult child of two parents with Alzheimer's. Many caregivers have no resources and no money, and the definition of relief is a shot of vodka or a snort of crank. As a therapist, in the less severe cases of abuse, I find myself ping-ponging between anger over incidents of abuse and compassion for the abuser.

Having two parents who lived long lives, my father dead at 96, my mother alive at 101, I have come to understand the poignancy and the exhaustion of the role of a caregiver. I have also found the potential for fiduciary abuse to be appallingly high. My mother, at age 101, cannot understand money any longer, but she does have ample financial resources. She is able to and desires to get out of the house a few hours every day, and I take her all over the East Bay area for fun outings: coffee houses, cafés, bookstores, ice cream parlors, the planetarium (yes, she loves the planetarium), the city parks. We do chores—groceries, personal shopping, doctor appointments, pharmacy—and I use her credit card, the one for Pauline Farrell, for all of the items I purchase for her. Whether my mother is with me or not, her credit card, in my hands, has never failed me. I can purchase anything with it.

Every once in a long while someone asks to see my ID and I show them my ID proving that I am, indeed, John Farrell. The clerk may have done a conscientious job of proving I am me, but has ignored the fact that I am not Pauline Farrell. One time, in my mother's favorite bakery where I was buying my mother a coconut cake, the woman who waited on me, upon completing our transaction, while staring at my mother's credit card, said, "Thank you, Pauline."

"And thank *you*," I said to her. I can rightfully and experientially say that fiduciary elder abuse is a piece of cake.

....

"What happens if you do kill Tommy Rosa?" I asked.

193

"You misunderstand. I'm not going to kill Tommy Rosa."

"What are you going to do? Shove him in a locker?" I asked. "If you hit him you could kill him."

"I want Tommy Rosa to know what he did to me, how he affected me, what a horrible human being he was in my life, less than a human being. And, yes, I want him to know fear, the fear that I could hurt him if I wanted to."

"You can't do that without risking violence," I said.

"Violence is entirely up to Tommy Rosa."

"No first strike, then?" I asked.

"No first strike. I'm not going across the country to fight somebody. I'm going there to make it clear who Tommy Rosa is and who I am."

Michael and I went around in circles again, this time for a half hour: I said Tommy Rosa could get hurt and Michael would not feel any better, he said Tommy Rosa would not get hurt and Michael would feel fine. I told Michael not to act rashly, to think this out, he said he had thought this out and the next reunion was five years away. Michael did convince me that he would use his fighting skills as a last resort, only in self-defense, but I knew he would never back down from that fight.

My hope was that after 30 years, Tommy Rosa had changed. Some bullies do. Many bullies have been bullied by bigger, badder people than they are, often by violent parents. The bully attempts to hide his own fear by tormenting others. After years of suffering, years of living with their own painful experiences, some bullies change; some even make amends, apologize. But many do not. I saw a couple in their '60s and the male was ruthless in his constant belittling of women who were overweight. His wife was included in his derogatory remarks. "Look at that fat woman eating an ice cream cone in public. What a pig." Oddly, he was quite overweight himself, more so than his wife, but no less was his derisiveness of her and all women like her. He never missed an opportunity to belittle a heavy woman.

Michael did not meet my criteria for a Tarasoff warning. I was

194

convinced that his character and his taekwondo training had made him fearless, but I hoped, disciplined. He did reassure me that even in the times he had lost control of his temper, like the one time he repeatedly pushed down the man who had thrown beer on his wife, he had never struck anyone, never kicked or punched anyone, which he acknowledged could do significant damage. I was aware of the possibility that his discipline could break down in some circumstances, and that the event in front of him was as provocative as any he had faced in his life. I was not without worry. His main intent, I believed, was to talk, not fight, but I was by no means certain Tommy Rosa was just a talker.

"I'm going to ask a favor of you, Michael," I said. "I want you to call me when you get back from your reunion and tell me what happened, good or bad."

"You'll be the first to know," he said. "The only one to know. I've never talked about this with anyone."

"Not even your wife?" I asked.

"Especially not my wife," he said.

"I think it would be a healthy thing to do. I think she would appreciate your very normal human trials. To me, they add much to your dignity."

"We'll see when I come back," he said.

"She, of all people, knows what you have accomplished in life, what you have to give, and what you have to lose."

"We'll see when I come back."

. . . .

I was told by Laura's attending physician that Laura would be hospitalized for observation, so Laura and I had more time to develop a safety plan. Everything she owned was in her little, inherited house, even her purse and wallet. Laura had a nasal fracture, but, remarkably, no other fractures. She would most likely be discharged within 24 hours.

"The police are looking for Rodney," I said. "Is he likely to go back to the house?"

"The police will never find Rodney," she said. "He knows the ranch lands out there too well. He'll ride out to the middle of some field and sleep there until this whole thing dies down. He'll be expecting me to forgive him and go back to him."

"What do you want to do?" I asked.

"I am done with Rodney. I need him out of my life forever but he'll never leave me alone. He'll kill me first. He's said so many times."

Laura could have been right about that, Rodney might kill her rather than let her go. As I talked to Laura I realized she had very few resources, fewer without a job. She had no friends because Rodney would not allow her to have friends, no savings because Rodney cashed her checks and kept most of the money in the house, and no family—not exactly no family. Laura remembered an aunt, her mother's older sister, who attended her mother's funeral, whom she had met on only that one occasion.

Laura remembered that her aunt apologized for having so little contact with Laura's mother and no contact with Laura at all. The two sisters had had a falling out, "a stupid, unimportant argument, and now I'll never see my sister again," her aunt told Laura. Laura remembered how her mother's sister cried uncontrollably and told Laura that Laura was the only family she had left. But that was years ago.

"I wonder if your aunt could be helpful?" I said to Laura. "I think now is the time to reach out to anyone who may care for you. You need a secret, completely confidential place to stay, someone to care for you, and help with food, clothing, and money. You need to be in a place where Rodney cannot get to you, and you may need to be there for a long period of time. Does Rodney know where your aunt lives?"

"I don't know where my aunt lives," said Laura. "Rodney doesn't know I have an aunt."

"Good," I said. "Let's start there."

Laura, like many women with a low sense of entitlement, could not imagine that her aunt would want to be burdened by her. I felt

196

differently. Laura was the aunt's only family and family sometimes comes through in an emergency, even distant family. Laura gave me her aunt's name, her approximate age, and the name of the small town in Texas where her aunt, Willa, might or might not be living. She gave me permission to find the aunt and to explain to her Laura's difficult and dangerous circumstances.

Laura was wheeled up to the inpatient unit to be attended to by the trauma team, and I made certain the nursing staff and the medical team on the inpatient unit were aware that Laura was on a blackout. Her only allowed visitor would be Dorothy, the warm and kind woman holding onto the gurney as Laura rolled into the unit. I told the staff about a violent boyfriend named Rodney who might try to enter the unit. Honestly, I would not want to be the man who tried to push through competent, capable nurses, dedicated women and men, to kidnap his abused girlfriend. I thought Laura was safe for the night and encouraged Dorothy to take care of herself now. Dorothy checked into the Marriott Hotel on our hospital grounds to stay close to Laura.

Through the miracle of modern internet searches, intrusive for sure but very helpful to the Crisis worker in need of finding family, I was able to locate Aunt Willa, a Ms. Wilhelmina Songer, who had recently moved from one small town in Texas to another. She was more than delighted to hear from me; she was grateful. She had been thinking about her niece, wanting to make contact with her for a very long time. She said she still had deep sadness over the loss of her sister and anger with herself for never repairing the relationship before her sister's death. She lived alone in a small, friendly town, had been widowed for several years, had no children, and was working as a manager at a local market. She volunteered that she had abundant room in her house and she could help Laura financially because her late husband's hard work and prudent lifestyle had left her in comfort. She was appalled by what had happened to Laura, and she was eager, without reservation or hesitation, for Laura to stay with her for as long as Laura wanted or needed.

197

There were no barriers and there was full-throttle enthusiasm in Aunt Willa's offers of help—time, transportation, money, anything. I gave Aunt Willa my name and contact number and told her I would call her the next day when I knew more about Laura's treatment and discharge plan.

The unfortunate circumstance of many women I have seen who have been beaten by their boyfriends or husbands, is that they do not have a go-to aunt like Aunt Willa, or a strong, confident friend like Dorothy. Laura did not know she had people who cared for her until all hell descended on her. Hospital resources or county resources are often too thin, but Sacramento and surrounding counties do have organizations willing to provide hidden shelter, crisis counseling, legal counseling, and practical resources to individuals courageous enough to take the leap and leave a dangerous relationship. Life is never immediately easy after the break, but a return to the abuser is always a high risk.

. . . .

Much had happened by the time I returned to work at 4:00 the next morning. Too much. Rodney somehow had gotten a call through to Laura's hospital phone by her bed, an unusual breach of a blackout, and he had threatened to burn down Laura's house unless she came back to him. He held his phone up to the crackling fire he had built in the fireplace. He gave her 10 seconds, counting down backwards, to make up her mind and promise to come home. She refused. He burned down the house.

Laura called Dorothy at 3 AM right after she hung up on Rodney. Dorothy called a friend, a neighbor, who drove to Laura's house and confirmed that the house was burning, almost completely burned to the ground, and the fire engine sirens were coming closer.

Dorothy was mad enough to go hunting with handgun and shotgun, but Laura was numb. It was the numbness that sets in when a woman knows that her relationship is truly over and life can never return to what it was. With a single act of spite, Rodney burned down a house and, in so doing, burned down his relationship. This defiant act was the shortest victory of his life.

The hospital discharged Laura that morning, beaten but not broken, and Dorothy gently helped Laura up into her truck and drove her all the way to a small town in Texas. I never heard from Laura or Dorothy after that, nor did I ever hear what happened to Rodney. Such is the nature of crisis work. I did, deliberately, run into Dorothy's daughter, the ICU nurse, and I told her that her mother was a saint, a brave and strong woman who saved another woman's life. She knew.

. . . .

I did hear what happened to Michael Foster. True to his word he called me back; he was a new man, a satisfied man, a victorious man. He told me he did what he went to do, rid himself of the curse of Tommy Rosa.

Tommy Rosa still lived in the Long Island town where he long ago ruled over the high school like a mad dog. He married a woman from that high school whom he came to know better at a rehab program to which both he and his future bride were court-ordered to attend due to their various charges of drug intoxication and drug abuse. Sometime in his 20s, Tommy Rosa had run his car into the side of a house while high on codeine and Valium, a house owned by his former high school football coach. The coach ran out of the house naked, having been in the shower at the time, to find Tommy Rosa sitting in the driver's seat with a goofy grin on his face. The coach slapped Tommy Rosa in the face repeatedly until the grin went away. Tommy Rosa was taken to the hospital, was found to have multiple fractures in both legs, and had been unable to stand or walk without a walker since. He was charged and convicted, and he spent a small amount of time incarcerated after which he was required to attend a drug rehabilitation program. It turned out to be the best penalty of his life, a sentence that pushed him into the arms of his future wife, Dolores.

Tommy Rosa and Dolores fell off the wagon many times in their first years together, and it was Dolores who repeatedly pulled

Tommy Rosa back up on the wagon. With the additional help of the town's First Presbyterian Church, they both got clean and stayed clean. Tommy Rosa became a janitor for the church, a slow but hard worker with his walker, his only steady job since high school, and Dolores, while working full-time herself, taught Sunday school at the church.

Tommy Rosa had suffered through a tough childhood. He was picked on, beaten, burned, locked in a closet for three days, stripped naked and locked outside of his house overnight, and abused in many other ways by his sociopathic, cruel, older brother. His brother was eventually placed outside the home into one foster care setting after another by the Child Protective Services agency who declared the brother to be a bad seed and faulted the parents for not protecting Tommy Rosa.

Tommy Rosa did not recognize Michael when Michael sat down next to him and his wife, Dolores, for the start of the reunion dinner, but he did recognize Michael immediately after Michael introduced himself. Michael needed to say no more because Tommy Rosa held nothing back. Michael played back the conversation to me.

"I have thought about you many times, Michael. I was a mean kid. Horrible kid. I did not know it then, but I know it now. I am really sorry."

"He was a real asshole in high school, even to me, and I married him," said Dolores.

"I was an asshole," said Tommy Rosa. "I lived in the gutter and never got out of the gutter. I was a filthy person."

"You did hurt me," said Michael. "Made me live with terrible fear every day."

"I know what that's like," said Tommy Rosa. "I would shit in my pants, actually shit in my pants, when my parents left me with my brother. I wanted to kill my brother all my life, because he tortured me and I think he wanted to kill me."

"I spent some time wanting to kill you," Michael said.

"I wanted to kill him, too," said Dolores.

"You both would have been doing me a favor," said Tommy

Rosa. "I wanted to kill myself."

Michael talked to Tommy Rosa during the entire reunion dinner. They both talked about how much better their lives were now that they were out of high school, and how much the love of a woman helped heal some of their pain. Tommy Rosa asked Michael for a very large favor, a favor that Tommy Rosa stated he did not deserve: would Michael forgive him? Michael did.

"You see, John, I didn't lock Tommy in a locker like you feared."

"Always bad form to lock a man with a walker in a locker," I said. "I didn't hear you call him Tommy before, only Tommy Rosa."

"He's Tommy now. That chapter is closed. I did need to go to that reunion. Even against the advice of my therapist."

"Nobody gives worse advice than I do," I said.

Can't Get In, Can't Get Out

Something has gone wrong when a man is tied up in a hospital office, day and night, tied with soft, thick cloth restraints to both feet and both arms and belted around his middle with a wide leather belt, his hands and deadly fingers gloved in cushioned, sub-zero ski gloves. Something has gone wrong with the hospital, the mental health system, or the man himself, when all we can do is subdue this dangerous, possibly suicidal trained killer, place him on a psychiatric hold, tie him up in one of our interview offices, and pray that an inpatient psychiatric hospital will accept him quickly.

He was too big a risk to our staff to keep him as our guest, and, with his suicidal declarations, he was too big a risk to himself to be safely contained in our little office. On day seven of his stay, our prayers remained unanswered. No transfer was imminent.

I was young and unafraid in my early years as a psychologist and clinical social worker, working and learning in the Crisis Clinic, doing psychiatric evaluations for the Emergency Department at UC Davis Medical Center, taking in the wonder of it all. I was optimistic about the value of our treatment, doing my best to help every one of my patients. I was happy and energetic working the 3 to 11 evening shift with nurses, social workers, and psychologists, all about my age, the age of the third-year medical students and the psychiatric residents who were assigned rotationally to our shift.

All of us were at our peak, not by the measure of maturation but by the yardstick of enthusiasm, a very attractive bunch I would say, playful and carefree with each other, confident and happy to be working an exciting, high-paying job. This was the job I was trained to do, the exact job I wanted to do, and now the job I was hired to do. It was a good time in my life and I looked forward to coming to work because my work was my life, both professionally and socially.

We all practiced the "work hard, play hard" philosophy, and we ended shifts with an en masse march to someone's house for an after-work party that went well into the early morning hours. We may just as well have lived in one big house together because the routines of our lives were so entangled.

This family of exuberant mental health professionals cared for our tied-up mental health prisoner on the critical 3 to 11 p.m. shift, the busy hours, the social ones including the dinner hour, and the relaxation hours before the sleeping hours. We were too social a group to exclude our captive from our lives so we made him an active part of our lives—played poker with him, watched television with him, and had two potluck dinners with him, although he was a poor contributor to the feast. We trusted he would not kill us even if we veered away from the exact protocol set by his main treatment psychiatrist, the clinical director of the Crisis Clinic, Dr. Henry Novak.

Our detainee was Norman Dupree, an extra-wide, extra-tall, bald, white man with beet-red skin like that of a homeless man without shelter, a 28-year-old veteran of the war in Vietnam, a former decorated Green Beret, a captured POW who escaped his captors, who survived in the jungle for three months, who sustained multiple injuries and lived with severe pain, and who crawled back to a friendly base camp and made it home, back to the USA alive. His military job, as he told it, was that of a "surgical executioner." He was trained to kill, he excelled in killing, and he could kill with a single finger, could almost kill with a stare. We were told never to stare at him. That was one mandate in a series of critical rules set up by Dr. Novak to keep us all alive.

"I was trained to locate my target, get in, rescue, get out, kill anything that tried to stop me," Norman said. "I have ripped out a man's trachea with my fifth digit."

"Which finger is that?" I asked.

"Little finger," he said. I wondered what he could do with his first digit.

Everyone who worked in the Crisis Clinic, every last staff

member, and all the support workers, like the housekeeping and cafeteria workers, had been briefed about Norman Dupree, told to keep a safe distance, instructed never to look into his mesmerizing, bewitching stare, because he was capable of hypnotizing and disarming an enemy instantly with that gripping stare.

Dr. Henry Novak, a dedicated man with a good heart and a steadfast belief in leaving no mental health patient behind, took it upon himself—even though he was our program clinical director and not generally self-assigned to treating patients—to treat, and if possible cure, Mr. Dupree of the severe, violent flashbacks from his war trauma. This was the worst and most deadly case of what is now called post-traumatic stress disorder that Dr. Novak had ever seen.

Every interaction with Norman Dupree was dictated by a strict set of safety precautions prescribed to prevent injury from one of Norman's unpredictable flashbacks. Norman was to be fully secured at all times: hands, feet, trunk, fingers. Every interaction with Norman was to be completed in pairs and any interaction that involved changing his restraints was to be executed while the UC Davis Police were in a back-up position. We were to take our step-by-step care of Norman very seriously. I honestly believed Norman liked us on the evening shift and he regularly warned us if he was losing control over his temper or if he was coming close to exercising his violent powers. He was the one who requested that we slip a comfortable blindfold over his eyes so he would not hypnotize us. He seemed genuinely concerned for our welfare.

Each evening as we spoon-fed Norman his dinner, we lifted his gurney to a sitting position which allowed him to have a little more freedom of movement than the protocol allowed. We also cheated a bit by giving him snacks, chips and pretzels, because he like them so much, but we were careful with our fingers as we approached his mouth with a snack. Norman had told us about one account of his killing a man with his bare teeth.

Because he was comfortable around me, Norman told me details about the tricks of his killing trade, like his ability to penetrate someone's mind with his voice alone. Once, out of concern for me, he instructed me to gag him so he would not subdue me with the beguiling tone of his voice. I took my chances because I could not bring myself to gag a man, not even at his request. It was not in my training.

Norman had many scars testifying to the incidents of torture he had endured, and he lived with chronic pain. The psychiatric nurses on our shift were carefully instructed on how to administer doses of oral pain medications, mainly by using long spoons and a lengthy straw for water. While giving medications, nurses were accompanied by muscular medical technicians who stood by as a safety precaution. We sometimes called upon as many as four sizable men or women to untie and retie one of Norman's limbs, as we followed the protocol given to us. No action, no treatment, no maintenance was without risk, and Norman had the decency to regularly warn us of that risk. If he feared a knot on a soft restraint was coming loose, he told us to tighten it, if he thought the young woman with the long spoon feeding him was too close, he cautioned her to back up. He did not want to hurt us, but, as he consistently warned us, he had no control over his violence.

The real problem for Norman and for our staff was his normal need to use a bathroom. He was carefully sponge-bathed every day while secured in restraints and his teeth were brushed as best we could, although obviously flossing was out, but a bedpan for bowel movements was particularly tricky and poor Norman could not go in public on a bedpan. Between the constipating effects of the pain medication and his humiliating exposure when using a bedpan, he failed to have regular, comfortable bowel movements. Also, he could not abide a nurse wiping him and cleaning him. He may have suffered many humiliations in his life, but he could not surrender the freedom to wipe his own ass. Norman proposed his own solution for this problem, and he recruited the considerable talents of Dr. Novak to help him execute the solution.

Norman explained to Dr. Novak that the operatives in his military company who were the most capable of hypnotizing others were also, ironically, the most susceptible, pliable, and obedient subjects when they were induced into a hypnotic state. Dr. Novak was a talented hypnotherapist, had undergone many sequential courses in hypnotherapy, and was aware of the powerful potential of a deep hypnotic state. Dr. Novak, after repeatedly inducing Norman into a hypnotic trance, came to feel confident that he could, for brief periods of time, 5 to 10 minutes, safely control Norman's violent thoughts and actions.

The plan was for Dr. Novak to induce Norman into a deep state of hypnosis and introduce into Norman's unconscious world a code word which would subdue and pacify him for the 5 to 10 minutes. Armed with an effective code word, we could untie him, escort him to the bathroom, return him from the bathroom, and safely restrain him on the gurney again, but if we went over the 10-minute mark we were at risk. Norman chose his own code word to be introduced into his unconscious mind; it was "Godzilla," and we used it on multiple occasions, twice by me, as I saw, on Norman's return from having a bowel movement, some signs of his awakening from his state of calm. Each time I said "Godzilla" he crumpled to the floor like a heavy elephant, and he was as difficult as a heavy elephant to lift back onto the gurney.

. . . .

At an all-staff case conference focused on the care, treatment, and maintenance of Norman, Dr. Novak filled us in on Norman's background, patiently recorded from hours of Dr. Novak's psychotherapy sessions with Norman, and on Dr. Novak's approach to treating Norman. Norman Dupree was born in Kansas City, the son of a former small-town Kansas mayor as his father and a former beauty queen for his mother. Norman described an idyllic childhood, brought up with principled Midwestern values, with commitment to family, church, community, and country, and with exuberant enthusiasm for high school football. He was the high school varsity quarterback all four years and took his team to the state championship game twice, victorious each time. He was a town hero, admired by everyone, adored and favored by his parents, and

206

worshipped by his disabled younger brother.

Norman won full-ride scholarships to colleges all over the country, some academic, but most for football. But his high school days were during the late 1960s, turbulent times, and Norman owed a debt to his great nation and he intended to pay it. He became a member of the special operations force of the United States Army, the Green Berets. He was stationed and trained at Fort Bragg in North Carolina, and he went off to fight in the war in Vietnam. He was well-trained in unconventional warfare, and he specialized in hostage rescue which ultimately led to his capture behind enemy lines twice and his subsequent escapes.

"I rescued plenty of them," Norman told Dr. Novak, "but when it came to me, I had to rescue myself."

Due to his multiple injuries, repeated torture, and subsequent chronic pain, Norman was honorably discharged from the army, and he landed on the streets of San Francisco, homeless, penniless, and in need of pain medications.

"I'm not mad at my country," said Norman, "but this country is fucked. I died 100 deaths and killed 100 Viet Cong. They owe me better."

Dr. Novak thought Norman was a haunted man, a shell of the man he once was, broken down by the enemy and dumped on the streets by the army. Norman wandered from homeless shelter to homeless camp, finally making his own camp along the American River where he was picked up by police after he asked a passing bicyclist to call the police before he killed himself. The police brought Norman to the Emergency Department, but he required no medical care, so he was ushered straight to our Crisis Services. At that time we did not board psychiatric patients in the ED for days at a time because Sacramento County operated a county psychiatric hospital and was obligated to take all of our patients, at least theoretically. When a Crisis staff member told Dr. Novak that Norman Dupree, a former Green Beret, a man who could kill with his fifth digit, was having an active flashback in our Crisis interview room, and was threatening to explode and kill, Dr. Novak called our UC Davis Police to restrain Norman so that no one was hurt.

It was Norman who told Dr. Novak just how dangerous a patient he was, how he was trained to kill instantly, and how, in the middle of a combat flashback, he had hurt innocent bystanders. It was Norman who instructed Dr. Novak about the extent to which Dr. Novak and his staff needed to take precautions to ensure their safety. And it was Norman who helped Dr. Novak develop the careful protocol for his care and maintenance so that no one was assaulted and injured during his hospital stay. It was Norman who imprisoned himself.

Dr. Novak immediately phoned Sacramento County's psychiatric hospital, called Live Oak, and told the admitting doctor that Norman Dupree was the most lethal patient he had ever seen and Live Oak needed to accept him immediately. Norman was described as a high-risk patient to himself and to all staff members of the Medical Center, and Dr. Novak was ready to transfer his patient, the paperwork was completed. The admitting doctor at Live Oak, however, while thanking Dr. Novak for his honesty and cautionary comments, declined to accept Mr. Dupree saying they had a nursing staff shortage and the absence of an available seclusion room. Over the next seven days there was no let-up in the nursing staff shortage and no vacancy of seclusion rooms, consequently, no acceptance of Mr. Dupree. The private hospitals in Sacramento were not required to take our patients, and none of them would take this patient. Understandable.

This is how Norman Dupree came to live in one of our only two interview rooms during my early days working in the Crisis Clinic. By day seven, Dr. Novak seriously regretted his honesty in his report to Live Oak. He mumbled to others, to anyone passing by, that he "never should have described Mr. Dupree as the most lethal man he had ever seen." Given the opportunity for a redo, Dr. Novak would have described Norman as having "occasional hostile impulses."

Personally, I enjoyed Norman's company. Occasionally, at night, when I assumed the role of caring for him, I would untie both his hands, give him a large bag of barbecue potato chips, his favorite, roll his gurney into one of our personal offices, actually Dr. Novak's office because that was where the television set was, and watch reruns of MASH with him, a program he requested. Four or five times I went to the staff lounge hotplate and cooked Jiffy Pop popcorn for him. During the daytime, with Dr. Novak and other important staff present, there was a return to the careful, safe protocol that even Norman insisted be followed on that shift.

After our houseguest stayed with us for us for a full week, and as we walked in and out of an office daily where this poor man was bound on a gurney, our new life became the new normal. "Hi Jim. Hi Mary Ann," I would say to fellow staff when I came to work. And then, "Hi Norman." Carefully walking around a self-imprisoned, heavily restrained, pain-medicated killer, was simply ordinary.

Each shift had its own peculiar way of living with Norman. The day shift was preoccupied with following strict rules for everyone's safety. Dr. Novak carefully supervised the day staff while he also focused on writing a potentially groundbreaking article on the effects of war trauma. He was preparing a psychiatric grand rounds presentation starring Norman Dupree to be delivered to the larger professional psychiatric community in Sacramento. The evening shift, me included, was in social mode, relaxed in rules, casual about safety, sloppy and loose with restraints.

The night shift was completely perplexed and off kilter. During the slow nights, the night staff ordinarily liked to sleep in one of the two interview rooms, and the new guest, having taken up residency there, made that impossible. They became grumpy, even more reclusive and less communicative with other shifts than they usually were, and they usually were. The big problem for the night shift was that they were leaderless. Jerry Douglas, the strong, charismatic, if not strange, leader of the night shift was on vacation, off on another wilderness, survivalist backpacking trip, by himself, as always, just Jerry and his closest comrade, his handgun, Mr. Friendly. Without Jerry, the night shift was confused, disoriented, and now sleep-deprived.

Norman talked the most intimately with those of us on the evening shift because we were the shift of conversation, not the shift of sleep like the night shift, nor the shift of treatment like the day shift. After passing the one-week mark, Norman confided to me that he enjoyed living on my shift the best. The night shift, he said, was unfriendly, and I could understand that because most of us who overlapped with them thought the same. And as time went on and patience wore down, the day shift no longer allowed Norman to take charge of his own treatment; it was like they were trying to set the rules for him—not his rules, their rules. Norman was beginning to state outright irritation with his lack of control over his treatment. After all it was he who called the police and told them to take him to an emergency room. It was he who divulged he was a dangerous man and needed to be restrained. It was he who demanded to be admitted to a psychiatric hospital.

As the days slowly passed, he became more upset that we had not successfully admitted him to a psychiatric hospital, yet he was told by Dr. Novak that he was too dangerous to leave our emergency room. He was stuck and we were stuck in a stalemate of poor treatment in a false psychiatric setting, no setting at all, just a room which began to smell in spite of Norman's daily sponge baths. Norman was a houseguest who had stayed too long, a guest who captured our professional imaginations at first and enjoyed the attention we gave him, but a guest who became bored with us in time as he started to take a hard look at where he was and what he was doing.

. . . .

While Norman was stirring with irritation and discontent over his new life in the ED, I realized that life was returning to normal for me when my regularly unscheduled patient, 24-year-old Amber Lydell, walked into the ED, this time as a voluntary patient, asking to see me. Amber was usually an involuntary patient brought in by police, fighting, spitting, and biting, but this time she skipped the middlemen, slipped through the locked entry doors, and walked directly back to my office to visit me. I considered her voluntary, walk-in entry to be a significant and positive treatment step for her, and I favored it over her more dramatic entrances. Her most famous and frequent suicidal method involved her remarkable ability to hang by her fingertips from her second-story window while threatening to jump. Occasionally a new friend, usually a man, often a fantasy boyfriend, would bring her to the emergency room hoping to unload this stick of dynamite that regrettably had come into his life.

Amber was wild, uncontrollable, vivacious, violent, sexy, smart, primitive, exuberant, brash, beautiful, exhilarating, and episodically, suicidally depressed, sometimes all in the same day. Amber was a borderline personality disorder.

Her behaviors in life were often outrageous. Before I ever knew Amber, I was told that psychiatric inpatient hospitals did not want her; she used them for shelters and respite, refused to do the work of treatment, seduced men on the unit for her own advantage, refused medications other than the "good kinds," used screaming as her normal talking voice, provoked fights among the patients, threw any object in her room at anybody in her room, and physically fought with staff and other patients. I was told, above all else, never to admit Amber to a psychiatric hospital, never to place her on a psychiatric hold, because Live Oak would never forgive me. Over the years I admitted Amber to Live Oak many times.

Amber could fool me, and she could make a fool out of me. I could not always tell how serious she was about suicide. When paramedics first introduced her to me, they alerted me that she had regularly threatened suicide by hanging from her second-story apartment, on possibly dozens of occasions. By law, if not by sympathy, they took her gestures seriously and assumed that she could hurt herself accidentally if her fingers gave out while she was hanging there. They repeatedly brought her to the Medical Center, but she was rarely admitted for these jumping gestures because they were rarely a true sign of her suicidal intent.

But one time she made a suicide attempt by overdosing on her medications, and she told me she was fine afterwards, that she wanted to go home. I discharged her when she was medically cleared, only to find she had overdosed again before she left the hospital with drugs she had hidden in her pant-leg cuff. It was a serious overdose which required an intensive care stay. I was the one who discharged this woman who did not even make it outside the doors of the hospital before she collapsed. I was the one to point the finger at when the ED attending asked, "Who the hell discharged this patient?"

I visited Amber on the ICU when she was lucid because I was concerned about her and I was concerned about me. She was lying in bed covered with a bedsheet, and she greeted me with her large bright eyes and a big smile.

"I understand you less the more I know you," I said to her. "Why don't you just tell me when you're really going to kill yourself?"

"What fun would that be?" she said. "It would take all the mystery out of it."

"I have no stomach for mystery," I said.

"I knew you would come and visit me. Maybe that's why I do these things."

She told me this as she was looking into my eyes intently, trying to observe where my eyes might wander, as she removed her bedsheet, slipped off her hospital gown, and walked her young naked body to the bathroom, never taking her eyes away from my eyes. She peed with the door open, walked back to the bed and slipped under the bed sheet, eyes still fixed on my eyes.

"Why do you do that?" I asked with irritation.

"Do what?" she said.

. . . .

I am a skier, a good skier. I should be a great skier because I have skied for over 50 years, and I would be a great skier if I were bold, reckless, unafraid to fall, and unafraid of injury. I am not bold and I do not wish to be injured so I am a competent skier, able to conquer

212

any mountain timidly, but drawn irresistibly to the big packed bowls, the blue runs, not the black-diamond runs. When I do try to tackle with gusto a frighteningly steep, triple-black-diamond slope fraught with deep moguls, and I fall badly, skis flying down the hill without me, me tumbling down the hill without grace, limbs akimbo, I regret it. I reconsider my life as a bold skier and envision my life with a spinal cord injury. The best skiers do not think about a bad fall. After they have one they slide downhill or climb uphill with smiles on their faces, collect their skis, step back into them, finish the hill and return to that hill, and conquer it. I do not do that. I leave that hill because that hill defeated me. It not only knocked the wind out of my lungs—I could recover from that—it knocked the confidence out of my mind, heart, and soul.

A skier without confidence is a broken skier, prone to conservative decisions, likely to make mistakes, overcome by self-consciousness and fear. It is a terrible thing to lose spontaneity and instinct. The only way I can effectively collect myself and work my way back up the steep hill of confidence and courage is to return to a very easy hill, a beginner run, to pick up the pieces that were torn away from me. Bit by bit, easy hill by easy hill, I can work my way back up to the big, smooth, packed bowls. I find the pieces of myself I lost and I put myself back together.

A therapist needs confidence, too. A tentative therapist is a nervous one, one who remembers all his mistakes and is destined to make more mistakes. When I fall as a therapist I lose confidence, become timid, and no longer trust my instincts. I play a more conservative game and end up making even more mistakes. I get more cautious, and that will cause me to start admitting patients who are using me or using the hospital inappropriately, patients who do not really need to be hospitalized. Therapists rarely get sued for admitting patients who do not need to be admitted, but we may well be sued for discharging patients who do need to be admitted. If I lose my instincts, I lose, perhaps ever so slightly, my ability to distinguish the close calls between patients who should be admitted and those who should not.

I made a mistake by discharging Amber the day she overdosed twice, and, as a consequence, I stopped listening to the voice of Live Oak telling me not to admit her. For the future, I was free of the pressure from Live Oak; my fear of falling again was stronger than their demands. I was more conservative in my assessments of Amber, and I tended to listen to her carefully when she said she needed to be admitted. I tended to admit her whether she needed it or not. But as our relationship progressed, Amber was more honest, less gamey with me, and I was more comfortable accommodating her.

Some therapists follow the letter of the law. They admit patients to a psychiatric hospital whenever patients say they are going to kill themselves, and they do not admit patients to the hospital when patients make no such claim. For the letter-of-the-law therapist, gravely disabled means precisely what it says, a person is not able to provide for his or her food, shelter, and clothing as a result of a mental disorder. I operate with a broader definition of gravely disabled. In my mind some very psychotic patients, people who are suffering terribly, who are severely frightened, delusional, disorganized in their thinking, hallucinating, out of touch with reality, and exercising poor judgment, are in need of psychiatric admission even if they are wearing clothes, living in a garage, and eating food. I still place them on a psychiatric hold as gravely disabled because I am not a letter-of-the-law therapist, I am a meaning-of-the-law therapist, although I confess that, like all therapists, I do my own interpreting of the meaning of the law.

Some patients just cry out for a psychiatric hold. I do not even have to think about criteria. The police once dropped off at our emergency room a man who was walking down the freeway naked, and he walked for miles all the way to a Macy's parking lot. He had a birdcage over his head, he was hearing voices and talking a stream of gibberish to himself, and he had watery feces running down his buttocks and legs. A manager at Macy's called the police to say he was disturbing the shoppers. I would guess so. This man had clothes in a bag, was eating candy bars when approached by the police, and had a room in a board and care facility. Technically, he had food, clothing and shelter, but he was a severely decompensated schizophrenic patient who required psychiatric hospitalization. The criteria I used for his admission was not literally consistent with the letter of law, a danger to himself or others, or gravely disabled; my criteria was, "Shit. That doesn't look good at all."

This man did not want to be admitted to a hospital—many severely psychotic patients do not—but my sacrifice of his freedom is the price I exact to relieve his misery. Based on the obvious, I will sometimes deviate from the literal interpretation of gravely disabled. Some therapists will not.

Unlike my birdcage patient, some people will visit the ED, desperately attempting to get into the hospital having rehearsed all the right words—yes I am going to kill myself, yes I am going to kill other people, no I cannot provide for my daily needs—when in fact, they do not need psychiatric hospitalization and do not benefit from it. There are many reasons why people seek out hospitalization, reasons other than pain, injury, and illness. Some people have no place else to go, some want to escape the rain, others are cold seeking warmth, hungry needing food, lonely wanting company, frightened pursuing safety, or rejected by a partner, searching for kindness. We cannot keep everyone in the hospital, shelter everyone, feed everyone, comfort and treat everyone—only the most severe. Like every city, Sacramento needs other resources for all those people who are not so severe as to require psychiatric hospitalization, places of respite with kind staff to help them handle the overwhelming demands of daily living. Is it wrong to seek hospitalization when you are wet, cold, hungry, and frightened if there are no other resources in the city? It is not wrong, it is understandable, but attempts to get admitted to the hospital for these reasons are often met with staff irritation and downright hostility. We are all too proud to be "manipulated."

....

Amber Lydell is a revolving-door patient, a "frequent flyer" well

215

known to all the Crisis staff and many of the ED staff. Crisis services has a folder of frequent flyers, each patient with a strategy for treatment which, if read carefully, exposes a subtle direction or push toward a specific kind of treatment which would discourage the patient from coming back to us. As a group of mental health professionals, we are not mean, although we do have our mean days; we are trying to push chronic patients into more stable, comprehensive, outpatient, case management services—wrap-around services that respond to all the crises that erupt in a patient's daily life. Wrap-around services, for example, Turning Point in Sacramento, offer a broad range of programs to each of their patients: psychotherapy, pharmacotherapy, day treatment, social and job skills development, housing, transportation, drug and alcohol services, and crisis respite. On many occasions I have been grateful to the surprisingly upbeat staff from Turning Point when they come to the ED at all hours to pick up their troubled and difficult patients. I would be surprised if a therapist from the private practice community came running as quickly, but, in fairness to them, they are rarely called upon to do so.

I tried to convince, even coerce, Amber to join the treatment community of Turning Point. I tried to persuade her to do many things I thought would be helpful for her, but my track record on that score was dismal. Amber lived in her own world, a world punctuated by powerful tornadoes and erupting volcanoes.

I met Amber in the first week I worked for the Crisis Clinic, and I met her dozens of times that year. She came to prefer seeing me over other staff largely because I was the new guy. She would ask for me, even in the middle of her volatile eruptions in the ED. She would spit on one nurse and ask another if I was working that night. Crisis work in an ED can be just like outpatient psychotherapy if the same patient keeps asking for you. You get to know them pretty well. They come to treat you more kindly than the rest of the staff, and the rest of the staff is happy to avoid them and save them for you, thinking you have a special way with them. "She does not spit on you," my Crisis coworkers would tell me about Amber. "She likes you. I have scars from the scratches she gave me when I last saw her." All Crisis staff workers have their own caseloads of returning patients who prefer seeing them over anyone else, and all of us "anyone else" staff are happy to accommodate that patient request.

Amber was a wild child, a stormy adolescent, and an uncontrollable young adult, always pretty, precociously sexual, popular with boys and competitive with girls. Amber separated people into two camps, all friend or all foe but no in between, and friend could become foe in an instant with her slightest perception of betrayal. Her father was an attorney, a kind one, not a combatant, a man who worked hard at compromise and reconciliation. Her mother stayed home, providing the most support and love she could to a child both parents realized was troubled.

"Amber has too many emotions," her mother once told me. "Too many, too strong, too quick to ignite." Amber kept her preschool habits of biting, scratching, kicking, and hitting other children all through the primary grades, and consequently was referred to counselor after counselor and a handful of child psychiatrists. She was first diagnosed with ADHD and placed on Adderall, which she was fond of, as many teens and young adults are, but Amber liked it at the age of six.

She was later diagnosed with a conduct disorder, still later with oppositional defiant disorder, and after that with borderline personality disorder. Along the way to adulthood she displayed many instances of severe anxiety and multiple episodes of depression, and she was typically prescribed anti-depressant and anti-anxiety medications which she used for suicide attempts. She cut herself periodically, not to kill herself but to bleed the angst out of her.

Amber was sexually active early, at the age of 13, and was on birth control pills at 15. She had many boyfriends; they were easy to acquire but not easy to keep, and she was invariably angry with them and then full of rage when they tried to leave. She was a beautiful girl, "So beautiful," said her mother, "if she would only stop with

217

the tattoos and piercings." Her parents were kind, loving people who lived their lives for her happiness, but did so unsuccessfully. Their daughter rarely had sustained happiness and was chronically in a crisis.

Amber became irrationally hateful toward her parents during adolescence, but they had patience and a saintly tolerance with her. I talked with Amber's parents many times and we got to know each other well, often after the police brought Amber to the ED on a 5150, usually after a suicide attempt following a break-up with a boyfriend, a fight with the landlord, or a volatile state of intoxication. She could not hold onto a boyfriend, an apartment, or a state of sobriety, and there was much interplay among the three. She would get drunk, trash her apartment, and attack her boyfriend. But she did not always need intoxication to trash her apartment or attack her boyfriend.

Amber would change friends, boyfriends, jobs, and apartments like other people changed clothes, jumping out of one thing, usually with a push, and jumping into another. She would join lively groups of homeless youth as a member of their tribe, and she would feel wanted and loved by them for a while, but the fires of rage would burn down her relationships with them, and she would find herself alone again, sometimes turning to her parents, sometimes to me, sometimes to suicide.

She liked to keep me informed about her life and she did not object to my keeping her parents informed. She once called me from Eugene, Oregon, saying she was getting married to a man she met on the street in Ashland while he was playing his guitar and panhandling. He was one of the many charismatic Pied Pipers of the homeless, a good-looking, guitar-playing street artist with no job, no money, and an eye for a pretty girl. They moved to Eugene because he said they let homeless youth live on the streets and in the parks there. It was a paradise.

Amber excitedly put him on the phone with me to say hello, and she introduced me to him as her best friend. In his first sentence to me he said hello. In his second sentence he asked me to send them some money. Amber apologized for him, and I think she hit him with his phone because I heard a whack and then the call was dropped abruptly. Amber borrowed and stole, but she never begged.

A year later I heard from Amber when she was living in a park in Grass Valley, California, with a group of homeless young men and women, "the best friends I ever had." Amber's attachments in life were quick and powerful, and her detachments ugly and potentially lethal. Separation, rejection, loss of love, abandonment, whether real or imagined, sank her into the deepest, darkest hole where she saw no value in herself and no reason to live. Perceived loss of love from another meant, for her, a complete lack of self-love and self-care, and she possessed very few lifelines, few bridges she had not burned, perhaps none but those with her parents, who loved her always and never gave up on her, and me, her link to the world of mental health.

Amber needed but resisted the kind of services that would be most helpful to her for all the years I knew her. The gold standard for unstable borderline patients would be residential treatment, a treatment environment that would focus on the whole package of psychiatric treatment, medications, relationship skills, and job and living skills, an environment which would bring daily routine to constant chaos. The world of mental health resources was available to her through the willing and generous support of her parents, but residential treatment was never as compelling to her as a beautiful man in the park playing his guitar. As Kris Kristofferson said, "Freedom's just another word for nothin' left to lose."

There were brief moments in time, usually after the devastating break-up of a relationship, when Amber was lost in emptiness and self-hatred, that she recognized the need for help. During these brief interludes when she was too tired, too sad to fight, she would walk into the ED when she knew I was there, and she would ask me for help. She would not have been in treatment or on medications other than her self-treatment of daily marijuana and alcohol, and, at these times, she was slightly more open to the idea of prescribed medications. However, many of her previous psychiatrists were aware that she functioned only marginally better while on prescribed medications if better at all. Pharmacotherapy did not appear to be Amber's road to recovery.

....

When Amber showed up to see me this time, walking in on her own with no police accompaniment, I took her into our one available interview room because the other was still occupied by Norman. I sat down to talk with her and was pleased to see she was sober, calm, attractively dressed, and youthfully clear in the eyes and face. She looked like a lovely and happy young woman. She asked me if we could take a walk because she wanted to introduce me to someone, so we did. She introduced me to Charles, her boyfriend, possibly 45 years old to her 24, the owner of a beautiful new BMW which we stood beside as we talked.

"I wanted you to know that I am happy and doing well," she said. "And I wanted you to meet my boyfriend."

Charles was shy, eyes down, but he stuck out his hand and said, "Nice to meet you."

"Very nice to meet you, Charles," I said.

"Charles knows that you saved my life many times," Amber said to me. When we get settled, we want to have you over for dinner."

I knew I had not saved her life many times and knew I would not be getting together with them for dinner. I was worried that Charles was another faulty life raft adrift and sinking slowly. Amber loved her men, wanted to move in with them quickly, talked to them of marriage way too soon, and eventually wanted to murder them. Marry or murder, little in between for Amber, but it was never the men who were in danger after fleeing, it was Amber. I also worried that Charles was a postponement of real treatment for Amber.

Effective treatment for a borderline patient 40 years ago was anemic at best, but since then good faith efforts have been made in psychotherapy, medications, day treatment, partial hospitalization, and residential treatment. For example, in the late 1980s, dialectical behavior therapy, or DBT, was added to the repertoire of therapy

220

strategies for the borderline patient.

I am no great wrangler when it comes to corralling a wild horse; I keep my distance. But if I had the power to force Amber, that furious runaway steed, through a narrow treatment gate, it would be the gate of residential treatment at an isolated, bucolic, western ranch that had a comprehensive DBT focus. No phones, no computers, no drugs, no alcohol, no ability to run away, and no bull-shit except the kind steers plop on the ground. DBT is part psychotherapy, part classroom learning, and part practice, and it teaches people to work with their waves of emotion, their tidal waves of emotion, emotions so hot they burn the patience right out of family, friends, and lovers.

If I ruled the world, Amber would be living in Middle-of-Nowhere, Texas, many miles and a long hike away from an antique payphone that did not work anyway. In today's world of psychotherapy, practitioners are doing better at treating borderline patients with the assistance of the right treatment in the right setting, better at more productively channeling the borderline's impulsivity and energy, better at helping them pour self-love into their empty cup, and more effective in helping them contain the intensity of their rage. The fires of hostility and the feelings of worthlessness can be self-soothed and expressions of affection can be learned, but there is a catch, a catch that eliminates most potential clients, a catch that eliminated Amber: Amber had to walk through that narrow gate by herself, because I did not rule the world, not her world.

. . . .

Toward the end of my shift I was paged by an ED physician to consult on a patient brought to the ED by ambulance from Sacramento International Airport. She had been steps away from boarding a plane to Mexico when she became suddenly ill and collapsed. The ED doctor told me that she had been driving from Seattle, where she lived, to the Mexican border to undergo treatment that was not available to her in the United States. Since she was brought directly to a university-quality, major metropolitan hospital, she decided to share her story with the doctors here.

Christina Martinez, a 53-year-old Latina, told the doctor she was eight months pregnant and that her baby was shrinking in her body. She also reported that her own sexual organs, her clitoris and her vagina, were disappearing. She had a disease that no doctor was able to name, let alone cure, even after many medical consultations. Ms. Martinez was terrified for her baby and worried about herself and frustrated that previous doctors had not helped her or would not help her. Concerned relatives in Mexico told her of a fine clinic in Mexico City with different kinds of doctors who treated illnesses that were not treated in the United States. Ms. Martinez withdrew all the money she had in her bank account and started out in her car from Seattle with the intent of driving straight through to Mexico City. Her car broke down on a Sacramento freeway and a kindly man, stopping to help her on the side of the road, drove her, at her request, to the airport. She would never see that car again.

Ms. Martinez possessed, in a large beach bag, three bottles of a homemade, thick, soupy, smelly concoction she had created herself and drank regularly to help her baby grow. It was her exclusive source of nutrients because she feared regular meals would bring back the nausea and vomiting she had suffered for weeks. She sipped this murky liquid as we spoke.

"The doctors seem to think you are doing much better," I said. "Are you feeling better?"

"Much better. Can you take me to the airport?"

"It is quite late, Ms. Martinez. I don't think you would get any flights out tonight. I think we should plan on taking care of you here at the hospital tonight, and then we can help you tomorrow morning."

"My baby is very ill, doctor. I need to get going right away."

"Let us take care of you and your baby for right now," I said.

"No, the doctors here won't help me. None of the doctors here will help me. They are like all the rest of them. I have to go now."

"No car, no plane, late at night. Where will you go?"

"I-5 goes all the way to Mexico. Could you take me to I-5?"

I do not like to smash right through someone's delusions; it is ineffective and impolite. But when a patient is in a hurry to place herself in harm's way, I cannot afford to be passive in my treatment approach.

"Let's get somebody to help you," I said. "A friend, family? Do you have a husband?"

"That's not important," she said.

"Anybody I can call for you? Someone who knows you."

"No," she said, a little louder.

"Where do you live, Ms. Martinez?"

"That's not important," she said.

"Maybe if I called your doctor she could call our doctors to help them help you. Who is your doctor?"

"I don't have a doctor. I'm trying to get a doctor. Can you take me to I-5?" she said, now insisting.

Ms. Martinez had registered as a patient and we did have an address in Seattle and a phone number that she had given to the registration clerk before she was treated. She did not want anyone called on her behalf, and she did not want anyone to know she was here at our hospital. She no longer wanted our help and she no longer trusted our help. But I intended to call the one phone number we had for her, against her wishes, a clear yet legal breach of confidentiality. It is a legal breach because I need to know whatever I need to know to protect Ms. Martinez if I believe her safety is at risk due to a mental disorder.

Having excused myself from Ms. Martinez, having lied to her about my intention to explore transportation possibilities for her, I called the phone number she gave registration and, in a moment's time, was talking with her husband. His gratitude was extreme, his relief palpable; I could feel it over the phone. Over 20 days had passed since he had heard from his wife. He knew for certain she was once again on a hopeless journey to save her imaginary baby. For the last several years dark delusions had seeped into her mind and body, dreadful thoughts of being eaten away from the inside, strange beliefs that the baby she miscarried in her 40s had been placed back into her body by the God who forgave her. In Ms. Martinez's mind, her prayers had been answered, her little girl was on the way again, the girl who would complement her five sons.

On three different road trips over the last three years, each time close to the Thanksgiving holiday, close to the anniversary of her miscarriage, Ms. Martinez headed out to find emergency medical help for her dying little girl. She frantically sought out one doctor after another, most of them dismissing her with, "It's all in your head," and sending her out with no psychiatric consultation and no call to her husband. The road trip would end when she ran out of money, ran out of gas, ran out of energy, was exhausted and broken, and unable to move forward. Twice she was placed on psychiatric holds and transferred back to Seattle to continue her psychiatric care. Once she made it all the way to Florida because she heard there was a clinic in the Bahamas that could help her. Time was running out for her because she believed her sexual organs were being eaten away and she would no longer be able to carry a baby.

Ms. Martinez resisted treatment in hospitals and avoided treatment outside hospitals, convinced that her pregnancy was real and that her disease, the insidious wasting away of her baby and her sexual organs, was obvious and urgent. When a woman knows that her symptoms are true, and when her loving but exasperated husband tries to talk her out of what is true, when her own large, caring family and her husband's supportive, sympathetic family both side with her husband, and when the entire medical community of Seattle thinks you are crazy, it is time to leave town by foot, thumb, car, train or plane and get to a place where people understand you and will help you. So far, Ms. Martinez had found no such place.

. . . .

False beliefs are a common symptom in many psychiatric illnesses: schizophrenia, bipolar disorder, depression, dementia, even high stress states. But the diagnosis, delusional disorder, is used to describe a unique presentation: less disorganized with less break from reality than schizophrenia, without the depth of depression or the exhilaration of mania in bipolar disorder, less organic and cognitively impaired than dementia, and more entrenched than high-stress states. I might not know that the man sitting next to me on a bus had a delusional disorder, not even on a cross-country trip where time would enhance observation, but I would know if I was sitting next to an untreated schizophrenic or bipolar person. The false beliefs of the delusional disordered patient are circumscribed, limited to real-life fears, conflicts, and issues, untouched by hallucinations, by disorganized speech and behavior or severe mood swings, all commonly seen in schizophrenia or bipolar disorder.

Ms. Martinez was surrounded by loving, caring, hopeful people, a close community of Latino family members who prayed for her. All through her 40s they prayed that God would bring into her world the little girl she had always wanted, a girl who would round out her family of five boys. She was a good mother to the boys, but she wanted a little girl. In her early 40s she miscarried; she knew in her heart she had miscarried a little girl, a little girl sent to her by the generous God to whom she prayed, and taken away from her by the cruel God she could not forgive for a long time. Years after the miscarriage she went back to the church she had rejected, back to the priest, back to confession, and asked God to forgive her sins and to give her back her baby girl. There was a bitter stain on her soul that she could not erase and needed to cleanse.

When, at the age of 50, she announced to her large extended family that she was pregnant with a little girl, they were stunned but they believed her, they rejoiced with her, and they looked to the heavens and celebrated the miracle, the great love of God Who returned to Ms. Martinez the blessed daughter she had lost. They had parties with many gifts, and as Ms. Martinez advanced in her pregnancy, noticeably advanced, they treated her like a queen.

There was nothing wrong with Ms. Martinez, everything was right. She was happy, sweet, and affectionate with her children, and she was responsive to and appreciative of her large, extended family. Using Ms. Martinez as an example, her priest spoke to his congregation of the miracles of God.

At the six-month point of her pregnancy, with Ms. Martinez looking very pregnant indeed, Mr. Martinez began asking his wife questions about how the pregnancy was going, what the doctor was saying, and who the doctor was. Ms. Martinez would not tell him anything. She thought it would jinx the health of the baby, and she became increasingly irritated with his questions. It was not until her eighth month of pregnancy, when he rushed her to the hospital after her water broke, that he ever talked to a doctor about his wife's health. The conversation with the doctor was the most painful conversation of his life.

"Mr. Martinez," said the doctor calmly, "your wife is not pregnant."

"Oh my God," he cried out. "We lost the baby again. This is going to kill my wife."

"What I mean to say, Mr. Martinez, is that your wife was never pregnant."

Mr. Martinez was incensed with the doctor. He raised his voice in a threatening manner and said, "Of course she's pregnant, just look at her! And her water broke. I saw it."

The doctor was kind and soft in voice, but he did not sugarcoat anything. "I have seen this before, when a woman is very sad and when she desperately wants to have a baby. The body follows the wish. The body gets bigger, the stomach gets bigger, and the dream becomes a reality in the mind of the dreamer."

"But her water broke," said Mr. Martinez.

"Your wife appears to have lost control of her bladder."

Mr. Martinez told me he was never quite the same after that exchange with the doctor, and since that time his wife was never quite sane. She exploded in the hospital, physically attacked the medical staff, needed to be restrained by medications, and was hospitalized on a psychiatric hold. Mr. Martinez drove home a broken man, severely depressed and confused about what to tell his boys, his family, and her family. He pulled his car over and stopped three times on his short ride home because he could not drive on. He sat in his car and cried—powerful, heaving sobs unfamiliar to him in all his life. He could not bear the truth, but he was not a man to lie. He told his children, his family, and her family, "We lost the baby." He said no more, they asked no more. They could see his pain.

Over the next three years, Ms. Martinez's fixed belief that she was pregnant and that her pregnancy was at risk cursed her and doomed Mr. Martinez to a joyless life of worry. She ran from doctor to doctor, hospital to hospital, city to city, then state to state, seeing the wrong doctors and receiving the wrong treatments, or often no treatment at all, until she became convinced that she needed to leave the country to get the cure she needed.

· · · · · · · · · ·

The disease of a delusional disorder can hit the young or the old, for reasons not clear. I have seen a number of women during the involutional years, from 40 to 55, move into this debilitating but not totally disorganizing state, without any prior psychiatric history, or at least any known and treated psychiatric history. Forty years ago we had a special name for the phenomenon when post-menopausal women became depressed and delusional; we called the disease "involutional melancholia." It was the sweetest sounding, most mellifluous diagnosis in psychiatry and as a young man I liked saying it: "involutional melancholia." But I would not want to live it.

Delusional disorders come in many forms, all with varying degrees of risk and life dysfunction. I tried to treat a young man with a delusional disorder who was referred to me by his employers. He worked in a spacious open area of a large office where many people passed his desk during the course of the day. He became acutely aware that each man or woman who passed his desk somehow amassed the dust that naturally exists in the air and pushed it in his direction. He could feel the film of dust in his throat after they passed by him. When the sunlight came in through the office windows illuminating the dust, he became intensely apprehensive, although he said nothing of his fears to his fellow workers. But he knew without a doubt that his coworkers would be collecting that dust in preparation to their pushing it at him like a wave. He was certain his office coworkers were talking about him and plotting against him, and that they had hatched a plan to make him ill through dust exposure.

When he could no longer tolerate the dust in his face, mouth, nose, throat, and lungs, he screamed at coworkers and reported them to his supervisors. His supervisors did nothing to protect him. In fact, they did not believe him, and they demanded he submit to a psychiatric assessment before he returned to work.

I saw this man three times before he noticed, quite abruptly during our third session, that I, too, was pushing dust in his direction. He told me that he was very disappointed and angry with me, now that he understood that I was working in concert with his coworkers to destroy him. He left my office abruptly, and he never came back. It was interesting to me that after he left I could see, from where he was sitting, the illumination of dust created by the sun shining through my office window shades. Dust exists everywhere. I can only imagine how I would feel if people were using it as a weapon against me.

I was once called in to do a psychiatric assessment on a woman in her 30s who, like Ms. Martinez, started by visiting one doctor in her hometown and progressed to seeing nearly 100 physicians over a period of years in consultations about the parasitic invasion of her skin. She saw many highly-respected dermatologists all over the country. She tirelessly searched for the cure for her parasitic infestation, a condition which caused her skin to erupt in rashes with itching, burning, blotching, and scabbing. She searched libraries and internet sites for the cause and cure of her infested skin, and she compiled a suitcase full of articles proving she had what she had: bugs in her skin.

She demanded that I read that suitcase full of articles. Her search for a competent dermatologist had gone on for years, and they all said the same things and they all ruled out the same things. She did not have bugs in her skin, no scabies, no bedbugs, no mites, no fleas, nothing. She knew they were wrong and knew they were stupid. She would continue her hunt for a smart doctor.

She had never used methamphetamine, a common cause of delusional infestation; she stayed away from all drugs. She did have the markings of a woman who mercilessly scratched and dug at her skin searching for the cause of her affliction.

Occasionally, dermatologists would recommend that she see a psychiatrist for what they strongly believed was delusional parasitosis, a unique and torturous subset of delusional disorders. When the doctors came to that conclusion and made that referral, she walked out the door cursing them, but she soon entered another door to tell her story to a fresh face. I was the fresh face that day and, knowing I would see her only one time, I also suggested that psychiatric help would at least reduce the stress she encountered from her chronic condition. She walked out of my door cursing me.

I saw a woman in her 70s who was convinced that her neighbors, who lived in the other half of her duplex, were harassing her, trying to intimidate her so she would move out. They danced on her roof all night long with heavy shoes, sneaked into her house and rearranged her clothes closet as she slept, sent putrid gases into her house through the heater system, altered her drinking water to make it dark and muddy, and placed chemicals in her food to loosen her bowel movements. She called the police regularly, and the fire department, the gas company, the water company; they all knew her well. They suggested she move out of the duplex, but she had experienced similar problems with other neighbors in other houses at earlier times and, in fact, she had gone through three sets of neighbors in her current duplex and they were all involved in harassing her.

Patients with delusional disorders might seek out medical doctors, or they might hire lawyers, they will complain to the police or other agencies of authority, but they do not march into psychiatrists' offices. They do not believe their problem is "in their

229

head," they do not want and will not take anti-psychotic or anti-depressant medications, and they do not return for psychiatric treatment. I cannot talk delusional patients out of their delusions, and to try to do so pushes them further away from me. It is certain that these patients need treatment, but they do not see the need for psychiatric treatment, and they usually do not meet the criteria for involuntary treatment. We cannot admit them to a psychiatric hospital, so their endless search for a cure, their search for justice or peace, continues, sometimes for many years.

. . . .

Ms. Martinez was certainly adequately dressed, she had a warm home of welcoming, concerned family members, and she was taking in nutrition, albeit a dark, murky-looking liquid something-or-other, so she technically had food, clothing, and shelter. She was not trying to hurt herself or anyone else, quite the opposite: she was running to save her life and the life of her baby. She did not meet the criteria for a psychiatric hold according to the letter of the law. But, again, the letter of the law is not the law, not if I do not believe it to be, and at that moment in time my clinical judgment was not guided by the letter of the law. Taking into consideration her intention to flee for her life to a foreign country, her severe somatic delusions, her exhaustion and fragile health, her self-concocted potion devised to restore the health of her imagined baby, her avoidance and fearfulness of normal food, and her lack of money, transportation, or a safe plan to get anywhere after she left the hospital, I placed her on a psychiatric hold. I did not feel she had the judgment to care for herself, and I thought she would be in harm's way the moment she walked out of the hospital.

Ms. Martinez was very angry with me and said I had as good as killed her and her baby, and she added that I would rot in hell. Mr. Martinez, however, was very grateful. We hospitalized Ms. Martinez in a private hospital in Sacramento while her husband flew to Sacramento to be close to her. At a more stable point in time she would be transferred back to Seattle to be treated close to home, close to the extended family who loved her and worried about her and hated to see her so haunted and tormented.

. . . .

I believe I made the right decision in admitting Christina Martinez to a psychiatric unit. Conversely, I never felt confident about whether I was doing the right thing or the wrong thing when I admitted Amber Lydell or when I let her go. I could not read Amber very well: sometimes she begged me to admit her to the hospital only to change her mind quickly before she was actually transferred, and sometimes she ran from the hospital when she was acutely suicidal. All I asked of her was that she clearly tell me what she wanted so I could accommodate her, but I was assuming she would always know what she wanted or needed, and that was not true for her. There are so many levels of intensive treatment in psychiatry, some settings with no freedom and other programs with great freedom. They vary from involuntary to voluntary hospitalization, from partial hospitalization to intensive outpatient care including board and care placement and wrap-around services, and from isolated residential care out on a ranch, farm, or wilderness area, to community residential care. But I never could seem to land Amber in the right slot at the right time; she had serious trouble with her landing gear.

I cannot always place patients into the programs that would be most beneficial for them even if they have ample follow-through motivation, because the right programs do not necessarily exist in every community, and insurances do not always cover them if they do. But due to generous parents, Amber had the world of mental health services available to her. She had resources to manipulate and enhance the two great forces that affect us all, our biology and our environment. She had the best medication consultations and the most perfect residential treatment programs available to her. She needed only to ask for them.

I have seen some borderline patients benefit from a change in living environment alone, usually a change into a highly structured lifestyle, like the military, or an isolated work environment, like a Native-American reservation or an Alaskan oil rig. Some borderline patients do not do well living with normal freedom and independence, yet they make progress with their maturity and stability in these alternative, regimented settings. Some people do very well when freedom is at a minimum and life activities are dictated down to the minute.

Amber could choose to enter the best psychiatric treatment and the most advantageous living environment, but she was not willing to surrender freedom and submit to structure for the promise of a better life. She did not see the value in structure, only the disadvantages, and she could not envision a better life, so for her the exchange of freedom for the promise of treatment was a bad trade. If she wanted forced help at all, involuntary hospitalization, it was on her terms, not the hospital's, and she only wanted forced help briefly. She committed to treatment impulsively and quit treatment immediately.

. . . .

It was the end of my shift, past the end, after I admitted Ms. Martinez to a psychiatric hospital, and so I attempted to spend some time with Jerry Douglas, who was just arriving. He returned from his backpacking vacation with a full and long beard, which was curious, because he had no beard when he left. Werewolf, I thought. No one who knew Jerry, and few people did, doubted that he was in charge of the hospital when he was in the house, on the premises. He was not officially in charge, not by title or by assigned position, but he was in charge. Upon returning, Jerry did not like the look of things. There was a man tied up in the one office his night shift personally used for sleep, apparently some natural-born, professionally-trained killer taking up his space. Jerry was an irritable person by nature, now extra agitated because he was back at work and not in the woods where he belonged. The man Jerry carefully, slowly looked over, who was fully restrained, ski gloves on each hand to prevent a death blow by a single finger, was clearly not where he was supposed

232

to be. Jerry was in no mood to be social with me, so I went home.

....

The next afternoon I returned to a whole new work setting, a different Crisis Clinic, one relieved of a terrible burden. The elephant in the room was gone, discharged in the early morning hours by Jerry Douglas. Everyone was shocked, most of all Dr. Novak who, when I saw him, appeared confused and lost, perhaps a little deflated. His patient was gone, the most dangerous man in the world was wandering the streets. Jerry Douglas had let him go, had no permission to do so, sought out no input before he did it. I was not as confused as Dr. Novak because I knew Jerry conducted his life as an independent agent, no permission and no input required, needed, or welcomed.

Jerry, having spent his first life, his life before his odd decision to enter social work, in military intelligence, immediately knew that Norman Dupree had not spent one day of his life in the military. Norman was not a Green Beret, not a trained killer, not a decorated hero, and he did not suffer flashbacks; Norman lived in a fantasy world that came to life in many accommodating hospitals.

Jerry's staff did the research, called other hospitals and called Norman's parents, after Norman freely spilled the truth to a man to whom nobody lied; I do not know why, but nobody dared lie to Jerry Douglas. I tell Jerry the truth out of friendship, respect, and fear, but I do not know why other people succumb.

Norman was well-traveled in the world of mental health hospitals, having played out this fantasy scenario in many emergency rooms and many inpatient units in this state and in others, and the staffs he had burned with his fantastic story of lies were only too willing to elaborate on the scam he had ran on them. Norman was originally from Kansas City, that was true, but he was not the son of a former mayor and a one-time beauty queen. He was the son of two impoverished parents living on county welfare, and no one in his family had ever won any beauty contests, that was for sure. His honored Midwestern values included assisting his parents in stealing alcohol and cigarettes from their local market. He had no great commitment to God or country and he hated his family. He had an older brother, not a younger one, who escaped the family and left Kansas City when he was 18 years old by joining the army. Norman had not heard from his brother since the brother's enlistment. The brother, like Norman, wanted nothing to do with his family.

Norman had not played football, but he did go to football games to drink beer, usually alone, and to flirt with girls who never seemed interested in flirting back. He was not the apple of his parents' eyes, he was the face to the back of their hands. There were no scholarships, of course, no academic promise nor athletic prowess, no awards and no recognition. Norman led a remarkably uneventful life, left home after high school because there was nothing and no one at home for him, and learned to survive by the kindness and handouts of strangers, by an occasional drifter's job, and by the food, shelter, and clothing provided by county services.

Norman's scars were not the consequence of enemy torture—he had never enlisted in the armed services—his scars were the result of his self-inflicted cuts, a habit he started in high school to relieve his anger and sadness. His need for pain medication was part of his addiction, never a treatment for injuries. At first he went from one doctor to another seeking pain medication, but over time he developed an evolving, sophisticated life story of glory, glamour, and heroism, a life story to replace the one he tried to forget. From hospital stay to hospital stay he became the man he dreamed of being, a big man on the high-school campus, beloved by his parents, friends, girlfriends, and town, a war hero to his country, a country that did not appreciate him.

He enjoyed being tied up, preferred to be bound tightly, requested and enjoyed the hood that was placed over his head so he could not hypnotize anyone, was fond of being spoon-fed, and delighted in the sponge baths. It was all so exciting for him, titillating, exhilarating, sexual. He appeared to treatment teams to have no control over his illness, but in fact he was in complete control. He savored his days at a hospital, the decorated, wounded hero suffering the nightmarish flashbacks of the horrors of war, and he often, but not always, escaped or was discharged from the hospitals before his true story was found out. This theatrical presentation had become his life, replacing a bland and unremarkable one, and he had almost come to believe it himself. But he suffered no real delusions that could elevate his fantasy and give it life. He was an impostor, he knew it, with the goal to flee before exposure and live to enter another hospital.

. . . .

I have seen many inadequate men and women in the ED who told me their life stories, stories which were much grander than their actual lives, whose plot and drama often followed specific popular trends. For example, right after the Navy SEALs killed Osama bin Laden, several men and one woman came to the ED and reported that they were Navy SEALs. They could not tell me much about it because it was top secret, but they could tell me it was dangerous and they were lucky to be alive. One such man, who was exceptionally good-looking, was excessively well-attended to by several caring and loving female nurses, nurses I knew well, who were much more caring and loving that day than I had ever seen them before. Such is the right and privilege of a hero. Special forces are extra special for those who do not feel special at all. They fill the emptiness of an unlived life.

Even delusions follow current events, dictating whether the FBI, CIA, Mexicans, Russians, Chinese, or jihadists from Afghanistan are following the deluded, meaning them harm. It is important that therapists are up-to-date on the news.

I have been fooled by patients many times, patients who want into the hospital, patients who want out of the hospital, patients who do not tell the truth about what they want because they do not know the truth about what they need. Fool me once, shame on you, fool me twice, shame on me. So, shame on me, many times over. Some therapists are incensed by lies, but I don't mind. I am intrigued by the lies told by those who feel empty, and I am

235

particularly impressed by the elaborate lie. I say bravo. Great performance. I am sorry that real life has not brought to you the rewards you so clearly deserve in your fantasy life.

. . . .

I last saw Amber Lydell at the UC Davis Whole Earth Festival, a celebration of my people, tribal hippies of the glorious, consciousness-expanding days of the '60s. Psychedelic and world music pulsated from the grassy quad of the campus while marijuana smoke floated through the air in a low cloud. Amber had broken up with her older semi-father-figure boyfriend. It turns out he was married.

She was now joined up with a group of young neo-hippies who traveled from one awesome, mind-expanding festival to another, chasing the dream of the '60s: life without boundaries, love without obligations, or is it the other way around?

Amber was dancing in a Sufi-like trance, high on weed, whirling to the music in concert with several long-haired men and topless women who wore long, tie-dyed skirts. Amber was dancing topless herself when she shouted out to the brothers and sisters of her new family, "That's my therapist!" She ran straight at me, so happy to see me, hugged me hard, knocked me down, and landed flat on top of me, bare chest and all. She proudly introduced me to her new shaggy friends, some of whom reminded me of myself years before.

Amber looked young, healthy, and happy. She was a free spirit with a full life, too full at times, and I hoped for her, more than she knew, that she would find peace and love.

A Few Observations About the Profession

"I thought it was a normal shoe store, Dr. Farrell. I'd been there before with no problem. The switch came when I took off my shoes and tried on a new pair of walking shoes. That was my mistake. I never should have left my shoes unattended. The shoes I returned to were not my shoes. They had been swapped out and replaced by another pair. I didn't notice at first. They looked like my shoes. I don't know how the salesman could have made the switch so fast to a pair of shoes that looked so much like mine. But I could tell. The shoe laces were different.

"They were black. Mine were black too, but these were blacker. And the replaced shoes were heavier. Not by much, just a little, but I could tell they were heavier. I had a blood stain on my left shoe when I came into the shoe store—a round stain on the tip of the left shoe right over the top of my middle toe. The stain was higher after the switch, still over the top joint of the middle toe, but slightly higher. These people did a good job with the phony shoes, and they almost fooled me. It was after they swapped out my shoes that my feet started to smell."

Before Mr. Randolph told me about his smelly shoes and feet, courtesy of the "operative" pretending to be a shoe salesman, before he told me about the odorous, nearly identical pants which were secretly exchanged for his real pants while he was sleeping, by the same operative, before he told me in detail about the ever-so-slight differences between his own coat and the infected, nearly identical coat substituted from the back of his chair while he was doing research at the library, he told me about dozens of other details in his life that had been manipulated to make him sick and cause him to smell. He knew who was organizing this effort to torment him, he knew why she was doing it, and now the picture was becoming increasingly clear on just what she was doing.

Mr. Randolph, when he was five years old, teased his kindergarten classmate and neighbor, Denise Bristol, telling her she smelled. In response, she slapped him hard in the face and shocked him, not from pain but from disbelief. He never expected Denise Bristol to do that, she was such a shy girl. He said he was sorry and gave her the two, little, white powdered-sugar donuts from his lunch pail, and that was that, it was over; they played together again like nothing had happened.

It was not until Mr. Randolph was 31 years old that he realized it was not over, it had just begun. Subtle things at first: a nearly identical but different watch on his nightstand in the morning, and a baseball cap that looked just like his cap, but it had a little larger sweat mark inside the forehead and a slightly stale smell.

And then there were not so subtle things: his cereal was laced with a substance that made him sweat and gave him body odor, and his computer emitted a constant stream of malodorous magnetic waves. He could not escape his noxious environment no matter how many showers he took. He radiated impurities.

Mr. Randolph smelled just fine to me, although he apologized many times for the putrid odor which he said would attach to my office and attach to me, maybe forever, it was that bad. But I detected nothing but a worn-out and obsessively clean man troubled by an imaginary payback from a little girl he once insulted, a girl he had not seen since he was five years old. The persecution he faced was relentless and the story he told was endless; I was two hours into the excruciating details and his story was still coming at me, uninterrupted.

When I tried to interrupt him, he became agitated—not angry, because he was too constricted to express anger, but visibly agitated. When he lost his train of thought he would have to start his long record over from the beginning. If I did not know the whole story, every detail of it from the age of five to his present age of 31, then I did not know the story at all. If I did not know the whole story, then

238

I could not help him; he told me so. He told me that the problem with all his friends, his acquaintances, and his family, was that they would not listen to him. His therapists in the past would not listen to him. Nobody ever listened to him.

At the two-hour point into this psychiatric assessment, with no end in sight, as I was squirming in my chair with agonizing impatience, late to leave work having picked up Mr. Randolph as a patient at the end of my shift, I was losing all hope of escape, imprisoned by a delusional man with an obsessive-compulsive, circumstantial thought disorder, thoughts that were highly detailed, lined up in formation, marching out into speech that would not allow interruption. I have always believed in a balanced life, time at work and time at home. I wanted to go home. I began to sweat. I came to rival Mr. Randolph as the malodorous discontent in the room. I sought release, but one false move and I would set the needle back to the beginning of a record with no known ending point. There should be four criteria, not three, for a psychiatric hold: a danger to self, a danger to others, gravely disabled, and the therapist has to go home now.

"Please let me go home. Please," I begged silently. "I have a home to go home to. Your home may be booby-trapped by all sorts of devious plots, but my home is welcoming me and misses me very much. I got your point five minutes after sitting down with you and for the next eternity you batted away my interruptions like an angry baseball player. Don't make me press the emergency panic button right under this desk because the police will come running. They will."

That is what I wanted to say, but did not, to the paranoid man who sat across from me and pummeled me with infinitesimal details of his persecution. I did not say those things to him because I work hard at being helpful and professional, but sometimes the work is difficult.

. . . .

So many patients are enjoyable to see—poignant, courageous,

thoughtful—moving forward in their lives in spite of major obstacles, but I have been worn down by others. Not everybody likes their therapist either; usually patients do not come to the emergency room and ask to see me specifically, and I do not show up at work requesting to see them. It can be a forced marriage, their pain to my profession, and not every forced marriage is a happy one, even though some of them last a long time. For a long time I had a forced relationship with an angry man, Donny Weber.

"You are the worst therapist I have ever had," he told me. You don't understand me at all, you never have. You don't even try. And if you did try you wouldn't understand me anyway because you're stupid. Of all the therapists in the world I could've seen, they gave me the stupid one. I can't even look at you, I'm so disgusted."

Relative to other tongue lashings he had given me, Donny Weber was mild in his criticism of me that day, almost complimentary. Our relationship started badly the first time I saw him when I called him "Mr. Weber," his legal name and his hospital-registered name, because Mr. Weber was, in his mind, his father, not him. He hated his father. The relationship further soured when I called him Donald, again the name he registered under, but a name his classmates used in taunting him during elementary school after the class watched an educational cartoon featuring Donald Duck. He insisted on the name, Donny, always Donny, never Donald.

I thought our relationship hit bottom in the first five minutes of our ED psychiatric assessment when he asked to see a female therapist, "a pretty one this time, not the old hag I saw last time," and I told him I was the only Crisis worker on at that time. He called me a liar and pointed to the woman he wanted to see, "the one over there." As pretty as Karyn was, and she was an exceptionally beautiful East Indian woman, she was an ED nurse and not a Crisis worker.

"Then I'll see a nurse," he said. "Anybody is better than you."

I was premature in thinking that our relationship was at rock bottom. Our working relationship had no bottom, or none I had discovered. It was a black hole.

"I don't know why I come back here," Donny regularly said to me. "I feel much worse after I see you."

I did not know why he kept coming back to the ED to see me either. He was supposed to go to the outpatient clinic, and I repeatedly worked very diligently to get him there. He never made it to a single outpatient appointment, but he did keep coming back to the ED, a clinic where he had to register and wait a long time before seeing me, a therapist whose stupidity and ineptitude disgusted him.

"I feel for you, Donny, I really do," I said. "You walk into an emergency room, take your chances on who you might see, wait a long time before you're seen, and then you get me. And as you say, I haven't helped at all. The real work in psychotherapy, the progress, the movement, the promise of feeling better and doing better, takes place in outpatient psychotherapy, working with someone you respect over a longer period of time. Let's try one more time to get you from here to there."

"Been there, done that," he said.

"Let's do it again," I said.

Donny glared at me, the unmistakable glare of hatred. He stood up and walked out. Session was over, six minutes. It was not our shortest session. There were many short sessions, times when he rammed his head against a wall and threw things around the office, times when he threatened to hit me or went on and on shouting loud, vulgar profanities at me until our security guards came running to rescue me. And this was his normal behavior, not 5150 behavior.

I have a few rules for psychotherapy: no throwing objects, no violence toward me, no self-inflicted violence in the room, no extended, explosive screaming. Whenever Donny broke the rules, which he did many times, he would stomp out of the office. Sometimes, to his credit, he walked out of the office just before he broke the rules, showing some restraint and control.

Donny was theatrical, but he had more control over his behavior than he was willing to reveal. For instance, he never once hit me even though he enjoyed making me think he would. He waited patiently in the ED waiting room, even for hours on some busy days, because he knew he would be ejected if he caused trouble out there. His sole purpose for visiting the ED seemed to be to berate me. He was not interested in psychotherapy; he saw no need for it. He had no desire to talk about his symptoms, his feelings, or his behavior. Donny Weber lived in a cruel world, a world where cannibals ruled and he was a tasty morsel. The injustices he perceived and endured were unbearable, the abuse unyielding, and any suggestions I made that he had a part in creating his world were violently rejected. Donny walked into the ED to find me each time the worst of his worst calamities had befallen him, several days a week during his bad weeks.

The ED is the appropriate setting to address acute crises; there are other settings more appropriate for those with chronic problems. But Donny was in that third category of men and women who frequent emergency rooms: he was chronically in an acute crisis. I was there for Donny whenever his boiling point hit the dangerous mark, and it hit that mark frequently. I was the emergency parachute, the last brake on the rocket's plunge to Earth, a brake to slow the impact of an explosion. Donny exploded inside my office so he did not have to explode outside my office. This was a contract I accepted, and it was recognized by both of us, but never stated. Donny would not have wanted to state the obvious.

Whenever I suggested he stop coming to the ED, that he go to the more appropriate outpatient service instead, I was breaking our well-understood, unstated contract. I was telling him I did not want to see him anymore. I was abandoning him, and in so doing I was adding one more injustice to his unjust life. This pushing him away was a mistake on my part, not an error of judgment, but an error of character; it meant I was sick and tired of Donny screaming at me and I wanted him to leave me alone. To my credit, I always apologized after pushing him away; I told him I was human, a man with feelings, a man with fragile days, a man who was sometimes hurt by the intensity of his anger toward me. To his credit, he always forgave me and we resumed our lively relationship.

Some of what Donny said when he hurled insults at me was the truth: I have no corner on wisdom, no genius, no magic, no cure. I am all too human and I make mistakes. I work with people in pain who also make mistakes. People coming to me looking for God will find Him only in their imaginations, and they will be disappointed when the truth sets in. My advice, if given, is not all that brilliant, and what I say in psychotherapy is rarely memorable. If I have value, it is in my being there, wanting to help, seeing a patient through the eyes of hope. If I lose that, I have no value.

. . . .

There is stress in this field, there is joy in this field. When the stress is reduced and the joy is recognized and celebrated, the profession is one of the best on Earth. I was told by a fine mentor in my first year of work at the Medical Center to recognize the patients who boil my water and the ones who cool it off, that I cannot hand pick my patients, but I can recognize the effects each patient has on me.

He told me that I would see many hostile patients, full of anger, and their only target would be me. There would be patients who hated me irrationally and those who loved me without reason, patients who expected too much and gave little, and patients who gave too much and expected little. He told me I would have patients that I love and patients that no one could love, and that I had the same responsibility to both.

"Make mistakes, forgive yourself," he would say. "Make bad mistakes, get supervision, and forgive yourself. Get a life outside work, love a partner, love a child, love a dog, but mainly love yourself. Play is just as important as work, love is more important than work. Laugh a lot, cry enough, and don't be a psychologist at home." He also told me something that proved true for all my 43 years on the job: "If you enjoy your coworkers you will enjoy your job."

While Crisis workers cannot pick and choose every case, we can choose some and occasionally avoid others. Some therapists enjoy the challenge of working with angry patients and they are good with

243

them. Other therapists feel more stress when they are working with patients who overvalue them, who make them feel they are "the best clinician in all the world." The one thing most therapists have in common is that they like to work with patients who get better more than they like to work with patients who get worse, even though the therapist may not be responsible for the progress or the decline.

Healthy patients are fun. Remove a life obstacle or two for them and they quickly get even more healthy and motivated; they change, they face their fears, they tell the truth to themselves, they love themselves, and they love their therapists. Healthy patients are the patients we seek in a perfect private practice. The challenge of psychotherapy and much of the frustration is not in changing the people who want to change, it is in moving the patients who are afraid to move.

Much of psychotherapy, both in theory and practice, is focused on a patient's resistance to change. Some people stand in the same spot, and repeat the same mistakes that cement them to that spot, because they do not know how to move, or because they do not want to move. There are chapters in many books and some entire books written on the subject of "breaking through resistance." Symptoms can have value for people by blocking even greater pain and hiding unfaceable fears. Not everyone wants to surrender their symptoms. Bad feelings are stirred up when a therapist attacks symptoms and defenses without replacing them with something more stable. It is frightening to step out of an old life into a new one. The old one has built-in rewards, not the least of which is familiarity, something the new life lacks. Stepping into a new life is a leap of faith, an act of courage, which often involves looking inward where dark images live and hold imaginary powers. One of the great rewards in being a psychotherapist is the witnessing of fear losing power.

There are many other rewards in the work life of a therapist. Each patient I saw held up a mirror to me showing me something about myself that I could not otherwise see. I learned skills I could learn in no other profession, because few other professions are as intimate. I learned how to deal with aggravation from my aggravating patients; I learned to move with calm and confidence, rather than fear, straight toward the bully, the controlling patient, the narcissistic one.

And I was offered a clear vision of the bully, the controlling person, and the narcissist inside me by the mirror held up to me. I could choose to examine those qualities and do something about them. For every challenging patient I have had, I could choose to focus on what the experience did *to* me, or I could focus on what the experience did *for* me: the angry patient taught me not to take anger personally, the passive patient taught me to be active, the seductive patient helped me practice integrity, the violent patient allowed me to face my fears, the loving patient handed me a poignant gift every session. Be cursed by a patient or be blessed, it was up to me.

. . . .

There have been sweet spots in my life, times when all was going well at work and life was good at home, and then an angelic patient would come along to help me step out of my very good life and into an even better one. When all of life is good, there is little motivation to make things better. If I have a beautiful view of the mountains, I have no need to turn around to look for a better view; someone might have to come along and turn me around so I can see that better view of the ocean.

During one sweet spot, when I was particularly happy with my job, finding it fun, meaningful, and fulfilling, and I was even more happy with my girlfriend, certain she was my life partner, perfect in every way and much better than I deserved, I faced an issue threatening my freedom and independence. I was living on my own, completely free to live impulsively. I worried little about money and was traveling to exotic places, and I was playing at work rather than working at play. I went to work to see the people who were my closest friends. I was free to fully appreciate the bounty of my life, free to indulge myself, free to attend to my every need, and free to give leave to my narcissism and let it run wild.

245

At just that time the woman I loved thought she was ready to consider having children. That thought had been far from my mind. "Freedom," I told her, "travel, time, leisure, life for us, us first." The view of the mountains was glorious to me, and I could not see her view of the ocean, I had no need to look her way and did not want to, and I could not be easily talked into a shift in perspective.

My first glimpse of the ocean came in the form of an eight-year-old boy, Matty, a boy in the third grade who struck another student on the buttocks with a yardstick ruler when the other student dumped a big blob of black paint onto Matty's precisely drawn map of South America. Matty said it was no accident, and I believed him. Matty MacGregor took his art seriously because he was good at it, but the school he attended had a zero-tolerance policy for violence, so he found himself sitting in my office at the University Psychiatry Center, the outpatient clinic, with his father in tow, awaiting his fate for his violent transgression.

Matty was embarrassed and ashamed, and reluctant to talk with me, and it is possible that he was the cutest and sweetest little boy I had ever seen. Parents generally love their children, warts and all. Friends of parents try to love them and often fail, but strangers have no obligation to even try to love them. If you are a lovable child to a stranger, you are truly a lovable child, and Matty MacGregor was a lovable child. He did not try to defend himself to me, did not state his case, did not say anything at all our first session, but I was on his side, no doubt about it.

What kind of mean teacher would not handle this problem internally, without handing the little prisoner over to the principal, the gatekeeper of the sacred rule of zero tolerance for violence? That kind of teacher turned out to be a substitute teacher, not Matty's regular teacher. The regular teacher, home sick with a cold just before the Thanksgiving holiday, was replaced by a no-nonsense parliamentarian who took her job of keeping order seriously.

Matty had bigger problems to worry about than whacking a kid in the butt with a long ruler. According to his father, Matty had been sad for many months over the separation of his parents. His mother had recently, with little warning, moved to different state to live with another man and this man's two young children. She intended to remarry as soon as her divorce was final. The new man was apparently very important, and he had been recently promoted to a job which held vast responsibilities and required him to move across the country. Ms. MacGregor went with him.

It was mutually decided by Matty's parents that Matty would stay in Sacramento with his father, at least until the end of the school year. Mr. MacGregor, a successful real estate broker, was shocked and saddened by his wife's affair, and then her decision to move out of the house, followed by her move across the country, but he was doing his best to put anger aside and to channel all of his loving energy into Matty. He was alarmed and in disbelief over his son's school behavior because Matty had never shown even the slightest hint of hostility toward anyone. Mr. MacGregor was compliant with the principal's suggestion that Matty undergo counseling before he returned to school, and I was able to see Matty the next day after his suspension, the Wednesday before Thanksgiving.

Mr. MacGregor had flexible work hours as a real estate broker, and he was willing to do whatever was necessary for his son's health and happiness. I talked with Ms. MacGregor and she was not as surprised as Mr. MacGregor that her son had acted out in school. Ms. McGregor was aware that Matty was having a difficult adjustment to all the changes in his life, and her own psychiatrist had encouraged her to get her son into treatment.

Ms. MacGregor was in training to be a psychologist herself; she was an ABD, an "all but dissertation" candidate, having completed all of her coursework at a respected professional school of psychology. She was not just interrupting normal psychotherapy— once-a-week therapy—when she abruptly left the state of California to live with her future husband, she was abandoning her commitment to psychoanalysis—four or five sessions a week— which she believed in wholeheartedly. She had been undergoing her analysis with a psychiatrist in Sacramento, and changing analysts is not as easy as changing other therapists, not easy for the patient or the analyst.

It was her analyst whom Ms. MacGregor respected the most; she respected him like a wise saint. And it was her analyst who suggested to her that her son enter child analysis during the difficult transition after leaving her husband. Her analyst was suggesting putting Matty into the rigors of analysis for years. Mr. MacGregor did not think Matty needed that, not at all, but Ms. MacGregor's analyst was persistent, even insistent.

"The damage done at an early stage has implications for the years ahead," her doctor told her. Ms. MacGregor insisted that Matty start child analysis and Mr. MacGregor refused. This was one more cause for conflict and bitterness between the two.

An eight-year-old boy has never entered my office and said, "Dr. Farrell, I've been having some problems lately and I was hoping you could help me. I'm experiencing some significant losses and I think this is affecting my mood." An eight-year-old boy more typically comes into our big children's play-therapy room, sits on the floor far away from me, and stares at his shoes.

My experience has been that making contact with and engaging an eight-year-old boy comes one slow step at a time, each new step initiated by the failure of the previous one. Step one is talking directly to a young child. That always fails me. Step two is suggesting a play activity with the child meant to promote interaction and to yield information. That almost always fails me. Step three is sitting in the play room with the child and playing with the toys by myself. I can do that.

I believed that the problem, from Matty's perspective, the problem that somehow had landed him in this awkward position, was the wanton destruction of his beautiful, colorful map-in-progress of South America, with fruits, vegetables, and little animals painted in, by another child who could not, himself, paint, and did not care for kids who could. So I started to paint in the playroom. I whistled while I worked, made many self-congratulatory comments about my work, gave myself high fives as I progressed, and proudly taped my painting to the wall when I was finished. I proclaimed the word "magnificent" three times.

Matty walked over and looked at my painting.

"It's really good, isn't it?" I said. "Best one I've ever done. What do you think?"

"I like the blue," he said.

"Yes, I did the whole painting in blue. Blue is my favorite color. All my paintings are in blue."

Matty looked at my painting very closely. He studied it, and then he asked me in a barely audible voice, "What is it?"

"It's a painting of the person I admire most in the world," I said. "Do you know who it is?"

Matty was hesitant but he ventured this guess: "It looks a little like a horse," he said.

"What! A horse! That's my grandmother," I said. "You think my grandmother looks like a horse?"

"No," he said softly. "But the painting looks a little like a horse."

"To tell you the truth, my grandmother looks a little like a horse, too."

Matty diagnosed my painting ability immediately without saying a critical word. I cannot paint or draw, not a bit. My drawings of people are stick figures, my houses are boxes, my trees are lollipops, and that is when I put my best effort into it.

"Well, you paint something," I said to Matty. "Paint my grandmother."

"I've never seen your grandmother," he said.

"Just as well," I said. "Draw me someone like my grandmother. Somebody you think I would really like."

It did not take long for Matty to draw for me a detailed picture of a beautiful woman, not a stick figure, and he used the colored pencils to make that woman come alive. I would recognize her if I saw her in person.

"That is one of the loveliest women I have ever seen. She does not look anything like my grandmother, though. But she does look like someone I think I would really like."

I hung up his drawing right next to the one of my grandmother and said to Matty, "I'm going to call your mysterious woman, Josephine. That's my grandmother's name."

"Her real name is Miss Hall," Matty said.

"Fair enough," I said. "Miss Hall it is."

Miss Hall was Matty's third-grade teacher, not the substitute teacher, far from, but his regular teacher. The Monday after Thanksgiving I called the school and talked directly to Miss Hall who was back from a cold but with lingering signs of a hoarse voice. As I talked to Miss Hall I was holding Matty's loving picture of her in my hands—it was like using FaceTime—and I could hear in her fragile voice the sweet intelligence of the person whose picture I held.

The whole ruler incident never could have happened on Ms. Hall's watch. She was acutely aware of the changes and the sadness that Matty was going through, and she protected him like she would her own child. She was aware of his crush on her, and she filled me in on the cranky history going on between Matty and the other boy who coveted Matty's artistic talents.

"We really do try to help every child in the arts," said Miss Hall, "but some children are born artistic and others need a lot of work."

"Tell me about it," I said.

Miss Hall wanted her favorite child back in her class, and I called the school principal that day to say Matty was fine to return to school. The school principal was used to being in charge of things and wanted to be in charge of this decision.

"Do you think he is safe to come back?" the principal asked me.

"Yes, I do. He is safe to come back," I said.

"How can you say that? Can you guarantee he will not strike anyone?" she asked.

"What kind of guarantee do you have in mind?" I asked.

"I need to know he won't hurt anyone again," she said.

"I have complete confidence he is not going to hurt anybody," I said. Such a blanket statement of prediction is worthless, of course.

"I think with so little time going by," said the principle, "Matthew may not understand the seriousness of his behavior. He may not have learned the appropriate lesson."

"It is my professional opinion that Matthew has learned too many serious lessons too soon in his young life. It is time for him to go back to school."

The principal did relent but it was a struggle, and she made it known that she would hold me responsible if Matty hurt anyone. I accepted that statement although I was confused as to what the consequences would be for me if he hit another child in the butt with a ruler. Maybe detention.

I saw Matty six more times in the next three weeks. He painted and drew for me a dozen pictures of people he thought I would really like so I could hang them all in my office, but they all looked like the sweet, beautiful, and intelligent Miss Hall, whom I had never met, but whom I knew so intimately from the paintings.

As we both painted, side-by-side, as Matty precociously instructed me on methods that would improve my painting, and as he encouraged me to keep working at it, he also dropped little comments about his life. He did not know if his mother would come to visit him at Christmas. He was not sure if his mother was going to be a mother to other children now and not to him. In one of his pictures it looked to me like Ms. Hall was holding hands with his father.

While there may be Freudian aspects to a child's loss of his mother to a distant man, I was able to convince Ms. MacGregor that her son was precious beyond belief, superior to normal, and not in need of psychoanalysis. It did not take much convincing, just confirmation. Miss Hall made great progress with Matty and his former envious enemy by teaming one gifted artist with another who needed a boost. My own artistic ability was actually improving, not made good, but improving, due to an eight-year-old boy with patience and teaching talent.

Miss Hall never fulfilled Matty's fantasy of her holding hands with his father, but Ms. MacGregor, the real mother he yearned for, did come home for Christmas vacation, came for the whole two weeks. Ms. MacGregor called me after Christmas, weeping, and told me that the hardest thing she had ever had to do in her life was to leave her own child to be a stepmother to two new children. She ached to be with Matty every day she was separated from him. I told her that planes were fast and distances were short these days, and there were unexpected rewards for the frequent flyer.

On our last session, the week before Christmas, Matty and I celebrated with cupcakes that I had made and decorated, with Matty's favorite ice cream, peppermint, and with the chocolate chip cookies I baked, the burnt part scraped from the bottom. There is no end to my love of baking sweets nor my ability to make the same baking errors over and over again. I gave Matty a Christmas present, a very professional-looking set of water colors. Matty came in with a present for me. He had painted a picture of me that looked exactly like me, that was remarkably detailed and accurate with one artistic flare: it was painted completely in blue.

"Your favorite color," he said.

"My favorite color and now my favorite painting," I said.

"Do you know who it is?" he asked.

"I think so," I said.

"It's your grandmother, Josephine," he said, and he laughed heartily like I had never seen him do before.

I sent Matty home with all his drawings and paintings because they were so stunning, and I wanted Miss Hall to see them. Matty asked if he could borrow the painting of me so he could introduce me to Miss Hall. The first day of school after the holidays, I got a call from Miss Hall who said Matty had given her all the pictures he had drawn and painted, all the beautiful representations of her, and also a painting of some blue guy. Miss Hall was emotional in our conversation, I thought maybe tearful, as she told me what a sweet boy Matty was. She asked me if I knew of anything she could do to help him through his hard time ahead. I told her there was, indeed, something that would be very helpful to him: she could continue being the kind, loving teacher she could not help but be.

As for me, Matty turned my head when persuasion and polemics could not, from the beautiful mountains to the exquisite ocean, and my head never turned back. I wanted a child like Matty one day, boy or girl or both. I got lucky. I got both.

. . . .

Not all patients boosted my happiness and joy like Matty did. Not all mental health work in a university medical center was adventurous and fun, not all as exhilarating as heading into the Wild West, the untamed ED, with your posse behind you and your badge over your heart, pledging to clean up the psychopathology in town. Not all of my work gave me the great charge of racing out in the mobile unit to rescue a lost soul. Life was also about living with middle managers. The work of seeing patients is challenging, richly emotional, and occasionally frustrating; work with middle managers is just frustrating, not always but often enough. It has been my observation that the clinical cream of the crop does not always rise to the top. The top is heavy with former line workers desperate to get off the assembly line—the controlling, self-promoting, and self-inflating therapists who wish to avoid doing psychotherapy, the ambitious people who seek entrance into an elite club that removes them from real work and takes them away from the skills and practice they need to supervise others.

I can concede that UCDMC had some skilled, smart, capable people at the top of the managerial chain, but many of the middle managers needed work, literally needed some meaningful work to do so they did not mess up the meaningful work of those they supervised. Too often, I believe, people with mediocre clinical skills lorded over Crisis Services and made poor and uninspired decisions with bad results for the talented team.

Having stated my resentment and to honor full disclosure, I confess that I held middle manager positions several times during my 43 years of work at the Medical Center. I was a proud middle manager but not a good one. Some people I worked with, people I supervised, liked me too much, or they appeared to. They treated me differently starting from the very first day I rose to the position, a friend and colleague one day, honest and undefended with me, and then cautious and fawning the next day. I was the same person, but the relationship changed; it was less honest and laden with faux

253

respect. My most common phrase to colleagues became, "Don't talk to me like I am your supervisor, just talk to me."

When I was a middle manager people liked me so much, or they appeared to, that they made a more special deal out of my birthday than they did with the birthdays of line staff. I got a better cake, a bigger cake, a homemade cake. People sang "Happy Birthday" a little louder; I suspected some people were afraid not to. I could imagine a worker nudging a coworker whispering, "Sing goddamnit, he's the manager."

When I was a middle manager people liked me so much, or they appeared to, that they were extra sympathetic over my sad losses. I happened to mention to a staff member one day that my hamster had died. The next day I got a card signed by almost everyone I supervised lamenting the loss of that demon rodent I hated so much, whose bites I regularly suffered. I was glad to bury that angry little monster. But there I was, reading a card:

"We are so very sorry for your loss. We know the value of a furry friend, the love they give us, the love we give them in return. We know he is in a better place."

He was in a better place. He was six inches under in my back yard. He did not even love me when I handed him raspberry yogurt· chips, his favorite snack; he bit me. At least I could count on Jerry Douglas to be straight with me. He said, "Your fucking rat died. What do you want, a casserole?" I told him it was a hamster. "Same thing," he said.

When staff members were not liking me too much, they were disliking me too much. They blamed me for the stress of the job, the episodic heavy workloads, the conflicts that erupted between themselves, and the hardships of their daily lives. I became the common cause of all problems—work and personal—and I became the common enemy of the people. Occasionally, staff members raised the cannons and fired at me, and then worried about serious repercussions, like getting fired, but that fear never became a reality because I appreciated and understood the frustrations of the job. But people seemed irrationally fearful of me after they were intensely angry at me, and this was uncomfortable for all of us.

The life of a middle manager was not for me. I never identified with or much supported the higher-level management teams; I identified strongly with the clinical staff. I did not want to be friends with the management team; my friends were out there doing clinical work. I did not enjoy the work of a manager, the long secret meetings, the role of rating the clinical staff in the yearly evaluations. I enjoyed seeing patients and teaching students to see patients. Each time I became a middle manager I worked my way back to clinical and teaching positions, usually with the help and the push of the larger management team.

I did miss the higher salaries of middle management. Top managers, CEOs, and their coterie, have influence over their own pay and the pay of all those below them. Theoretically, salaries have to do with value, and if salaries are set by self-evaluation of value, then the biggest salaries will go to the most inflated egos. Managers at the top have exorbitant salaries and colossal bonuses reflective of those egos. They reap obscene incentives for accepting positions and are doled out offensive payouts for leaving them, all in the name of "attracting the best," and "staying competitive," and "what the market will bear." There is terrible greed at the top and the top people are setting salaries for themselves.

The best clinicians and the best teachers are often ignored on the pay scales, so the job of clinical work, the role of a line worker, has to be reward enough. No one will ever say, "What a talented clinician. Let's pay him a lot of money." I will admit that some top managers are great people and probably deserve their generous salaries and bonuses. A good manager can make the job better for everyone, they can inspire us all, and I have known some great managers, but still far too few.

. . . .

I think there is no profession outside of mental health that examines so obsessively both the inner workings and the outer world of the people it serves. We diagnose, pigeonhole, make generalizations about, predict behavior of, learn to hate, and learn to love our patients, and we informally do the same to our coworkers and ourselves. The study of human beings, how we think, feel, and behave, must necessarily involve the microscopic investigation of both the little capsule of life which carries our genetic coding, and the world which that capsule encounters from the first day on Earth. We study nature, we study nurture, and we will for many years to come because both are complicated. I have profound respect for the powerful influence of my parents' haphazard gift of genes because I can clearly see images of my parents in both of my brothers and in me. My mother and father were very different people, but they both stamped their unique footprints on all three of us.

My father was almost a different species than my mother. He was a bold, reckless, temperamental, hard-working, tireless, friendly warrior to my mother's gentle, peaceful, loving spirit. He was a genuine E-ticket roller-coaster ride, and he walked this Earth like he owned it. Laws and rules were there for the benefit of other people, but he did not require their guidance. He was a magnet for excitement and for trouble. He was notorious for his competitive aggression, and no bowl of chips or television set was immune from flight or damage when his sports teams were not doing well.

He was a successful business man, once the president of Hires Root Beer, but for most of his working life he was the head of his own wholesale foods company. I think of him as a natural-born leader, the man in charge who could not work well with others. My brothers and I were born under the protective umbrella of prosperity and security, but this was not so for my father. He was not born into prosperity; he had to create it, bare-fisted, and as a big underdog. My father was a fighter for his family so his family did not need to fight. The defining theme of his life was hard work.

He played in life pretty damn hard, too. He was an adventurer, a high-energy buccaneer. I have vivid memories of him barreling down waterslides in Maui and of his clumsy attempts at surfing in Waikiki. If the kids could do it, he could do it.

His enthusiasm was infectious, his appetite for food was

enormous, and his oozing of charm, especially with women, was over-the-top. He had absolute faith in his immortality, and he made 10 year plans for himself when he was in his middle 90s. He was a self-declared expert in all political fields, and he was certain he would be a better president of the United States than whichever one was in office, but he was too busy to be president; he simply did not have the time.

In the last 25 years of his life he rediscovered the one true passion that became his magical elixir, his fountain of youth: Dixieland jazz. Starting in the 1970s, after lying dormant for many years, Dixieland jazz reemerged to enthusiastic crowds—tens of thousands of people, a sea of white-haired devotees, a religious movement waiting for the second coming—and it came right here to Sacramento. My father was reborn. Dixieland jazz was the music of his youth, the music he heard growing up in New Orleans and at the clubs he later visited in New York, the music that made him feel forever young. Over the course of the next 25 years my brothers and I accompanied my father to nearly 100 Dixieland jazz festivals as the music caught fire from city to city and festivals sprang up all over the country. One hundred bands from all over the world played their unique brands of Dixieland jazz at the Sacramento Dixieland Jazz Festival every Memorial Day weekend. They played to audiences much older but just as enthusiastic as any rock crowd I have ever seen.

My father would defy the aging process during these festivals; he would hold a fat Polish sausage in a roll stuffed with sauerkraut and onions in each hand while yelling, "Go, go, go!" as a band heated up. He danced up and down the aisles with 1920s flapper-clad women in their 80s who twirled colorful umbrellas. He shouted, clapped, danced, and cheered from early morning to the next early morning for four days running, and then he would collapse at home. His sons learned to love Dixieland jazz, which was no easy feat for us coming from the psychedelic '60s; it was a forced love in the beginning and a learned love in the end.

My mother had to raise three boys, so nomination to sainthood was automatic. She still lives at the age of 101, and her mother and grandmother died in their 90s. I consider myself to be middle-aged at 68. My mother made motherhood look easy, and her three boys grew up in the company of her loving laughter. She would laugh at the slightest provocation and her laughter made me laugh. All three of us inherited the laughter gene, and I suffer today from periods of irrational laughter and inexplicable joy. I do not even want to think about diagnosing that.

My mother would see the best in us and ignore the worst. I received my driver's license on my 16th birthday, the first day allowed, and I racked up five speeding tickets before I was 17. My mother kept trying to figure out if something was wrong with our speedometer. She forgave us everything, overlooked our negatives, held no grievances, spoke poorly of no one, judged nothing harshly, and embraced us and loved us, of that we had no doubt.

The concept of mental health and normalcy is mystical, hard to define, and imprecise in measurement, but most of us who work in the field intuitively know that growth, happiness, and healing are dependent on love and meaningful attachment. Oddly, I have found some psychotherapists to be suspicious of happy people. They believe that happy people do not understand the gravity of the existential crisis they face. Happy people are in denial; they have suppressed and repressed their pain. A good therapist can unleash that pain and return patients to the misery they deserve, the misery that belongs to them. After all, how can anyone respect happiness born of ignorance?

Fathers sometimes receive a free pass or a casual glance in a patient's psychotherapy, but a thorough therapist will make a serious hunt for psychopathology in the mother. A distant mother, a detached one, a selfish or needy one, a resentful mother, a displeased one, a mother incapable of love, a mother who smothers with love, will be rooted out in psychotherapy and exposed. Imagine the disappointment of the therapist when no such treasure is found.

During my Ph.D. program, I was required to undergo 25 hours of psychotherapy, an experience useful to all therapists—sitting in

258

the patient chair. It was a calm time in my life, and I did not have some of the trying problems I had faced earlier in my life or later. I presented no great frontier of exploration necessary for successful therapy. I saw a psychiatrist at the time, a man in his 70s who had recently married a woman in her 20s. He was a young-at-heart man, no doubt, but still in his 70s, and he possessed a sharp mind and a quick wit. In the later stages of my therapy work, my psychiatrist grew tired of my incessant contentment. He failed, or believed he had, in finding the conflicts I hid, ignored, or denied, so he dug deeper and deeper in search of the usual primary cause of all problems, the motherlode, the mother herself.

My psychiatrist expertly probed the correct vulnerable territory: did my mother expect too much of me, did she expect too little, what were the conditions of her love, how did I fail to meet those conditions, why did she set the bar so high for me, how did she feel when I failed to jump over the bar, how did she express her disappointment, how did she feel if I did poorly in school, how did she handle her embarrassment about me. My psychiatrist attempted to do what he was paid to do, get the job done, find the dark source of hidden sadness, bring it to the light, and let me see more clearly the mother who failed me. My psychiatrist was clever. He explored all the islands with potential buried treasure. I think he got tired of fruitlessly digging up all that sand.

Toward the end of our psychotherapy we were discussing a time when I was really disappointed in myself. In the seventh grade I entered a science project, or I should say a poster, into the all-city science fair. It was a poster of the solar system, to scale, very accurate, full of detailed hand-painted planets revolving around the sun, or so it was supposed to be. Something very weird happened to the black background of my poster; it inexplicably grew like a weed and ate up all the planets and stars, leaving me with a big, black, amorphous, cardboard nothing with faint hints of color where planets once orbited. It was a six foot by six foot splotch of blackness.

It was too late to withdraw from the science fair so, when the time came, I stood there beside my project, prepared to explain what I had learned from my hard work and how my project communicated what I had learned. They placed my project right next to the extraordinary work of a genuine boy genius who had built his own telescope, who had built his own camera that he attached to his telescope, and who had taken unbelievable, magnificent pictures of the solar system, which he had developed himself.

"Your mother must have been very disappointed in you," my psychiatrist suggested.

My mother told me my entry was the best science project of the whole fair. I thought this was a stupid thing to say, and I felt angry with her and asked her how she could even think that. It was a big, black, ugly nothing. I remember her response to me quite distinctly, because she said it with sincerity: "Your poster was so black that it was the only project in the whole room that made me feel like I was truly in deep space."

That was my mother. She defeated my psychiatrist. He told me in our last session he was retiring soon and he was happy he could go out having heard the story of one good mother.

My older brother, Bob, has many of my father's finest qualities. He is bold, fearless, adventurous; he has energy that never runs down, curiosity that never lets up, and a vision of himself and what he can accomplish that is confident and expansive. He travels the world taking beautiful photographs. He is the new head of the family, the natural-born leader who works well at the helm of his own ship and works poorly as a servant to others. He has been a superb athlete in many sports, the life of the party whose wit never fails him, and a great role model for me. My mother says he has always been that way, from the start, practically from the womb: "Just like your father."

My younger brother, Glenn, five years my junior, is a sweet, kind, honest, loving boy, and I will always see him as a boy although he is over 60. He runs a foods company, the one my father founded, but he could not be more different from my father, nor more similar to my mother. He is a man everyone loves, nobody argues with, everyone respects—a gentle man always giving to others. He has possessed his core qualities since birth, according to my mother, and I personally remember his gentleness and sweetness from the time he was a toddler to the present. He is his mother's child.

When my mother was in her middle 90s, when her memory for her childhood and our childhoods was still sharp and accurate, she told me many stories of us as children because I was finally interested in hearing them. She described how active Bob was, how he never liked to sleep, how he was always exploring the world, climbing out of his crib, wandering away from his parents in department stores in Manhattan. Bob's early life was one adventure after another. He was on the go, not easy to contain. My mother also described how my brother, Glenn, was an "easy baby," probably a relief for her after raising her first two sons. Glenn was happy, sweet, content in his crib, always smiling, and affectionate. He liked to sleep and he slept well. He was easy to carry, not fidgety at all, content in my mother's arms.

My mother was full of stories about Bob and Glenn. When I asked her about me she was thoughtful and she put great effort into remembering what she could, but she couldn't. I was not extremely adventurous like Bob, but I may have been somewhat adventurous, she thought. I was not affectionate and sweet like Glenn, but she vaguely recalled I might have been kind of sweet. I was, in fact, a child who was hard to remember, a child of no extremes. I was a child born into the middle point of the continuum between Bob and Glenn, and I live at that point today. Such is both the power and the range of genetics. I am the child who can pretend to have the finest qualities of my brothers, Bob and Glenn, without actually possessing any of those qualities.

I do not want to sugarcoat the attributes of my parents. My father's vast energies sometimes turned to powerful anger, and my mother's constant love converted, at times, to irrational worry about her family. But the job of a parent is a difficult one, and one I did not appreciate until I became a parent myself. All parents were children themselves and parenthood does not necessarily make us wise or mature, competent or strong. Parents are vulnerable children in bigger clothes, actors playing the role of responsible adults, imposters hiding their fears from their children who see them as all-powerful. Like children, we parents love candy, cookies, cake, and presents; we need to be praised, we need to be forgiven, we need someone to sooth our pain. The job of parenthood is a big one, and nobody knows just how big until long after they have accepted the position, perhaps a little too late.

Parenthood is all about giving and little about receiving, for a long time; it is selfless work and it exposes our narcissism immediately and chips away at it for the rest of our lives. Saintly parents, be there such a thing, accept bad behaviors and bad attitudes from their children with patience and even grace. I was no easy child.

When I was eight years old my main reading material was comic books. In the 1950s one or more comic books advertised a product I was desperate to buy: a monkey in a cup, a real monkey, one so small it would fit into a cup. I did not know where the monkeys came from, I was not aware of what horrors went on behind the scenes in acquiring them, but I wanted one badly. I envisioned myself having the best little friend in the world, a smart little guy who I would carry to school with me in his little cup. We would eat lunch together at noon, and he would sit in his cup and watch me play baseball after school. He would likely cheer for me.

The monkey in a cup cost a fortune: $5.99. I used all the money I had and borrowed the other five dollars from my grandmother and sent away for my monkey in a cup. I did not tell anyone my monkey was coming, certainly not my mother, because I feared my mother would not let me keep my monkey. I skipped after-school baseball for two months, running home from school to head off the mailman and greet my new monkey in a cup. Day after day, the monkey never came. I had some harsh words with the mailman and, he assured me, he did not want and did not take my "stupid" monkey. And then it dawned on me what must have happened: my mother took my monkey.

"Where's my monkey, Mom?" I demanded.

"What, dear?" she said.

"You took my monkey," I said.

"I don't think so, dear. Where did you leave it?"

I am not sure how the conversation took such a bad turn but I do remember demanding and screaming, as an eight-year-old, "I want my damn monkey!" I was more shocked at what I said than my mother was. I explained to her all about my monkey in a cup that was to be sent to me by a reputable comic book company, Archie Comics. My mother explained to me that she did not think they actually sent little monkeys through the mail, but I knew better. A big company like Archie Comics was not going to lie.

I never gave up looking for my monkey. When we moved from Linda Vista, California, to Wayne, Pennsylvania, four years later, I made sure my mother left our forwarding address with the post office so they could reroute my monkey. Every few years I would say to my mother, "Mom, I know you took my monkey. Where is it?"

A person never gets over a loss like that. When my mother was 99 years old, young enough to remember, too old to lie, and I was 66, I asked her gently, as she was falling asleep, "Mom, did you take my monkey?" She looked confused, like she could not remember. I had waited too long. I should have asked her when she was 98.

. . . .

It helps to have a good partner if you are a parent. I have done few brilliant things in my life but I am proud of my choice of a wife. I chose a woman who is by far more intelligent, patient, and kind than I am, whose heart is more expansive than mine. I have spent all of our years together hoping she does not discover who I really am. A certain kind of child can also help us survive parenthood. My best advice to prospective parents is to give birth to children who will forgive you later in life. You will make mistakes, you will need forgiveness.

263

The contribution that parents make to the health or to the psychopathology of their children is rarely underestimated in the field of mental health. Parents provide the genes, and then they create the environment. A good psychodynamic therapist leaves no stone unturned in the search for family secrets, and a good pharmacotherapist knows the importance of genes. So parents beware when your child enters psychotherapy; the spotlight may turn toward you.

But parents should take some comfort in their child's desire to understand and forgive them, and to understand and forgive themselves. Most therapists I know are good and kind people who enter the profession with noble intentions and practice with worthy ethics. They advocate well for their patients, they care about them, and they are pulling for them.

One big reason I entered this profession is because I love the stories people tell, and there are few professions with stories so critical, so important. A good story takes a listener to a foreign land with all the benefits of exotic travel and few of the hardships. The trip can be a short one or a long one but any trip at any time can be intense, exhilarating, frightening, risky, and fulfilling. There are no guarantees of a happy voyage: the boy does not always get the girl, the hero is not always recognized or rewarded, the loose ends are not neatly tied up in the final weeks. But for me, each trip was worth the price of the passage, the price of caring and committing. Just like in the movies, I came to appreciate and understand the actors.

. . . .

I had a rocky start with my entrance into the profession. I took my first psychology class during my freshman year at the University of California, Berkeley. There was just me and about 1000 other undergraduates in the class. I studied earnestly a course that I expected to be fascinating, a course that turned out to be, for me, plodding and dull, full of endless minute facts irrelevant to my interests and my world. How could a course which introduced psychology be so uninterested in people? I thought I was a smart student, but it turns out I was not; with all my hard work, my rote memorization of what seemed to be a million facts, I received a grade of "C" in the course—satisfactory, average, nothing commendable here. Apparently, all the facts I dutifully submitted to my short-term memory bank did not make it to the final exam; they simply refused to show up.

No problem, I thought. I went to plead my case to my teaching assistant, whom I did not know, whom I had never met, but who seemed more accessible to me than the far, far away professor who lectured in the front of the big auditorium. It was the teaching assistant's job, I thought, to assist me, to support me, and, upon seeing my enthusiasm for the profession, to usher me into the club of wonderful people who wanted to become professional psychologists. My teaching assistant, a doctoral candidate in psychology at Berkeley, never patted me on the back—he was too neurotic to touch anyone—and he quoted a study to me: "In a large nation-wide review of hundreds of subjects completing an 'Introduction to Psychology' course, it was found that students who received a 'C' grade or below in the course had virtually no admissions to quality Ph.D. programs in the field."

I was doomed; he said so, the study proved so. But he was not aware of my personal study of one subject, me, which hypothesized that people who hated Berkeley's "Introduction to Psychology" class would ignore and reject its teaching assistant.

I am not a Pollyanna. Every day at work did not bring me growth, fulfillment, and meaning. I had a conversation with Jerry Douglas just before he retired, a conversation that reflected the wisdom of his decision to retire, and it made me think about hurrying my decision. With slight exaggeration, the conversation went like this:

"You know that guy you saw yesterday, Jerry, that bad guy, violent with staff, huge guy, weighed about 350?"

"No, what guy?" Jerry said.

"You know, the professional wrestler, the immense man with bright orange hair. Wore nothing but a speedo bathing suit. Very scary."

"Which guy?" Jerry asked.

"Really? Which guy?" I said. "The guy last night. Big, big guy, boa constrictor tattoo going four times around his trunk."

"Snake tattoo, huh. I've seen a few of those."

"Come on, Jerry. You had to run up to the fifth floor of the East wing when he set fire to the trash cans."

"I saw a lot of people last night," he said.

"You tackled him. You put him on a 5150."

"I would imagine so," said Jerry.

"Well, he wanted you to have this picture of him wearing his championship wrestling belt," I said.

"Oh yeah, that guy. I remember him."

Cases blur together, I understand that. That is why I jotted down personal notes, a few observations about some of the interesting patients I have seen over the years. I do not want to forget anyone. I genuinely root for the recovery and relief of my involuntary patients, and I have seen many of them walk out of the darkness and into a hint of light. I applaud the initiative of those voluntary patients actively seeking help for their symptoms and those searching for meaning in their lives; I am one of them. We are all on this planet together circling a big ball of explosive light not knowing where we are going, but the journey is not as frightening in the company of others. A good therapist is the company of others.

John Farrell is a psychologist and clinical social worker who worked for over 43 years at the University of California, Davis, Medical Center, a teaching hospital and a level I trauma center in Sacramento, California. He spent most of those years working with Psychiatric Emergency Services and Crisis Services in the heart of the hospital, the Emergency Department.

Dr. Farrell also worked for twenty years, concurrently, as a part-time faculty member at California State University, Sacramento, in the Health Department and the Psychology Department. For his whole professional life, he enjoyed teaching what he practiced and practicing what he taught.

Made in the USA
Coppell, TX
11 September 2020